SLAVERY IN
THE CLOVER BOTTOMS

SLAVERY IN THE CLOVER BOTTOMS

John McCline's
Narrative of His Life
during Slavery
and the Civil War

Edited by
Jan Furman

Voices of the Civil War
Frank L. Byrne,
Series Editor

The University of Tennessee Press / Knoxville

The Voices of the Civil War series makes available a variety of primary source materials that illuminate issues on the battlefield, the homefront, and the western front, as well as other aspects of this historic era. The series contextualizes the personal accounts within the framework of the latest scholarship and expands established knowledge by offering new perspectives, new materials, and new voices.

Frontispiece: John McCline in Santa Fe, ca. 1940. Courtesy of Mrs. Karolyn Roberts.

Library of Congress Cataloging-in-Publication Data

McCline, John, 1852–1948.
Slavery in the Clover Bottoms : John McCline's narrative of his
life during slavery and the Civil War / edited by Jan Furman. — 1st ed.
        p. cm. — (Voices of the Civil War)
Includes bibliographical references (p.) and index.
ISBN 1-57233-007-4
1. McCline, John, 1852–1948—Childhood and youth. 2. Afro-American soldiers—Biography. 3. Soldiers—United States—Biography. 4. United States. Army. Michigan Infantry Regiment, 13th (1861–1865) 5. Slaves—Tennessee—Nashville Region—Biography. 6. Plantation life—Tennessee—Nashville Region—History—19th century. 7. Nashville Region (Tenn.)—Biography. I. Furman, Jan. II. Title. III. Series: Voices of the Civil War series.
E514.5 13th.M38 1998
a973.7'415'092—dc21
[B]   97-45254

For Senta, Kara, Lucile, and Jay

CONTENTS

Foreword
Frank L. Byrne, Series Editor   xi

Acknowledgments   xiii
Editor's Introduction   xv

SLAVERY IN THE CLOVER BOTTOMS

Introduction
  by H. J. Hagerman   2

I. Before the War   11
II. During the War   51
III. After the War   107

Appendix I. Thirteenth Michigan Volunteers   113
Appendix II. Slaves Referred to by McCline   119
Appendix III. McCline's Will, Remembrances, and Obituary Notices   121

Notes   125
Selected Bibliography   149
Index   153

ILLUSTRATIONS

FIGURES

John McCline in Santa Fe, ca. 1940	xxv
John and Bertha McCline in Santa Fe, ca. 1938	xxvi
James John Hagerman Mansion in Colorado Springs	3
John McCline at the Home of Percy Hagerman	4
Home of Gov. Herbert J. Hagerman in Santa Fe, 1906	6
H. J. Hagerman at the Governor's Residence in Santa Fe, 1906	6
John McCline at H. J. Hagerman's Home in Santa Fe, 1934	8
Mrs. Hoggatt	13
1860 Slave Census Showing James Hoggatt's Chattel Property	15
Extant Slave Cabins at Clover Bottom, ca. 1920	19
Clover Bottom Mansion Restored to 1859 Italianate Style	29
Col. Michael Shoemaker of the Thirteenth Michigan Infantry in 1863	54
Col. Joshua B. Culver of the Thirteenth Michigan Infantry, ca. 1863	55
Dr. Foster Pratt of the Thirteenth Michigan Infantry, ca 1863	56
A Quartermaster's Wagon, Belle Plain, Virginia	57
"Crack Team" of the 1st Division, 6th A.S., Near Hazel Run, Virginia	58
Wagon Train Crossing a Pontoon Bridge over the Germana Ford	69
Sherman Hotel in Chicago, ca. 1880s	109
Palmer House Hotel in Chicago, ca. 1871	110
Lindell Hotel in St. Louis, Missouri, ca. 1874	111
First Page of Last Will and Testament of John McCline	124

MAPS

Clover Bottom Plantation in 1860	12
1871 Topographic Map of the Clover Bottom Area	14
General Sherman's Carolinas Campaign	98

FOREWORD

The memoir of John McCline is the first written by a black American in the Voices of the Civil War Series. His recollections raise the same question of accuracy as any older person's autobiographical narrative; a question to which Jan Furman's careful editing—including comparison when possible with the written record—gives a reassuring answer. McCline's memoir tells of his boyhood on a large plantation near Nashville, conveying a sense of slave life with its community and frequent brutality. He early developed an interest in horses, and he would work with them during much of the rest of his life.

After the coming of the Civil War, he ran away and attached himself to the Yankee invaders. His memoir of his association with the Thirteenth Michigan Regiment is a unique account of the life of an officer's servant and teamster. While telling a little about battles, he says much about Sherman's marches through Georgia and the Carolinas as seen by a black youth. Besides describing his coming of age, he illustrates the transition from slavery to freedom.

As he accompanied one of his officers to the North, he was part of the minority of ex-slaves who left the South early. (He did, however, return to Tennessee to attend a school for freedmen.) Developing his skills with horses and in household service, he was able to make a living by working for members of the Northern white elite and thus survived what an eminent historian termed the nadir for post-emancipation American blacks. Unusually, he ended his days in the Southwest, in the employ of a territorial leader who typed and edited this interesting and well-written autobiography. Implicit in it is much information about black-white relationships in nineteenth- and early-twentieth-century America.

Frank L. Byrne
Kent State University

Acknowledgments

The first phase of work on McCline's memoir began in the summer of 1994. I am grateful to the University of Michigan at Flint for financial support that summer and for underwriting a trip, the following spring, to New Mexico where McCline spent the last decades of his life. I am also indebted to the University of Michigan in Ann Arbor for the Rackham grant that paid for a trip to Tennessee where McCline lived his early life as a slave on the Hoggatt plantation near Nashville.

While in Tennessee, I met Steve Rogers, a talented historian and archivist by profession as well as by instinct. Steve is a historic preservation specialist at the Tennessee Historical Commission, the offices of which are located in the recently restored Hoggatt plantation house. Steve's archival research in Tennessee, Washington, D.C., St. Louis, and elsewhere has been indispensable in gathering and assembling information, photographs, and documents related to Tennessee, slavery, the Hoggatt plantation, and the Civil War. I am most appreciative of his generous and tireless assistance during our two-year collaboration. At the Tennessee Historical Commission, I would also like to thank Linda Wynn, and I thank Fred Prouty for his contribution to the Civil War research. In addition, I want to acknowledge Dorie Nugent of St. Louis and her kind assistance in researching portions of McCline's years in Missouri.

The Hagerman and McCline families and friends have been very supportive of this study. Berje Barrow, Bertha McCline's great-granddaughter, and William and Elizabeth Brooks, Bertha's grand nephew and his wife, filled in some of the blanks left in McCline's history. Mrs. Karolyn Roberts, who, as a young woman in the 1930s, was acquainted with John McCline, and her daughter Ernestine Lawrence have also provided significant details about McCline's life in Santa Fe. Katherine Kitch Hagerman, the Hagerman family historian and archivist, has generously assisted in documenting McCline's years with the Hagermans in Colorado and New Mexico. Her careful reading of the memoir and editorial comments have been most helpful.

Several university and state archivists and reference librarians have enthusiastically assisted my research: Paul Gifford, archivist at the University of Michigan at Flint; Grant Burns, director of Public Services at the University of Michigan at Flint; Charles Sherrill, director of Public Services at the Tennessee State Library and Archives; Robert Torrez, state historian at the New Mexico State Record Center and Archives; Austin Hoover, director of the Rio Grande Historical Collections at New Mexico State University; and David Orr, administrator at the Historical Center for Southeast New Mexico.

My gratitude goes to Elliot Sykes, who worked as my research assistant in the early phase of the project. I appreciate his intelligence and resourcefulness in tracking sources and locating materials, his unwavering faith in the work, and his friendship.

A special thank you to my daughters, Kara and Senta. They traveled with me, collected data, shared my frustration and joy, discussed my ideas, and gave affection and companionship when I needed it.

Editor's Introduction

> The genre of autobiography lives in the two worlds of
> history and literature.
>
> STEPHEN BUTTERFIELD,
> *BLACK AUTOBIOGRAPHY IN AMERICA*

When John McCline sat down in the early part of this century to record the episodes of his remarkable life as a slave and runaway in the Union army, he at once
became literary artist and historian, sifting the documented past through a sieve
of personal perspective. His own life became a paradigm for interpreting important historical events. Of course, his effort was not unusual. History and literature are natural extensions of each other, and memorable autobiography is expected to join the two. In that sense, McCline is one of the many who are prompted,
for one reason or another, to look back over the years. But McCline's subjects—
slavery and the Civil War—and his identity—a black man who experienced both—
make it possible and much more interesting to locate him in a context other than
the usual: he was writing a narrative of slavery and freedom.

McCline was one of the latest to practice a literary tradition that began more
than one hundred fifty years earlier with the publication in 1760 of *A Narrative of
the Uncommon Sufferings and Surprizing Deliverance of Briton Hammon, A Negro
Man*.[1] McCline's and Hammon's stories are, not surprisingly, as different as the
two men's lives or as different as any two lives separated by epochs of time.
Hammon briefly relates his "sufferings" caused by Indians who captured him in
Florida, his imprisonment in Cuba, and the jubilant return to his benevolent
master in England. McCline, writing about the enslavement he endured a century
later, condemns all slave masters as he chronicles the institution's inhumanity and
moral turpitude.

Having less in common with the eighteenth-century apologist, Briton Hammon,
than with the renowned nineteenth-century escaped slave and abolitionist,
Frederick Douglass,[2] McCline writes, to some extent, in the convention of classic
slave narratives, which developed in tandem with abolitionism in the decades
before the Civil War.[3] Although different in tone and style from classic narrative,

which, along with its literary ambitions, aimed to win allies in the freedom struggle by exposing slavery's crimes, McCline's narrative, written from the less polemical postwar vantage point of freedom and progress, will nevertheless be familiar to any student of the slave narrative genre. He highlights many of the same discouragingly unvarying themes and characters: deceptive masters, hypocritical mistresses, sadistic overseers, the inconceivable suffering of slaves, and the bondsman's will to be free.[4] Appearing as the narrative does now, near the end of a millennium—the last one hundred years of which have been progressively marked by social reforms culminating in the recent period of multiculturalism—McCline's narrative seems a startling and eerie reminder, lest we forget, of our not-so-distant (in the millennial context at least) past.

McCline spent about eleven years on the Hoggatt plantation in Middle Tennessee with his maternal grandmother and three older brothers. His mother and sister had died; his father, Jack McCline, had a different owner and lived nearby in another county. In some ways McCline portrays his childhood as unexpectedly ordinary: he went fishing and hunting on Sunday, his day off; attended church; was teased by his brothers; and he was comforted by his grandmother, Hanna. These were, in a sense, happy times, which never completely erased the near-constant fear of harsh punishment by Mrs. Hoggatt and the overseer, but which must have engendered the enthusiasm and optimism that charmed his friends in later years.

McCline reports on every aspect of plantation life. Writing retrospectively in old age, aware of the historical virtue of making note of a nearly forgotten time, he reconstructs a way of life. At its center was the "white house," the common name for the plantation house, where Dr. Hoggatt, his wife, and her two nieces lived. In charge was Mrs. Hoggatt, always equipped with the cowhide that she used often and indiscriminately to control her slaves. Her counterpart beyond the boundaries of house and garden was Richard Phillips, whom McCline characterizes as ignorant but cunning. Phillips (and his vicious hound) was hired in 1858 to replace a man named Anderson who had married and relocated. According to McCline, Anderson was a lenient overseer, but Phillips brought with him a regimented reign of brutality that may or may not have been mandated by the Hoggatts, but was certainly condoned by them. Caught between overseer and mistress were the blacks, whose labor made Clover Bottom plantation self-sufficient and brought in the cash crops that helped secure the Hoggatts' wealth.

McCline's description of the slave community is illuminating. In some respects black plantation life, in spite of its strictness, was defiantly independent. Both men and women had skills that would have been marketable in a free society. Resourceful black men owned guns, even though they were forbidden by Southern law. And there was always considerable interest in the politics of slavery and freedom. Yet, in the final analysis, it must be observed, any independence was ultimately subject to the strictures of slave authority.

Although *Slavery in the Clover Bottoms* takes its title and much of its subject matter from the plantation experience, it is mostly about McCline's thirty-month Civil War adventure. From December 1862 to June 1865, McCline "served" with the Thirteenth Infantry of Michigan. Company C of the regiment, on its way from campaigns in Mississippi and Kentucky, had marched along a road near the Hoggatt place, and McCline simply followed his boyish inclination to join their procession.

During the months that followed, McCline assumed ever-increasing responsibilities and maturity. At first a homesick boy regretting his impetuosity, McCline quickly adapted to daily life as a teamster in the regiment and transformed himself into a Yankee soldier. During the course of the war, he traveled many miles: from Tennessee to Alabama, then back to Tennessee, and eventually, in the final months of fighting, to Georgia as Sherman marched his army to the sea at Savannah. McCline was camped in North Carolina when Johnston's surrender to Sherman ended the war. Over the months, although not directly engaged in combat, McCline was close to many battles. At Murfreesboro and Chickamauga Creek, for example, he witnessed two of the most intense campaigns of the conflict.

When the war ended, McCline was only thirteen or fourteen years old, but much older in accumulated experience. Before the war, he had been no stranger to deprivation and gratuitous violence. The plantation system, with its irrational and abusive power, had been a more than adequate primer for the exigencies of war. Indeed, despite an initial abhorrence of the sheer numbers of dead and wounded, McCline in time took the destruction in stride, seeing it as the price of his freedom. But, ironically, he was not prepared for the routine alliances and affections that bind compatriots and engender life-long loyalties. With the exception of Major Culver, whom he accompanied to Michigan after the war, McCline most likely never again encountered the men of his regiment who had become friends and allies. But their influence on him was enduring.

So enduring, in fact, that a half century later—the exact date of the narrative's composition is not known, but McCline showed the manuscript to his employer, Herbert Hagerman, in 1930 and probably wrote it sometime during the previous decade—his memoir ranges no further than adolescence, as though these first thirteen years had been the most compelling, even for a man who had, by the 1920s, lived through the turbulence of Reconstruction, the First World War, and had seen up close the hateful territorial politics of the Southwest. Only at Hagerman's prompting did McCline add an autobiographical postscript to the war.

The intensity of his experiences may explain, to some extent, McCline's amazing recall of details in the narrative. It is fairly certain that sometime after the Michigan Legislature authorized publication in 1903 of personnel statistics—place of birth, dates mustered into and out of service, dates of reenlistment and promotion—on soldiers, McCline either began his project or finished the story he had already begun to write. Using these partial records as memory markers, he was able to regenerate the whole. That he was able sixty years later to remember and reconstruct events, places, episodes, and people from his childhood with such accuracy is testimony to their significance for him. It is not unlikely that his experiences remained clear and immediate because he related his adventure many times over the span of his years until, by the time he got around to writing it down, the saga was graphically imprinted. Time did not erase McCline's memories; on the contrary, the effect of time on childhood memories was panoramic: the narrow observation of a boy was transformed into a man's encompassing insight. McCline's recall was also aided by his apparent "cinematographic" memory. Every day of the life that he writes about became etched as impressions and images like a reel of moving pictures which he had only to recall and relate. Later, in his young adult life, McCline was proud of this ability. Living in St. Louis and working at a hotel hat check during a time when check stubs were not in use at finer hotel restaurants, McCline consistently, for nine years, returned the correct hat to its wearer.

THE MILITARY EXPERIENCE FOR BLACKS IN THE UNION ARMY

McCline's revealing personal history is also quite insightful as public history. In several significant ways his life in the military is representative of the black Civil War military experience in general and of Tennessee in particular. McCline writes primarily (but not exclusively) from the white Union soldier's point of view, but his hybrid life as runaway cum military civilian connects him to other perspectives as well. McCline's story takes on full meaning only in a large context.

Like McCline, slaves all over the South escaped from plantations to join Union camps (or contraband camps from which laborers and soldiers were recruited), especially in Tennessee, where widespread fighting by large contending armies blurred geographical boundaries between plantation and battlefield, disrupted work routines, and generally undermined slaveholders' authority.[5] Passing Federal armies often encouraged slaves to escape by declaring them free. And with masters and overseers gone to war in many instances, nothing prevented blacks from merely walking away. At Clover Bottom, for example, McCline was not the first slave to leave. Two of the ablest men, Henry and Abe, had disappeared earlier in 1862 and were assumed to have joined the army. As a precaution against future runaways, as many men as could be spared were sent to another farm at Murfreesboro owned by the Hoggatts on the pretext of being needed to harvest an unusually large cotton crop. McCline writes, however, that the men discounted the Hoggatts' explanation and understood very well that the farm's remoteness was meant to be a deterrent to escape. When exile did not work (at least one man, McCline's brother Jeff, and most likely others as well, escaped Murfreesboro), Mrs. Hoggatt tried beneficence—dispensing a few dollars of worthless Confederate money—but to no avail. No stratagem was completely effective in keeping blacks on plantations, not even the danger of retaliation facing family left behind.

Certainly, not every black Union soldier of record in Tennessee was a runaway or even a volunteer; many were forced to join the army, sometimes under brutal

circumstances. Statements of complaint from black recruits forwarded to the secretary of war describe kidnapping, violence, and even death for those who resisted
impressment. Writing from Nashville in September 1863, Maj. George L. Stearns,
a Northern abolitionist in charge of organizing black troops in Tennessee, called
the practice of impressment "Irresponsible": "The Colored men here are treated
like brutes," he wrote to Washington. "Any officer who wants them I am told im-
presses on his own authority and it is seldom they are paid."[6] Along with his report, Stearns sent as evidence the signed testimony of a man named Armstead
Lewis whose impressment ordeal began one Sunday morning after church. Lewis
was stopped on his way home by soldiers who demanded his pass and would not
return it. They ordered him to fall in, and he was marched from place to place as
they continued collecting men. All the conscripts were delivered to a camp about
a mile away and placed under guard. In Lewis's account, hundreds of men were
collected this way and imprisoned overnight in an outdoor pen, without blankets
or warm clothing.

Impressment was no doubt an expression of white soldiers' contempt for blacks,
but it also strongly reflected the legacy of incoherent government policy on blacks
in the military in general and former slaves in particular: in the climate of vacil-
lating commitments to emancipation and enlistment, field commanders had implicit authority to employ blacks as circumstances and need dictated. At the beginning of the war, public sentiment was overwhelmingly against the idea of any
black Union soldiers, whether they be Northern, Southern, free, or enslaved. It was
easy enough at that point to argue against the principle of enlistment on the dual
basis of white soldiers' ability to win the war and blacks' ostensible inability to
withstand the rigors of battle. More significant, black enlistment would have ob-
scured the Lincoln administration's war objective: preservation of the Union and
not emancipation of blacks. The latter was perceived as an obstacle to the former,
since many Unionists supporting Lincoln in the South (whose support was necessary to curb rebellion) were also slaveholders interested in preserving a Southern economy sustained by slavery. Lincoln could not free slaves without alienating their masters and endangering his goal. But as runaways entered federal camps
expecting protection, the separation of slavery and freedom became hard to maintain. Not all runaways, in the interest of separation, could be returned to slavery,
which was a practice early in the war. A partial solution to the dilemma of what
to do about runaways without antagonizing loyal masters was the Confiscation
Act of August 1861, authorizing the capture of all property used in defending the
Confederacy, including slaves. In targeting runaways used in the Confederate defense only, the act conveniently extended refugee status to many who needed it
without altering the government's position against emancipation. Despite its
shortcomings, the Confiscation Act was, in retrospect, the first step toward emancipation, and it was also an awkward step toward enlisting blacks. As the first official link between war and freedom, it provided a conceivable rationale and context for black soldiers: as weapons of war turned against the enemy.

What followed after 1861 was a graduated series of fragmented emancipation orders, each of which in its turn moved the army closer to black enlistment. The Second Confiscation Act of July 1862 declared all fugitive slaves of rebellious masters free, and the Militia Act of the same date authorized the deployment of blacks in any military or naval service. It was not, however, until enactment of the final Emancipation Proclamation of September 1862—expanding freedom to include all slaves in rebellious states as of January 1, 1863—that the government began enlistments. The first official recruits were recorded in November 1862.[7] In May of the next year the Bureau of Colored Troops was created to coordinate recruitment. Under its direction, recruiters, some of whom were carefully chosen, worked more or less successfully to raise black regiments in accordance with consistent policies. But as Stearns discovered in Tennessee as late as September 1863, old patterns of brutal impressment born in the previous months' policy vacuum were slow to change.

Remarkably, each act of emancipation sought to distinguish between the slaves of loyal and rebellious slaveholders, the former being ineligible for enlistment. Obviously, such a distinction was a practical impossibility. As Howard Westwood puts it, "Suffice it to say that the president and his government were very soon accepting black men into the armed services regardless of their status or home territory."[8]

Loyal Kentucky slaveholders complained about this failure to differentiate. A letter written to the president in January 1864 by nineteen Kentucky Unionists emphasizes these Southerners' allegiance to the government and their hope that the president "would not allow their negroes to be taken from them without at least giving them some timely notice, that they might prepare for so great a change." The letter expresses concern about "the establishment of a recruiting office for Colored Troops at Clarksville Tenne. . . . and the many inducements that are presented to the Negroes" which makes them leave their masters, all classes of them "no matter how loyal . . . [they] may have been." The dire case of B. C. Ritter of Christian County, Kentucky, is offered as evidence. Ritter, who had supported the Union with money and speeches, had recruited for the army, and had incurred the wrath of Kentucky Confederates by doing so, was, in the end, nearly destroyed by recruitment of "nine of his most valuable negroes." The slaveholders asked the president to order "the return of their Negroes" to the former status of slaves "at least long enough to enable them to prepare . . . crops for market."[9]

The situation was much the same in Tennessee. Taken over by Federals early in the war, the state was not considered to be in rebellion by the beginning of 1863 and was therefore exempt from the tenets of emancipation. Unionist slaveholders in Tennessee, in theory, were still slaveholders. In reality blacks who wanted to enlist did so, even those belonging to loyalists. Provisions, therefore, were made for such crises. In addition to enlisting "All freemen who will volunteer" and "All slaves of rebel or disloyal masters who will volunteer or enlist" in exchange for freedom at the end of their terms of service, the September 1863 communication on recruitment for black troops in Tennessee stipulated that "All slaves of loyal citizens with the consent of their owners will be received into the service of the United States in exchange for freedom" and that "Loyal masters will receive a certificate of the enlistment of their slaves which will entitle them to payment of a sum not exceeding the bounty, now provided by law for the enlistment of white recruits" (in Tennessee the bounty was three hundred dollars per slave).[10] In all, 39 percent of black men who were fighting age in Tennessee enlisted in the Union army. Of 51,809 men between ages 18 and 45 (1,762 free and 50,047 slave), 20,133 became Union soldiers.[11] (It has been estimated that as many as 2,000 black Tennesseans may have served in the Confederate army.) Three hundred blacks—35 percent of whom were born in places outside of Tennessee—applied for Confederate pensions in 1916.[12]

It should be noted that the uneven progress of black enlistment in the South was vastly different from the orderly (albeit reluctant) progress of enlistment in the North. Unlike the freedman's pervasive presence in the South, which made him inherently part of the war and which eventually led to his official status as soldier, northern freemen created no imperative. Keeping them out of the war was as simple as refusing their requests for service.

At the first sign of war, free Northern blacks had begun preparing to fight. A few who were light-skinned enough to pass joined all-white regiments as combat soldiers. Hundreds of others joined white regiments as cooks and servants.[13] But many enlistment advocates in New York, Michigan, Ohio, Pennsylvania, and Massachusetts petitioned the war department to organize all black regiments in order to, in the words of one petitioner, "display their patriotic zeal and unwavering loyalty in the most effective manner in this trial-hour of the republic . . ."[14] Some, like the Home Guards of Cincinnati and the Hannibal Guards of Pittsburgh, feeling the urgency of the times, enthusiastically formed units first and then petitioned for recognition. Blacks, like whites, felt the stir of public spirit. But they also knew the fight was an opportunity to prove themselves as able men to a society accustomed to thinking of them and treating them as less than able. Frederick Douglass, the black abolitionist positioned in the forefront of the struggle for black enlistment, described the matter well: black men "go into this war to affirm their manhood . . ."[15] Just as important, blacks viewed the war as a belated instrument of slavery's destruction. If the South fell, so would its peculiar institution. Again, Douglass phrased it best: "brave black men of the North, capable of bearing arms, shall come forth, clad in complete steel, ready to make the twin monsters, slavery and rebellion, crumble together in the dust."[16]

To all of these eager entreaties from willing blacks, the government in the beginning said no. Allowing blacks a role would send the wrong message about the reason for war. It took escalating conflict and the pioneering military courage of contrabands, among other significant factors, to change politics and public opinion on black enlistment. Finally, in February 1863, recruiting for the Fifty-Fourth Massachusetts Infantry began. It was not the first black regiment employed, but it was the most well known, the most widely recruited, and the one on which the hopes of Northern abolitionists, black and white, rested. Gov. John Andrew of Massachusetts called it "the most important corps to be organized during the whole war." Andrew had long advocated black enlistment, and when the time came prominent abolitionists under his direction raised money and a regiment. Influential blacks like Douglass, Martin R. Delaney, and William Wells Brown, former slaves and well-connected, articulate spokesmen for the black community, traveled the North and Canada as effective recruiting agents. Three months later one thousand men of the Fifty-Fourth, in the presence of an equal number of spectators and dignitaries, received state flags from Governor Andrew in a solemn ceremonious tribute to the regiment's historic importance. That was the beginning of black enlistment. Two years later, at the end of the war, more than 180,000 black men had served in the Union army.

Enlistment accomplished only the first phase of struggle. The second, becoming soldiers, was more formidable. Centuries of racial stereotyping blocked the way. In fact, once in the army black soldiers, especially runaways, were too often used as laborers.[17] Menial work had perhaps seemed inevitable employment for former slaves turned soldiers. Some officers reasoned that blacks were accustomed to deprivation and could be put to best use relieving whites of onerous duties. In the summer of 1863 the commander of Federal forces at Hilton Head noted that "In view of the approaching hot weather" relief details should be "made from the Colored Troops" in order to protect "the health and General efficiency" of his command. Another commander in the Southeast Missouri district requested that if a regiment of soldiers of "African descent" was organized, it should be sent to him because he "could use them to good advantage on the fortification and in the fatigue department."[18] In response many commanders of black regiments complained that, confined to fatigue duty as they were, black troops could demonstrate stamina, but not intelligence and courage. Col. Thomas Morgan, commanding the Fourteenth U.S. Colored Infantry (USCI) in Tennessee, asserted that his regiment was willing to do its part of army labor, but felt it "degrading" to be singled out for fatigue duty "while white troops stand idly by." This kind of treatment, he continued, "savors too much of the old regime, and if persisted in will utterly ruin the prospect of the work of making soldiers here of black men."[19]

Employed as laborers, black soldiers were also paid as laborers—$10 per month, from which $3.50 could be deducted for clothing when required. That was less than the total pay of a private, who received $10 *plus* $3.50 for clothing. Black soldiers requested more, sympathetic white commanders supported them, and the secretary of war even urged Congress in his annual report for 1863 to authorize equal pay. But Congress hesitated, and the secretary acquiesced. It was not until June 1864 that Congress finally granted pay equity retroactive to the date of enlistment for those who had been free on April 19, 1861, and to January 1, 1863, for all others. Contrabands, then, some of whom had been the first to enlist in South Carolina and Kansas, never received full back pay. Ironically, in many instances former slaves hired as civilian laborers fared better financially than soldiers. Assigned to quartermasters, commissaries, and engineers, laborers were generally rationed and paid wages equal to and often better than enlisted men. For example, advertised pay for most black teamsters—and perhaps as many as 10,000 of them were hired to haul supplies to and from ordnance stores—was $20 per month plus rations.[20] The Nashville quartermaster graded pay for black teamsters at the higher rate of $30 to $35 per month for those who drove 4 to 6 horses and $25 to $30 for 2 horses or mules. Cart drivers were listed at $10 to $15; general laborers at $35 to $40; wood choppers, $35 to $40; cooks, $30 to $35; adult messengers, $30; and younger messengers, $25. Not many blacks were hired at this generous pay scale, however. Only 4 are recorded on the quartermaster's list for 1864.[21]

Despite these problems the army offered advantages. For McCline and those like him with limited experience of the world, it brought travel, independence, and responsibility. In slavery McCline had been proud of his work as cowboy—turning the cows out in the morning and bringing them in at night. But pride inevitably turned to humiliation if the work was not done to the overseer's satisfaction. On one occasion, McCline, a child doing a man's work, was missing a cow at the evening count; his punishment was a brutal beating. Army discipline, for McCline, was not so capricious. He does write of being tied to a tree briefly and then sent to the guard house as punishment for overstaying a leave from camp. McCline was certain that he was the victim of injustice and that the mean-spirited lieutenant in charge singled him out because he could get away with it, but such treatment was not the norm. Having come to expect a rational use of authority in the military, McCline was more angry than fearful of the lieutenant and refused to submit to him as he had submitted to the overseer. The army also gave black soldiers opportunities for formal education. Almost every black camp had someone—a chaplain or officer's wife, for example—who offered instruction in reading, writing, and spelling. By all accounts soldiers took eager advantage of these lessons. McCline writes about coming upon a black camp in Chattanooga where soldiers took great pride in their appearance and demeanor, where many sat in tents reading, and where the chapel doubled as a classroom. (When McCline was invited to join the all-black regiment, he declined, explaining that he was probably too young and that, more important, he did not want to leave his friends from Michigan.) Although McCline received no formal teaching, he did learn the alphabet and simple reading with the help of a soldier in his company.

McCline does not address the contentious matters of black Civil War history directly. It is likely that, as one of two blacks in his regiment, neither of whom was an enlisted man, McCline was unaware of military policies toward blacks in general or of their predicament under certain commanders. For McCline, the Thirteenth Infantry was a microcosm of all military life. He may have believed that his congenial relations with white soldiers and commanders reflected similar relations throughout the army. Although proud of them, he did not, after all, identify entirely with other black soldiers, who came from the North in search of opportunity and from the South in search of freedom. Nor was he a laborer interested in wages. In a special category, McCline was at the time a child, working and playing at soldiering. His salary of eight dollars per month—more than black soldiers (in earlier years of the war) after they paid for uniforms and less than some laborers—which began during his second year with the Thirteenth reflected that uniqueness.

The personal and immediate, then, are McCline's focus. Even when his gaze shifts, as it sometimes does, to grander subjects of war strategy and statistics, the personal voice is not lost. The child, who cries himself to sleep, who plays marbles in camp, who talks to animals when he is lonely, and whose curiosity and tenacity know no bounds, remains.

McCline's Life after the War

After the war, McCline, still a boy too young to be completely on his own, spent nine years in Michigan living and working with various families. From there he went to Chicago, which was then under reconstruction and full of economic opportunity after the 1871 fire. In all, McCline spent sixteen years in Chicago and St. Louis (except for two years—1876 to 1878—when he alternately taught and attended school in Nashville) before moving to Colorado Springs. In 1906 he made a final move to Santa Fe, New Mexico, where he died in 1948 at age ninety-five or ninety-six.

One is left to speculate about why McCline's story remained unpublished during his lifetime. Once he had finished writing, McCline gave the manuscript to Herbert Hagerman, likely expecting him to use his influence and knowledge in getting the work into print. But for unknown reasons, the manuscript languished. Hagerman certainly made the effort: he wrote an introduction and prepared the text for publication. Perhaps death intervened (Hagerman died in 1935, the year after he finished his work on the narrative). At any rate, "Slavery in the Clover Bottoms" remained in McCline's possession until his death, when it was left with his widow, Bertha, whom he had married in 1938 when he was eighty-six. Bertha, age forty-six when they married, had a daughter from a previous marriage, and in later decades it was Bertha's great-granddaughter, Berje Barrow, who came to have possession of McCline's story, the only copy of which by then was Hagerman's typed version.

By ending his memoir at 1892, McCline left out twenty to twenty-five years of life (assuming he composed his story sometime in the 1920s), some of it noteworthy. From 1906 to 1907, for example, McCline managed the governor's residence for Hagerman before the latter was forced from office by political enemies. What was it like to be close to the major combatants in a fray that involved well-known leaders of the Republican party in New Mexico and the president of the United States? Any rendering of the people and events of this period would be no less alluring for readers than his recollections of plantation and army experiences.

Hagerman describes McCline as "deeply interested in what was going on during these strenuous days. . . ." But he was also "discreet . . . about politics and government." It is probable, then, that as a man of discretion, McCline believed that writing about important personages, many of whom were still in public life, would have been too presumptuous or too familiar to a local audience (and extremely awkward in the case of narrating his life with Hagerman and then asking Hagerman to edit that narration), and so the pioneering phase of his life in New Mexico goes unremarked.

It might also be that McCline's purpose in writing went beyond a recitation of history, public or private. He could have been in thrall to the act of creation. There is some sense, gathered from the narrative, of McCline as self-conscious literary

John McCline in Santa Fe, ca. 1940. The child with him is Kay Wiley Roberts, the son of a friend. Courtesy of Mrs. Karolyn Roberts.

artist. The effort to develop character and set mood, the metaphorical use of language and foreshadowing of episodes, suggest the extent to which writing was as much an exercise of the imagination as it was of the memory for McCline. In this process, chronicling recent events in Santa Fe, no matter how interesting, would not have offered the same opportunity for creativity as reconstructing the remote. Through the lens of time, childhood often enlarges beyond proportion to whatever else may once have appeared significant in life.

Successes in later life were dwarfed by slavery and freedom, the defining experiences of McCline's youth: starting out as a small boy in the universe of his grandmother's cabin, he soon encountered a new world on the pike intersecting the plantation, where he observed travelers headed toward destinations forbidden to him as a slave. Eventually, he too was on the move away from the planta-

John and Bertha McCline in Santa Fe, ca. 1938. Courtesy of Mrs. Karolyn Roberts.

tion and toward the much larger military world of unfolding landscapes and flowering consciousness. In the final analysis, *Slavery in the Clover Bottoms* is an act of creating the self of a young boy who endured and came of age. This is not merely the individual self of conventional middle-class success or the persona of the enduring rags-to-riches drama of American life and letters (which McCline chose not to represent). As the title intimates, McCline's self (as in most black autobiography) shares in the collective lives of a people who also endured and came of age and whose personal stories can only make complete sense in the context of American history and vice versa.[22]

Editorial Method

John McCline's handwritten copy of *Slavery in the Clover Bottoms* cannot be found. Whether Herbert Hagerman, McCline's employer and the manuscript's first editor and typist, returned it to McCline is uncertain. Neither man's heirs has the original. Without it, there is no certain way of knowing the text's accuracy: What did Hagerman copy verbatim? What did he change intentionally? What did he miscopy? My discussions with people who knew McCline, my visits to places he lived in New Mexico, Tennessee, and Michigan, as well as extensive archival and library research, support the truth of McCline's narrative and corroborate his marvelous recall of details. Yet, some inaccuracies exist, primarily in dates and occasionally in names. Not knowing if these are the author's memory lapses or the editor's typing errors, I have left the text as it is (except in instances of obvious errors, i.e., occasionally misspelled words which are otherwise consistently spelled correctly), and when needed, I have added a note of explanation. Consistent misspellings of the same word, which suggest intent, have been left in. I have also made no attempt to correct irregularities and inconsistencies in style; [*sic*] indicates the few passages in which missing words and casual punctuation interrupt the flow of text or raise questions about meaning.

Slavery in the Clover Bottoms

By

John H. McCline

with
Introduction
by

H. J. Hagerman

INTRODUCTION

BY

H. J. HAGERMAN

As this is written, in September, 1934, McCline is still with me. Not only that, but doing his daily tasks—actively, well, and with great good nature. He says he does not know just how old he is, but as, according to his memoirs, he was about ten years old in 1861, he must be eighty-three, or thereabouts, now. But you wouldn't suspect it.

Recently, at breakfast, he said to me, when serving a dish of his excellent hot cakes: "Mr. Bert, would it be perfectly all right should I take a day off tomorrow in celebration of a certain event?"

"Of course, Mac. But of what event? Is it a wedding anniversary?"

"No, Mr. Bert. Weddings now are but mere incidents in my recollection. But forty-two years ago tomorrow, I entered your employ."

Thinking back over it, it was, sure enough, forty-two years,—1892. Since then he has been for most of the time with me or some of my family.

At that time we lived in Colorado Springs, my father having moved there for his health a few years before, after an active business career in the East. He was then fairly opulent for those days; interested in mines, railroads, irrigation projects, and other enterprises. In 1892, I was still a student at Cornell University, but returned with a degree or two in 1895, and went into a law office.

Colorado Springs was charming in those days. No automobiles, not many tourists, few fences on the prairies to interfere with riding, nice people who liked each other and, also, liked horses.

My father built a big pink stone house on Cascade Avenue. (Now it is a swanky apartment house. Oh horrors! Why should so many old mansions have such a fate?) Mac had charge of the stable. He came to us from a riding-horse stable where he had been trying to make a go of it with a colored partner. His partner's sense of values wasn't all it should have been, as I remember. So Mac was glad to come to us.

How he loved his horses! He still talks of them now and then,—of Esther, Dick,

Joe and Harry, Jupiter and Mars. Joe and Harry, which belonged to my brother and to me, we both rode and drove. They were a wonderful little pair. I shall never forget how, when returning one night from Manitou, with Joe and Harry hitched to our pretty yellow and black four wheeler, a man driving down the wrong side of the street, evidently somewhat uncertain of himself for some reason or other, ran head on into us and pierced Harry's chest cruelly with the shaft of his buggy. Poor Harry gave an awful shriek, and bolted. When we got him back to the stable, Mac was heart broken and nursed the animal for weeks as he would a child. But Harry was never much good afterwards.

The driver of the catapulting rig, was, as it turned out, Major Llewelyn, of Las Cruces, New Mexico. That was before San Juan Hill and the Spanish War. I was destined to again run into the Major later in my checkered career, in a somewhat different manner. But that is another story.[1]

Quite accidentally and unsuspectingly, in July, 1898, I was appointed, through Senator Wallcot,[2] Second Secretary of the American Embassy in Russia. I stayed for nearly three years in St. Petersburg in that position. My first chief there, Ethan Allen Hitchcock, of St. Louis,—a grand old man,—was appointed Secretary of the

James John Hagerman mansion on Cascade Avenue in Colorado Springs. Courtesy of the Hagerman Family Archives.

Interior, by President McKinley. When McKinley was killed,[3] Mr. Hitchcock continued for a time in the same position, under Theodore Roosevelt.

Russia, in those days of the last Czar, was fascinating, brilliant and sad.[4] There was a lot going on in the Embassy due to the Spanish War, the Boer War, the open door in China, and much else. I had to resign and come home, in 1901, as my father's affairs were going badly. No one without a pretty good income can serve Uncle Sam as a diplomat. So I returned, and went to live in the Pecos Valley, in New Mexico, where my father had ranches, railroads, etc., the remnants of big investments. I lived there until 1906. We had cattle and sheep, with much ranch land; also apple, alfalfa, and other irrigated farms; all very interesting and absorbing, but quite unprofitable except for the middlemen and bankers.

John McCline at the home of Percy Hagerman, the brother of Herbert J. Hagerman, at 1306 Wood Avenue in Colorado Springs, ca. 1903. The child with McCline is Percy Hagerman's son Lowry. Courtesy of the Rio Grande Historical Collections, New Mexico State University Library.

During these years Mac had still been with the family in Colorado Springs. He never came to the ranch.

In 1906, quite suddenly again, and at the instance of Secretary Hitchcock, I was appointed by Roosevelt, Territorial Governor of New Mexico, "to clean the rascals out." I went to Santa Fe, and did so. Also a number of other things, which I think were more or less helpful. As was inevitable, some of those who disapproved of these proceedings got the President's ear, and started a big row.[5] This was especially true of Major Llewelyn, by that time an ex-roughrider, and very close to the Colonel's heart.[6] The President was very indignant when the flying chips hit the Major.

This was all pretty strenuous and a little disheartening. But during the year or so I was on that job, we (Mac and I) had a lot of fun.

The "Palace of the Governors", on the plaza, where the governors—Spanish, Mexican and American, had functioned for some hundreds of years, had just about that time been turned into a museum. As Mac remarked, "It has the most extensive display of governor's portraits of any public building in the United States."

The new executive mansion had not been built, so I got a little old house near the palace, built and formerly used as an officer's residence when Santa Fe was a military post, fixed it up, and lived there. Being single, I didn't require much room.

Mac came down from Colorado. I gave him a dress suit and installed him as "major domo" of this simple gubernatorial establishment. He was really delighted. He took the matter fairly seriously and did fine. Some of the statesmen and politicians fussed him a bit at first; but, in spite of the fact that horses, whose processes of thought and action are fairly reliable, had been his chief companions for a great many years, he succeeded in adapting himself quite admirably to his new environment and duties. I had a pretty good cook. At official dinners where the seating, especially of the "Ex's" and their wives was almost as confusing as at the embassy in St. Petersburg, Mac shone.

Before the first of these functions which I prepared for with a great deal of trepidation, I had told him to "announce" dinner when all the guests were there. He did so. Standing erect, his hand at military salute, he intoned slowly and impressively: "Your Excellency, ladies and gentlemen, dinner is announced!" I asked him afterwards where he got "Your Excellency." He said, as I remember, that he had read that in colonial times, governors were so addressed, and, even now occasionally—and that while it was a custom more honored in the breach than the observance, it was, one, he thought, which should be respected—especially in so old and historic a setting as Santa Fe.

Mac observed everything pretty carefully at that first official dinner.

Before the next one, I called him and discussed details with him. "Quite all right, Mr. Bert. But will it be with or without the finger bowls?" In explanation of this query, he added, that some of the gentlemen at the first dinner didn't seem to like the contents of the bowls.

Mac was always deeply interested in what was going on during these strenuous

Home of Gov. Herbert J. Hagerman on Lincoln Avenue in Santa Fe, New Mexico, 1906. Courtesy of the Rio Grande Historical Collections, New Mexico State University Library.

H. J. Hagerman at the governor's residence in Santa Fe, 1906. Courtesy of the Rio Grande Historical Collections, New Mexico State University Library.

days that filled my term as Governor. I often found him clipping news papers,—
"making history," as he called it. He always seemed to maintain a very philosophic
and discreet attitude about politics and government. When Major Llewelyn and
his friends "poured poison" in the President's ear and got me out, Mac was pretty
indignant.

For some years after this gubernatorial incident, I was again engaged in the
ranching business at Roswell; but, as President of the Tax Payers Association of
New Mexico, was often in Santa Fe, where I quite frequently saw Mac, who had a
good job which gave him quite a bit of leisure time.[7] In those days he started writing
his Memoirs, a process which, in his case, was naturally a pretty slow one.[8]

Again, in 1923, (one never learns by experience) I took another government job;
this time in the Indian Service, principally with the Navajos, and as a member of
the Pueblo Lands Board.[9] This took me again to Santa Fe. I got a little house, and
Mac came back to me again to take care of it. He has been with me ever since.

Mac acquired a little house of his own in Santa Fe, which he occupies, but every day he rides a bicycle to my place. There is a little lawn on two sides of my small
house, about the finest in town,—not a dandelion or weed in it. The neighbors
have become so imbued with Mac's lawn technic [sic] that they have emulated him,
much to the advantage of the immediate vicinity.

This Indian business, with the Navajos, Pimas, Papagoes, Pueblos, Apaches,
Walapi's,[10] was fascinating and absorbing, and kept me on the go in New Mexico
and Arizona for years; so I was away from Santa Fe much of the time, either working in the field, or in Washington wrestling with the Bureaus. But the little house,
under Mac's care, was always ready, and always spick-and-span. The Indian job
lasted about nine years, and was a most important one. I practically took charge
of the whole region. It ended, as do all Indian jobs, in another big row, with sena-
torial investigations and all that sort of thing. The Indian question has always been,
and always will be, the principal indoor sport of a lot of zealous and devoted
people. It will never be settled, for, if it were, a prolific source of eager controversy
would be dried up, a consummation however devotedly to be wished for—scarcely
conceivable. However, we accomplished a good deal during those years, and the
work we began is being carried on.

Mac was always discretely curious after my raids into the Indian country, or my
skirmishes in Washington. He always read the newspaper dispatches very carefully
during the worst of these troubles, but never referred to them except in a casual
and incidental way. He never seemed to think very highly of the Indians, and occasionally intimated that he thought they were being pampered a bit too much,
probably to their injury. A good many others are now of that opinion, what with
the many millions being spent on them. Mac finds the Mexicans more sympathetic
than the Indians. That is interesting in a Negro.

Mac is the Dean and advisor of the Negroes in Santa Fe. There are not many of
them here, or elsewhere in New Mexico, where their position, because of the Span-
ish-Americans and Mexicans, is not so very easy. He feels it quite keenly when any

of the colored colony here misbehave; and it must be said that they rarely do. There is a club which I understand, under his leadership, occupies itself more with religious philosophical and literary discussions, and an occasional picnic, than with politics.[11]

Mac is very fond of base ball, and never misses a game here if he can help it. He also has a little garden at the back of his house. He is not married. A colored pair live with him. The husband, a well-known barber of Santa Fe, and the wife a cook. They help him to take care of his little place. His one adventure into matrimony during his life, was not, I infer, very fortunate, though, on the few occasions when he has mentioned the incident, it was without rancor, and, indeed with a laugh.[12]

John McCline at H. J. Hagerman's Hillside Avenue home in Santa Fe, 1934. Courtesy of the Rio Grande Historical Collections, New Mexico State University Library.

This history, with its title "Slavery in the Clover Bottoms", dealing with his boy-hood life as a slave, and his youthful adventures as a muleteer and mess servant in the Civil War, is printed just as he handed it to me in manuscript, except for a few changes in punctuation and arrangement. The even tenor of the narrative seems to make incidents such as the killing of the slave, Austin, by the over-seer, Phillips; the march into Chattanooga of the starved and ragged soldiers after the battle of Lookout Mountain, all the more dramatic. The manuscript which cover [sic] some 300 pages, all in his own hand-writing, he first showed me some four years ago; but I was then so busied with Indian matters that I failed to appreciate the rather unusual document. Since then, however, I have read it carefully a num-ber of times, and find that in spite of certain monotonies and repetitions and, no doubt, inaccuracies, it holds my attention in a rather strange manner. It certainly seems to me worth preserving; and perhaps has some historical value.

The very fact that there is here, and now, in 1934, in the little city of Santa Fe, itself so saturated with history, a man living and puttering about in his daily tasks, cheerful and respectful; and in full possession of his memory—a man who was actually born and lived the life of a slave on a typical southern plantation—and then, nearly seventy years ago, participated in his humble way in great battles of the Civil War, and in Sherman's march to the sea, observing closely great events and insignificant events, that are now history—all this is, in a way, intriguing in the extreme. It makes one forget for the moment one's own complications, even the stupendous happenings of the last fifty years. For the moment it makes one forget time and trouble.

The last brief section of this little book, dealing with Mac's history after the war, is a compilation of things written by him at my request, and of talks with him, but all, too, in his own language, without much, if any promptings of any kind from me.

I thought the reader would be curious about his subsequent career. While the main narrative was written some years ago, this last chapter was compiled recently.

He is an unusual character, cheerful and optimistic, always curious and inter-ested in what is going on around him, not overly affected by rank and position. He has always found life worth living, quite amusing and worth while, and is, on the whole, quite a philosopher as well as a keen observer.

I

⚭

BEFORE THE WAR

THE HOGGATT PLANTATION

Dr. James Hoggatt was considered the richest man in Davidson County. He owned three splendid plantations and a hundred slaves on each of them. His sugar cane plantation in the State of Louisiana was doubtless his best paying property from a financial standpoint.[1] His farm at Murfreesboro was devoted chiefly to the raising of cotton. This fine estate of two thousand acres adjoined the Town of Slipup, eight miles west[2] of the City of Nashville, on the Lebanon Pike, and was known the country over as "Clover Bottoms", the Doctor's permanent residence. The house was splendidly built, a three-story brick of colonial style, and situated on a slight knoll perhaps a quarter of a mile from the pike. There were beautiful gravel drives running through the estate amply shaded by many varieties of trees. The view of the house from the pike was impressive. There were two ways of approach. The main entrance for friends and distinguished visitors, was from the north and through highly ornamented gates, the huge posts of which were capped by great round balls.[3]

On leaving their carriage, the visitors would walk up five white stone steps to the front door and ring the bell, which would be promptly answered.

The other route to the house from the pike was a wide dirt road, or lane, as it was commonly called, which ran southeast, clear across the place. A wide covered porch, the entire length of the house on the east side, and beautifully ornamented brick floors with many chairs and rustic seats scattered about. This was one of the most delightful features of the great house.

Dr. Hoggatt was a typical southern gentleman and, at the beginning of this history, about fifty years old. He was tall, slender, well educated, coming as he did from an old and distinguished family of that name. Smooth shaven, except for mere earlocks, faultlessly dressed in a suit of black broadcloth, he might easily have been mistaken for a minister of the gospel. Being a late sleeper he seldom appeared out of doors before ten o'clock in the morning. To see him at that hour, an awe inspiring figure strolling leisurely about the grounds of his beautiful and handsome estate, he seemed happy and contented. Though a regular physician, to the best of my knowledge he did not practice medicine outside of his family. His use of tobacco was confined exclusively to the pipe. The pipe of that date was a small affair, made of bright yellow clay with a long, thin cane stem, perhaps a foot and a half in length. His time for smoking was usually after meals, and the place,— comfortably seated on the long porch; and as matches were not then in use, he would ring for a servant who, when told what was wanted, would soon return with a red-hot coal of fire between a pair of bright brass tongs, taken from the fire place, the fire in which was never allowed to go out.

The Doctor's immediate family consisted of himself, his wife, and two nieces.

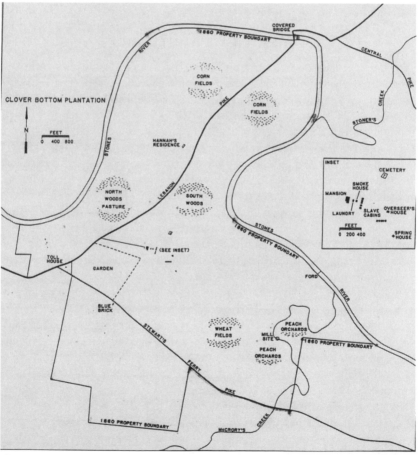

Clover Bottom Plantation in 1860. Courtesy of Steve Rogers, historic preservation specialist at the Tennessee Historical Commission.

Mrs. Hoggatt was a stout, handsome woman, about forty years old, and in appearance and action was much younger than her distinguished husband.[4] She was the most energetic and business like woman I have ever seen. While her personal interest on the great farms was confined chiefly to her fifty-eight acre garden and a dairy with forty milk cows, nothing on the place escaped her attention. She was an early riser and saw to it that the eight women who milked the cows, and as many boy assistants, were also on the job. A rough raw hide whip, three feet long with wrist band attached, was always in evidence and used unsparingly. When she struck one over the shoulders there was a stinging and lasting impression one never forgot.

The two nieces, Miss Emma and Miss Delia Gentry were sisters, ages seventeen

Mrs. Hoggatt, head of the household at Clover Bottom plantation. Courtesy of the Friends of Rock Castle and Steve Rogers, historic preservation specialist at the Tennessee Historical Commission.

and fifteen, respectively.[5] They attended a boarding school in the city of Nashville where they were taken by their aunt, in the family carriage, on Monday morning, and returned Friday afternoon. Miss Emma was of the dark type of southern beauty, with a splendid head of dark brown chestnut hair, beautiful large blue eyes, round plump cheeks, and a small mouth. She had many suitors, fine looking young men, and apparently men of wealth. They came, some in buggies and some on horse back, driving and riding the best of horses. Miss Delia, the younger sister was slightly inclined to stoutness, like her aunt, with plenty of light brown hair and rosy cheeks.

The Hoggatt plantation lay in the circle of Stones River, was bounded on the west by the Murfreesboro pike and on the south by the river.[6]

1871 topographic map of the Clover Bottom area. Courtesy of Steve Rogers, historic preservation specialist at the Tennessee Historical Commission.

NAMES OF SLAVE OWNERS.	Number of Slaves	Age	Sex	Color	Fugitives from the State	Number manumitted	Deaf & dumb, blind, insane, or idiotic.	NAMES OF SLAVE OWNERS.	Number of Slaves	Age	Sex	Color	Fugitives from the State
1	2	3	4	5	6	7	8	1	2	3	4	5	6
	1	14	m	B					1	27	F	B	
	1	25	m	B					1	16	F	B	
	1	10	m	mu			12		1	10	m	B	
James W Hoggatt	1	90	F	B					1	1	m	B	
	1	30	m	B					1	68	m	B	
	1	17	m	B					1	17	m	B	
	1	13	m	B					1	60	F	B	
	1	11	m	B					1	25	m	B	
	1	8	m	mu					1	35	F	B	
	1	42	F	mu					1	16	F	B	
	1	61	m	mu					1	16	m	B	
	1	33	m	B					1	60	m	B	
	1	27	F	B					1	22	m	B	
	1	6	m	mu					1	19	F	B	
	1	23	m	B					1	25	m	B	
	1	25	F	B					1	26	F	B	
	1	18	m	B					1	4	m	B	
	1	8	m	B					1	2	m	B	
	1	6	m	B					1	48	m	B	
	1	6	m	B					1	17	F	B	
	1	77	m	B					1	10	F	B	
	1	14	m	B					1	60	F	B	
	1	27	m	B				Wm B Lewis	1	80	m	B	
	1	27	m	B					1	55	m	B	
	1	22	F	B					1	44	m	B	
	1	2	F	B					1	70	m	B	
	1	1	F	B					1	57	m	B	
	1	17	F	B					1	34	m	B	
	1	23	m	B					1	28	m	B	
	1	41	m	B					1	23	m	B	
	1	25	F	B					1	22	m	B	
	1	12	m	B					1	28	m	B	
	1	9	F	B					1	28	m	B	
	1	22	m	B					1	26	m	m	
	1	23	F	B					1	12	m	m	
	1	3	F	B					1	27	m	B	
	1	13	F	B					1	27	m	B	
	1	1	F	B					1	10	m	B	
	1	31	F	B					1	10	m	B	
	1	22	F	B					1	12	F	B	

1860 slave census showing James Hoggatt's chattel property.

The great farm lay on both sides of the Lebanon pike. The pike entered the farm after passing through the toll gate at Slipup, then following its course, southwest for two miles, reached the boundary of the plantation at a long covered bridge which crosses the river at this point.[7] The hundred or more acres laying on each side of the pike, and on the river point were low and flat; and when the river overflowed its banks every Spring, this land was well fertilized. Corn being one of the chief products of the farm, was usually planted on these tracts.

The plantation was one of the best appointed and conducted in the state. There were a hundred slaves, and a thousand acres in cultivation.[8] The balance of the estate being pasture for grazing purposes. Stock of every kind, horses, mules, cattle, hogs, and sheep were plentiful.

Large slave owners, like Dr. Hoggatt, rarely speculated or dealt in slaves as a matter of profit. He never sold a woman, and if he disposed of a man by sale, it was because of some offense. It was the average poor and cheap farmer, with a few slaves acquired either by inheritance or shrewd dealing, who bartered in slaves and were always on hand at the auction block.[9]

MULES AND HOGS

One of the greatest and most easily marketed staple products of the large plantations of that date were the mules. The Doctor's chief hobby was the raising of mules. He owned the finest jack in Davidson County, and fifty brood mares. And from this source alone he realized a large profit. Every two years a hundred fine mules were sent to the Nashville market where there was a ready sale for them. The men on the place who thoroughly understood the business, would roach their tails and manes, and when they were sent to Nashville they were good to look at. There was a ready sale for them in Nashville, and they were usually bought by men for the states further south, where they were shipped by steamboat.

There were three mills on the place: a grist mill, a saw mill, and a gin mill; all operated in times of need. There were also, a carpenter shop, and a blacksmith shop, so that any ordinary building might be up and repaired by the slaves on the place.

The over-seer, Mr. James Anderson, was a good one,—kind, considerate, and well educated, and did no whipping. During his two years stay on the place the colored people were perfectly happy and there seemed to be no appearance of the existence of slavery.

Five hundred hogs and many cattle were fattened and killed every year, and the big smoke house was always well filled with curing meats for summer use. The hog killing season, the cold, frosty days of December, generally before Christmas, was a great event on the Hoggatt place. Three huge kettles set on a rock foundation, were filled with water, and fires were built under them. Great fat hogs were killed in a pen nearby and dragged to the kettles in which they were dipped to start the bristles, then quickly taken out, when several men with keen sharp knives, would scrape them until they were white. Then fifteen women, Grandmother Hanna, the oldest in experience, at their head, would be on hand with sharp knives and tubs, ready to scrape the lard from the guts. This was given to them. Also the chittlings, [*sic*] which they cleaned thoroughly and put away in jars. Mrs. Hoggatt was always on hand at these eventful times to look after the heavy leaf lard which was hers exclusively. She saw to it that it was carefully tried, strained and put away ready for the Nashville market. When the men had cut up the hogs, the hams, shoulders, sides of bacon, and all the largest parts laid aside for salting, there were hundreds of pounds of small scraps left over. These were also given to the women, and out of these the finest of sausages were made.

Many of these fine hogs dressed whole,—wagon loads of them, were sent to the market where they found a ready sale.

The smoke house, a substantial brick building forty feet long by thirty feet wide, stood perhaps 150 feet south of the main residence, which was commonly called the "White House."[10] Here the great number of hams, bacon, shoulders, were hung up, cured and smoked. For this purpose corn cobs and hickory chips were used.

A NEW OVER-SEER

The spring of 1858 was a sad and unhappy time for the colored people of the Hoggatt place. Mr. Anderson, the best over-seer resigned. He married Miss McRidley of an adjoining plantation and left the county. He was succeeded by one William Phillips—brutal, ignorant, and a perfect type of the poor white trash of that time.[11] His wife, a tall, thin, light haired creature, had a good education; and with some knowledge of medicine, was quite useful to the women on the place. The house, sparely furnished, which was occupied by the Phillips, was a large two-story frame building with a long covered porch on the north side. There was one large room on the second floor, facing south, containing two windows and one door. This room was used occasionally as a sort of jail where run-a-ways might be temporarily confined. Another large room on the first floor was used as a spinning room. Here the women who had young babies to nurse, were engaged with their spinning wheels, turning cotton, and sometimes wool, into thread for knitting and other purposes. The process of getting the wool into shape before it could be spun was a slow and tedious one. After it had been thoroughly washed and dried the women would take it between two hand cards and comb it out into a flat mass, then roll it into a rope like shape, when it would be ready for spinning.

The new over-seer brought with him, as evidence of the new reign of terror which was soon to begin, one of the largest and most vicious blood hounds I have even seen. He was a yellow, smooth skinned type; and only a little urging was necessary from his master to make him tear a man to pieces. Among his other instruments of torture was a ball and chain with band attached, to fit around the ankle. A pair of handcuffs, a double barreled shot gun, and a black snake whip that measured seven feet in length, the butt or handle, contained a pound of lead. This was of course for the purpose of knocking a man down should occasion arise.

Every man and woman on the place had special work laid out and was expected to do it or be punished. Stephen was head carpenter, also miller, with Austin as his assistant. Abe was the blacksmith. Daniel the painter. Uncle Jordan the head gardener. Wyatt in charge of the jack. The general work on the farm, such as planting, cultivating, looking after the stock, was attended by fifteen men, with David as the head. Just south of the White house was a beautiful strip of level land, containing about fifty acres and separated from the lawn around by the house by a high picket fence. This fine piece of land was Mistress Hoggatt's garden spot. The extreme south end lay along the Stewart's Ferry pike, and about ten acres of the plot were devoted to early apples and strawberries. All the women, and children large enough to handle a hoe or pull weeds, were used exclusively in the garden.[12]

VEGETABLES AND MILK

In the summer and vegetable season, a covered spring wagon, called a "carry all", drawn by two mules and driven by Richard, left the house every morning at four o'clock, loaded with all the delicacies of the season, and was taken to the Nashville market. Richard always made the sale and brought back the cash to the Mistress, which was in silver, carried in a sack. As this was the only kind of money I had ever seen, I naturally supposed it was the only kind of money in use. The fact was, the laws of the State of Tennessee at that time forbade the use or circulation of any other kind of money amongst the slaves, as they were not supposed to be educated, and hence were not supposed to know paper money or gold in denominations greater than $1.00.

In connection with the large profits secured from her garden Mrs. Hoggatt had also forty cows, milked by eight women and with four boys to care for the calves. The churning was done twice a week in three enormous churns used for the purpose. During the summer months milking began at five o'clock in the morning, and many times our lady, not fully dressed, her brown hair sprinkled with grey streaming down her back, with keys and wicked raw hide whip in hand, would appear on the scene. Four large cedar tubs with bright brass hoops around them, were placed on a wide board table in a corner of the fence, and into these the women strained the milk. Each woman used what is called in the South, a "piggin", to milk in, made also of cedar and having only one handle on the side and which would hold about a gallon. They were kept scrupulously clean and scoured until the hoops were bright as gold.

When Mistress Hoggatt appeared in a cow pen in the manner above stated, something was wrong, real or fancied, and some body would have to suffer. The first thing she would do on entering the cow pen would be to go and look into the tubs and see if the amount of milk was above or below the average; then she would go to Aunt Hanna, the head woman in the pen, and complain that the cows were doing poorly for this time of the year. The pasture into which the cows fed during

Extant slave cabins at Clover Bottom plantation, ca. 1920. Courtesy of Steve Rogers, historic preservation specialist at the Tennessee Historical Commission.

the day was fine, and they were not fed when driven out at night, nor in the morning before going to pasture. Mrs. Hoggatt, of course, did not know that this made a great difference with a milk cow, or that there was bound to be a lot less milk at the morning milking.

Every woman and boy in the pen was in mortal fear of her and no one knew when he or she would get a whack from the raw hide. Being strong and powerful, she never struck that she did not leave a mark, and it was quite natural, therefore, that every one kept out of her way as much as possible. She was never without her whip, in fact it was always in evidence and as much a part of her being as her pink sun bonnet.

Until the coming of Phillips, the spring of 1858, the colored people lived in cabins and houses promiscuously scattered about the place. Entertainments like quilting bees and dances, where people from the adjoining plantations might be invited, were permitted. In this he made a radical change. He said there was too much liberty amongst the slaves which would lead to a spirit of unrest. In the fall of that year, after the crops had been gathered and put away, two rows of cabins, ten in each row were planned and built. They were good frame houses, of one room each, the lumber of which they were built having been taken from the forests on the place. Each house had one big wide door which closed with a hook. The first row of ten were built just east of and within calling distance of the "White House." These were occupied by all of the servants engaged therein. The second row was erected some distance away, and west of the over-seer's house, and was used for the farm hands.[13] The beds used in these houses were the regular four poster kind, and were made by the carpenters on the place. The houses were whitewashed inside and out twice a year, and had a neat and comfortable appearance. Each had its twenty foot front yard space which was kept clean by sweeping. Mrs. Phillips looked after these, also the occupants, if any were sick. In some of them there was evidence of taste and means, but as this was not her affair she did not meddle or concern herself about it. The floors were thoroughly scrubbed with soft soap and water once a week, and were nice and clean on Sunday. When two houses stood close together one chimney would serve the purpose of each, each having a huge brick place. A large pot hook hung in each fire place so that cooking could be done with some degree of convenience. All had the usual dutch oven with cover attached, for baking purposes.[14]

THE LEBANON PIKE

The Lebanon pike, thirty miles in length, extending from Nashville, the capital of the state, and county seat of Davidson county, to Lebanon, the county seat of Wilson county, was the best known and most generally traveled in the state. Many of the richest plantation owners lived along this course. Lebanon, though a small village, was a place of considerable importance because it was the home of the Cumberland University, one of the chief educational centers at that time. The pike was a macadamized road, and the planters along its route kept it up to the highest point of efficiency. There were six toll gates and, owing to the heavy travel, a large revenue was raised from this source. As a rule, each toll gate was in charge of a man and his wife who occupied a house near by, furnished by the Pike Company. They were usually built close to the gate, with a long porch attached, so travelers might hand their fare to the keeper without leaving their vehicle. The regular fare from gate to gate, the distance being six miles, was ten cents for a person on horseback or a single horse and buggy. A person on foot paid nothing.

Two stages passed over the pike daily carrying the mail from Nashville to Lebanon, and many passengers. A good deal of heavy traffic, farm produce of every description hauled in great covered wagons and drawn by two to six mules, was also a daily occurrence.

MCCLINE'S FAMILY

I, John H. McCline, at the beginning of this history was about ten years old.[15] My mother died when I was two years old, leaving a daughter and four boys, I being the youngest of the family. Our sister, who I do not remember, died at an early age. The four boys, Richard, Jefferson, Armstead, and myself, were brought up by Grandmother Hanna, and all reached manhood estate. Jack McCline was our father, and belonged to one James Smith, living at Silver Springs in Wilson County. As early as I can remember, grandmother lived in a two-story frame house on the north side of the pike, and about a mile from the river.[16]

Buck, the shoemaker, and Betsy, his wife, and his son Frank, lived on the top floor. Frank and myself were chums, spending most of our time in and about the house carrying wood, water, and doing various kinds of work between milking times when we had to be busy keeping the calves away.

A FUGITIVE SLAVE

There were perhaps twenty acres of fine land around this house, and in those times it was planted in corn. It was early in the month of May, that a slave ran away from the Dotson place, five miles north of us and came to our house.[17] He was a friend of Buck's who took him in. He was concealed here for about ten days when his master got news of his whereabouts. It was one Sunday morning between ten and eleven o'clock, that six men, preceded by several blood hounds, rode up to the house and dismounted. Frank and myself were asked to hold their horses, and we did so, little knowing the object of their call. They drew their pistols, entered the west door leading into the main hall. Buck who had seen them approaching the house, from his window, realized their intention, and got his friend down stairs into the big front room facing the pike, and hid him in the fire place until the hunters had passed through and up the stairs, when he came out and made good his escape. The hunters in the meantime searched the house from top to bottom, and finally mounted their horses and rode away. There was a great deal of excitement which lasted for many months, caused by this incident. Late in the afternoon of the same day master sent for Buck to explain why he had harbored a run-a-way slave in his house, contrary to the laws of the state and the rules of his master. Now, Buck had never been whipped. He was a good shoemaker, and was the only one on the place that could read. He well knew the reason he was sent for. Rather than suffer the disgrace and the cruel whipping which he was sure to get, he ran away. A large reward was offered for his capture, and the poor whites whose main existence depended on this kind of employment, were in hot pursuit, scouring the country for miles around. They were, however, unable to apprehend him.

The corn fields along either side of the pike and along the river bank were beautiful in the extreme. The rows, which were a good half mile in width and perfectly straight, were the admiration of the traveling public. Wheat fields of more than a hundred acres, were situated about a mile southeast of the White House and along the Stewart's Ferry pike. As much of these was new ground, and too rough for the reapers, it had to be cut with the scythe and cradle. These things were crude and heavy, and required strong-armed steady men to handle them.

CORN HUSKING

The greatest event on a plantation like the Hoggatt place, and the one most enjoyed by the colored people, was the corn husking bees which were in vogue on beautiful nights. The method of cutting the corn in those days was to first go through and pull the leaves off the stalks and tie them in bundles, commonly called, pulling fodder. Then the corn was left to season and dry on the stalks. Later, in the month of September, it was pulled off the stalks, hauled and piled up in front of an immense crib where it was husked and thrown in. On the night when the shucking is to begin, fifty men, or more, women and many visitors from neighboring places would join in. Some one would start a song familiar to all present, and the good work would go on until twelve o'clock, when all would stop and adjourn to one·of the largest cabins where supper would be served. The supper was eaten with a relish, and the merriment wound up, as a rule, with a dance engaged in and enjoyed by all. Vann played the fiddle with dexterity and enthusiasm, and was assisted by Abe, with the banjo.

A NEW JOB

When Phillips came, my brother Jeff, who was then a cow boy, was taken into the White House as a waiter. Before entering upon my new duties as his successor, I had to report at the Phillips house every night for a week or so and take lessons in counting by Mrs. Phillips, who taught me to count from one to a hundred. When I qualified for my new job I was given a fine black mule to ride, named "Nell"; and early every morning I would drive the forty cows into two separate pens, where they were milked by eight women. After the milking, I would get my breakfast and, astride Nell's back, I would drive them to a large pasture two or three miles from the house. Here I left them to graze and feed at will until four o'clock in the afternoon, when I would return for them. Returning to the house after taking the cows to the pasture, I would hitch Nell to a cart on which was arranged a barrel, and with this I would haul water from a spring, a quarter of a mile from the house, for cooking, drinking, and other purposes. It took many barrels to fill the big tank that stood near the kitchen door, usually taking me until noon, when I would unhitch, feed Nell, go to grandmother's and get my dinner. My next important duty would be to take the men's dinner to them in the field—that is if they happened to be working a good ways from the house, as was frequently the case. To say that I was proud of my new job, can hardly express the pleasure I had in it. The fact that I was able to ride and drive a mule made me feel like a man, for it seemed to me that I was doing a man's work. Then, too, I was glad to get away from the house and grandmother who was forever calling for a bucket of water, a basket of chips, or a little sweeping to be done. All these domestic duties I had grown heartily tired and ashamed of because they seemed to me to belong to the other sex. Many times I had to drive the cows along the pike in order to reach distant pastures. This was a great delight to me because I could see new farms in the various new vehicles [sic], and the great traveling world—men on horse-back, heavy covered wagons drawn by two to six mules, were always a curiosity to me.

It is strange about cows—they have a sense peculiarly their own. It is characteristic of the women to give each cow a name. For instance, the bell cow was named

"Cherry", and the fact that she wore a bell gave her a feeling of importance or authority. When I drove them out in the morning she always took the lead, and with her head well up, she would move along with cow-like grace that was pleasing to behold. I had been on the job about a month, bringing them up on time without a hitch or complaint from Mistress or the over-seer. Naturally I began to feel a sort of security and independence in my new job. For about ten days I had been taking them into the North woods pasture across the pike, where they had a much larger range. It is rather precipitous along the river bank. No fence, and only an occasional path where they went down to drink. When I went for them I found them quite a ways from the pike and feeding quietly near the river. Several had been down to the rock-bedded stream to drink, and were returning, walking leisurely along the winding path from the stream below. I got them together and counted them several times but on this occasion could only make out thirty-nine. One was missing, that was certain. And which one it was I was entirely at a loss to know. After a vigorous search through the woods for more than an hour, without result, I drove the others home, worried and very much frightened. I reported the missing cow. The next morning, after I had driven them out to pasture, I returned and was crossing the lane to the stable to hitch up Nell to the cart. I met the over-seer. He walked up to me and grabbed me back of the collar, told me to stick my head between his legs. He was introducing, for the first time on the Hoggatt place, his brutal method of punishing small boys. After he had my head clasped between his knees he unbuttoned my trousers, pulled up my shirt, and with a keen raw hide three feet long, gave me a whipping on my bare back. That night when I went home and told grandmother, she took me in her arms and cried a long time, then bathed my poor aching back with water, soothed it with some kind of liniment, and put me to bed.

The churning was done on the porch of the laundry, the two-story brick building east of the kitchen in the White House and just across the driveway from the smoke-house. The churns were three great monstrous things, as big as a barrel, requiring a good deal of strength to move them; and twice a week, Jeff, Frank and myself, would report at nine in the morning; and on these fateful days, after Betsy had put long clean white aprons on each of us, we would proceed with our heavy job of churning. Mistress was always nosing around after we got started, and we were in mortal fear of her and that whip of hers. We would raise those heavy dashers with a vim that was painful to behold. She called me an impudent rascal once, without cause or provocation. I had no idea of its meaning, and am certain now that she did not. Never in my life was I impertinent to her. In the first place, I did not know how to be impertinent, and would have been afraid had I known. It was one morning while working in the garden that I heard the term for the first time. She had given me a garden tool, called a grubbing hoe, and told me to dig up a small hotbed near by. I have never done any work of this kind and, naturally, did not know how to go at it. Being stout and strong, she took the hoe from me and dug with perfect ease. She handed the hoe back to me and said: "Now do it just like that." I took the hoe, which seemed dreadfully heavy, and began to work. For the life of me I could not do it just as she did, and she became furious. She had in her hand a stick about three feet long and the size of a broom handle. She gritted her teeth and, while I was stooping over, she snapped out: "You impertinent rascal", and struck me a smart blow on the back and I fell as flat on the ground as if I had been shot.[18] She then left me and went to another part of the garden. I got up and began digging the best I knew how.

CHRISTMAS CHEER

It was now Christmas time. Time of good cheer, Peace on Earth, Good Will to all men. But little did we know of its real meaning—its good intentions. Of the hundred black souls on the place, I don't believe there was one who had ever heard of Santa Claus. The entire week was given us, and we certainly enjoyed it. At this time every man on the place was given a suit of clothes, consisting of coat, shirt, a pair of trousers, and a pair of shoes. The cloth of which the suits were made, was of cotton grown on the Murfreesboro farm and spun on the looms there. To dispose of the ugly grey of the cloth, it was dyed in the juice obtained from the outer shell of the black walnut, which grew in large quantities on the place. The women, and boys big enough to work out, were also given shoes and cloth enough to make dresses for themselves and their children. The cabins, or quarters, of the people on the place, were seldom visited by either master or mistress unless some one was sick. Neither, therefore knew of the elegance and prosperity displayed in some of them. None of the people were supposed to have money, or to know its use and power. The fact is many of them had some, and spent it in the usual way, just like people who had always enjoyed freedom, liberty, and happiness.[19]

On Christmas morning, each family would receive ten pounds of flour and two pounds of white sugar, called in those days, loaf sugar, which was scarce and considered a luxury. Grandmother usually broke it up in small pieces and issued it out to us boys in the form of candy.

All who cared to were allowed to go to church on the Sabbath Day. There were two churches, the nearest being two miles east of the Hoggatt place. This was a Methodist church. The Baptist church was three miles west of us.

UNCLE SILAS

In the beautiful summer season, when all nature was in its fragrant bloom, and smiling in sweetness from the sassafras and pompom trees, it was a pleasure and surprise to see the people turn out in their Sunday clothes—the men in their suits of broadcloth, and women in their silk dresses, hoop skirts and poke bonnets, so fashionable at that time. Here they were, all dressed in their best clothes, on their best behavior, going to church to worship the living God in spirit and in truth, praying to him for freedom from the cruelties of slavery and its humiliation.

Of the many ministers of the gospel who came to the Baptist Church to unravel the mysteries of the Bible for us, the best known to me and remembered, was the Reverend Silas Jones, called by us "Uncle Silas." He was of medium height, slightly inclined to stoutness, and was perhaps fifty years of age, of a light brown skin, he had keen eyes and a short, full beard sprinkled with grey. He came every fourth Sunday, as was the custom of the time, astride a big bay mule, he called "Maggie." Her gait, so well known to all of us, was a slow pace. As a rule, he reached the neighborhood of the church on Saturday night and put up wherever it was convenient. He had often visited our place and, on two or three occasions, had spent the night at Grandmother's. Many a time have I met him on my way after the cows, and to me he seemed a mystery. He went about with perfect freedom, and I never learned whether he was a slave or a freed man. Whenever we met he was always kind and friendly. Taking my hand in his big one, he was soft and tender, never forgetting to tell me to love and fear the Lord. Beside his Reverence, which old Maggie carried with perfect ease, were the usual heavy and well stuffed saddle bags; one side of which contained the Bible, and the other a clean shirt and perhaps a small bottle, merely for his stomach's sake. The big hickory stick, carried in his right hand, had become worn smooth from constant thumping of the old nag's sides.

One Saturday afternoon I was riding leisurely along the pike, and just before reaching the point where I was to turn in to the pasture for the cows, I stopped and was in conversation with a half dozen men who were repairing the board fence, when Uncle Silas rode up. There was the usual hand shaking all around, and then he questioned each one of them about his family and his sins. And the reports of all were bad enough as to their sins, but he thought they might be worse. He had started off when one Austin, one of the men present, stopped him and asked him if the "Good Book" said anything against chewing tobacco. Now Uncle Silas was a vigorous chewer of the weed himself, but answered hastily, saying: "Certainly. He that is filthy, let him be filthy still," and rode away.

It was now February, 1859, and because of the high winds and a good deal of snow, work for the men out of doors was difficult and unpleasant in the extreme. A good deal of heavy timber had to be cut however, during the winter months, and the great heavy logs had been hauled to the mill to be sawed into lumber. The small and inferior ones had been split and made into rails for the repair of fences. It is characteristic of young mules to be restless, and as they roam about the place a great deal during the winter, it was quite natural that they would be jumping fences from one pasture to another, so the fences had to be built ten rails high, and then stapled.

THE WHITE HOUSE FIRE

It was one bright sunny morning along about the middle of the month, that fire was discovered on the roof of the White House.[20] The alarm was given and every one grabbed a pail, or anything that would hold water, and ran to the big cistern near the kitchen door. Hundreds of people came from the village nearby and helped with a spirit of good will, but the cistern was soon dipped dry; and, as there was not possibility of checking the flames which had gained headway owing to the lack of water, the men were told to go in and bring out such things of value as could be saved without danger to themselves. Nearly all of the oil paintings and chairs from the parlors on the first floor were saved. Dr. and Mrs. Hoggatt's bed rooms were in the basement, and on the north side of the house. His beautiful library and study were situated in the northeast corner of the house. The fine, large dining room and kitchen were on the north side. Miss Emma and Miss Delia, who occupied rooms on the second floor, fortunately were at school and knew nothing of the calamity until the evening when they were notified and arrangements were made for them to remain in the city for a time. The great house was completely gutted. Nothing but the walls and chimney were left standing. About two inches of snow lay on the ground and it was a strange sight indeed to see household furniture of every description scattered about over the snowy lawn.

It was the first time I had ever seen an oil painting. The one which had so particularly attracted my attention, was of a handsome young woman, it was standing on a small bureau and I stood looking at it a long time. What seemed most strange to me was that, no matter which way I turned, the face kept looking at me. Well, I finally walked away with a feeling that there was a lot I had to learn about oil paintings.

Everything was finally removed from the snow covered lawn and temporarily stored in the adjoining houses on the place. Master and Mistress made their home with the Phillips until April, when they went North and remained two months while the house was being rebuilt. The same spot was selected, and most of the old walls, which were found to be firm and in good shape, were used. Many men were employed, most of them white, in the rebuilding of the house. Most of the men were brought from the City of Nashville, and the work went on with great rapidity.

WE HEAR OF JOHN BROWN

News of John Brown and his activities in Kansas and Virginia, was being whispered about at this time.[21] Strange how the people, especially the men, got hold of the fact, which was the cause of so much excitement on the place and in this neighborhood.[22] We boys, always playing around, and eavesdropping, would steal up when we saw three or four men in close conversation. After many close calls of having our ears boxed, for listening, we learned that John Brown's plan was none other than to free the entire Negro race held as slaves in the Southern states. His idea, as we understood it, was that every able bodied man was to provide himself with a gun, pistol, or weapon of some kind, and conceal it until a certain time. The word would be given to organize. They with their weapons were to get in line and march up to the master's door and there demand of him their freedom. If he refused to grant their request, they were to shoot him on the spot and, in a body, escape to the mountains where they would be joined by thousands of others.

Strange and futile as the plan seems to us now, not only the slaves, but the masters themselves, believed in it. Up to this time, and as far as is known, there were only two shot guns on the place,—the one brought by Phillips, and the other used by Stephen to shoot a fattened steer occasionally. But a few weeks later every man on the place had one.

The rapidity with which the plan appealed to them was remarkable. Instead of attending church, as formerly, they were off to the woods in bunches of twos and threes, to practice. Many secret meetings were called by the great plantation owners, like Donaldson, Dotsons, McRidleys, and others. The plan of these secret meetings was brought to light. As a matter of precaution and to prevent any possible surprise or outbreak among the slaves, the masters had decided to organize a company of patrollers whose business it would be to scour the country and pike at night, and apprehend or arrest any negro, or negroes found armed; and if they could not give good account of themselves, they were to be held until the next day, when further inquiry would be made concerning their conduct. As there were many poor whites living in the neighborhood, without work or regular employment, here was a golden opportunity for them. Those who were too poor to furnish a horse, gun and bull whip, were provided with them by the masters within the vicinity where they were to operate. The over-seers on all large plantations were notified by the owners to thoroughly search all cabins and quarters for arms. And if any were found they should immediately confiscate them, and the owners be severely punished.

We were also informed by Phillips that there would be no more night visiting from one plantation to another without a pass from the master or over-seer. Even though armed with a pass, under no consideration were we to have in our possession weapons of any description; and if so caught, a terrible whipping would be the result. As Phillips could neither read nor write, the appeal for a pass was made to his wife, and was readily granted. On nights when no passes were issued, the over-seer would call at all cabins, about eight o'clock, and inquire if all were within; and having satisfied himself, would retire for the night. The patrollers usually went about in parties of two or three, closely watching the lanes and paths leading out to the pike from the cabins.

The young men on the place went about as freely as ever, and doubtless felt that they knew the country too well to be caught off their guard. When they did have passes, they were secured for the purpose of attending a big Saturday night frolic at some of the neighboring plantations and, on such occasions, they usually took the pike, as the patrollers were extremely vigilant on such nights and often went to the place and looked around. When they were halted by the patrollers, they would be asked their names, their owners, and then a demand was made to see their passes; and, all being satisfactory they would be allowed to proceed. The patrollers were also required to visit the cabins once a month; which visits, as a rule, were made late at night; the purpose, of course, being to catch, if possible, the people off their guard.

We boys who had to retire early, were naturally afraid and never dared to venture out of doors after nine o'clock. Late one dark and rainy night, two of these men came to our house. Grandmother was up moving things about, as the roof leaked a little. The one who attracted my attention most, and the first to enter, was a dark complexioned, thick set man, with a full black beard. He wore a broad-brimmed hat, and a red flannel shirt. His long black whip, similar to the one carried by Phillips, was wrapped about his shoulders. On entering, he said "Hello, Granny, what are you doing up so late?"

"Oh, just moving a few things so they won't get wet." There were two cedar chests in the room, sitting on each side of the door. These she used as a sort of bureau in which she kept clean linen, dresses, etc. Into these he plunged, turning everything over from top to bottom. In one of them he found a bottle of whiskey. He took it out, held it to the light, removed the cork, smelt of it, and said, "Dog bite my time, if the old gal aint got some good liquor." Then he took a big drink and passed it to his partner, and went out.

No changes were made in rebuilding the White House. The original architectural plans being carried out in the rebuilding.[23] The beautiful porch, extending the whole length of the house on the east side, still remained. Here many easy chairs and rustic seats were placed, and here, the family spent much of its time. An excellent view of the pike was obtainable from the north end of the porch, and Mistress Hoggatt could witness every move in the garden, from the south end. They were doubtless greatly benefited by their trip North. Many new ideas, which they called "yankee notions", were introduced on the place as soon as practicable. Buckwheat, oyster plant, spinach, and cauliflower, unknown in that country, were planted for the first time in the Clover Bottoms.

Hitherto a good deal of money had been spent for garden seeds in the spring. This plan could now be improved upon by saving and curing the seed right there at home. The carpenters had put up a nice little building, twelve by twenty feet, as a temporary work shop, in the garden just west of the gate. This was to be left standing and used in the future as a seed house.

THE WHITE HOUSE REBUILT

In the fall of 1859, the White House, new, and imposing as ever, had been built. The family moved in, and the work of arranging a lot of new and artistic furniture, including a Grand piano, all of which had been purchased in the North, was finished. In about three weeks a great party was given, to which all the wealthy planters in the country were invited; also many merchants from the city. It was a great event, and the popularity of the "Clover Bottoms" was the talk of Davidson county.

Many changes were made, which seemed necessary at this time. The chief, and first of importance, was the retiring of Richard as the market man. He had served faithfully for many years, in fact had grown old and rheumatic in the service. He was succeeded by an Italian, named Zukervilla, a man forty years old, who had a

Clover Bottom mansion in 1997, restored to original 1859 Italianate style. Courtesy of Steve Rogers and the Tennessee Historical Commission.

large family.[24] Mistress Hoggatt saw in him many advantages over Richard. He was a White man, spoke good English, and could read and write. He naturally, therefore, appealed to her as being better suited for the job of driving bargains in garden products. An old two-story brick that stood in the extreme west corner of the garden was put into perfect repair, and here he moved with his family;[25] and on the first of the year 1860, he took charge of the truck wagon. Soon after he became settled in his position, he and Phillips had become fast friends,—his work on the wagon would be much easier on this account. When Richard had charge of it, he was expected to help load it, and to care for his team. With Mr. Zuccorilla, however, this was different. He would walk over from the house, at four in the morning, carrying a small lantern which had been furnished; and, on reaching the White House, would find the wagon loaded, his team hitched, and all he had to do was simply to step in and drive off.

Returning late in the afternoon, he would drive into the yard, step out, and his team cared for by a man waiting for the purpose.

THE DOCTOR BUYS A NEW COACHMAN

Another important change that attracted much attention and comment, was the Doctor's purchase of a new coachman, Lawson, who had served in this capacity for as long as any one on the place could remember was also retired, being so old and worn that new livery could no longer improve him in looks, or fit in with the new order of things. There must be a younger and better looking man on the seat of the new carriage. New silver mounted harness, and a magnificent pair of spirited mules. As none of the young men on the place seemed fit for this responsible position as coachman, there was no other alternative than to buy one.

It was one fine day in June, Doctor called for his fine trotting horse, "Tige," a handsome dapple bay, with two white hind legs, and drove in to the city. While there he bought a fine looking, brown skinned chap, named "Jesse". He was about twenty years of age, born in Nashville, and was an experienced coachman. He was familiar with every part of the city, and was a steady driver and made a striking appearance on the box in new livery. As none of the younger chaps on the place had ever been in the city, it was a great pleasure for them to meet and know Jesse, and learn from him what a big city was and what it looked like. He smoked an occasional cigar, something few of us had ever seen before. Among the many beautiful things he had in his possession, was a pearl handled dagger, the first I had ever seen.

PHILLIPS AND AUSTIN

Phillips had been on the place now eleven months (February, 1860) and during this short space of time had brutally beaten many men, women and boys. Indeed, he had been so active in violence, with his monstrous whip, that it was generally supposed by the colored people that Master had given him free hand. But there was one man on the place he had never struck with a single blow, and of whom he was mortally afraid. This man was Austin, a mulatto, tall, and of powerful build. He carried concealed about his person a keen knife, and was often heard to say: "This is for Phillips, the day he strikes me with that whip, unless Master is there and says so." That Phillips, by some means or other, heard of this there can be no shadow of doubt. For besides the great whip wrapped about his shoulders, he carried his double barrel shot gun; and whenever it was necessary to go into that part of the field where Austin, with others might be at work [sic].

ABRAHAM LINCOLN

Just now there was much excitement and political talk over the possible election of Abraham Lincoln as President of the United States. We learned a good deal from Jesse, whose duties as coachman brought him into the city many times during the week. Until these exciting times, the Doctor would dispatch a servant to Slipup for the mail, dropped twice a day by the two stages. But now he went in person and, to us, the mail seemed to be much larger than usual. It seemed a settled question among all that if Lincoln was elected over Breckinridge or Douglas, there would be a civil war in the country, that he was against slavery and would use every means in his power to crush it.[26] There had been many political debates between students of Cumberland University and Lebanon; and, judging from the many duels fought between them, it was evident that they were not all of the same mind. I had often met many of the young gallants on the pike, when in search of the cows, and was generally afraid of them because they were up to all kinds of mischief. On one occasion a bunch of them—and they always went in a crowd of a dozen or more, riding the best of horses—they met an old white man riding a horse that was so poor it was scarcely able to carry him. They stopped this old man, forced him to dismount, shot his horse, cut him open, put the owner inside and sewed him up, leaving his head exposed of course so that the poor man could breathe. They paid him well for the horse that was really better off dead than alive; but their cruelty, and seeming painful lack of sportsmanship, showed that they were equal to and would stop at nothing to satisfy their craving for mischief. The old man was in this ridiculous state for an hour or so when the stage approaching from the west and heavily loaded with passengers, stopped and released him. He stated that the young rascals had their fun and seemed to enjoy it, but paid him well for it.

THE MURDER OF JORDAN

It was on one of those beautiful days in April, when all nature seemed to smile and be happy in its new spring dress of green, and the sun, high in the deep blue sky flirted with a few fleecy clouds, that a murder was committed on the Hoggatt place. The awful crime was perpetrated in the seed house, and Jordan, the head gardener, was the victim. He had gone there early in the morning with Cynthia, a handsome young black woman, as his assistant, for the purpose of assorting seeds soon to be planted. He had been struck over the left eye, and his skull fractured by the blow. The instrument used, as was divulged later, was a pestle, or wooden hammer, in common use by the carpenters. He had been stabbed also, in the left breast, a little below the nipple. Judging by the instruments used by the murderer, it was not vicious and brutal, he seemed to realize that the blow on the head was not sufficient, and then the knife was brought into play. The discovery of the terrible crime was made by a daughter of Jordan, named Laura, at about eleven o'clock. Laura was a waitress in the White House. Mistress wanted him and had made several inquiries, but no one had seen him or thought of going to the seed house. So on returning to the house she called Laura and told her to go there. She went, and on reaching the door which opened to the west, and seeing her poor father lying on the floor cold and dead, she screamed, and fell in a dead faint. This, of course attracted the attention of every one around the premises, and there was a rush for the seed house to learn the cause of the alarm. The poor, old man lay in a pool of blood, with his head toward the door. There were two hand work benches in the little house, one on each side of the door, with a narrow passage between them, so that two persons could have room enough to work and not be in each other's way. These were covered with seeds of various kind, but there seemed to be no sign of a struggle. Cynthia was the only person seen in company with him that morning, and no one on the place had ever seen or heard of any trouble between them. That she had struck the fatal blow, there can be no shadow of a doubt. The men came and the body was taken to his cabin and prepared for burial.

When Master, who had driven in to the city, returned and heard of the facts in the case, he sent two men to look for Cynthia who had disappeared. She had wandered down to the lane to the gate leading to the grist mill which stood in the middle of a large peach orchard, and here she was found, sitting on the fence, crying. She was brought to the house and was locked up in the laundry. Later in the afternoon, the remains of Uncle Jordan were placed in a new cedar coffin, then put in a cart to which Nell had been hitched, and followed by every soul on the place, we laid him to rest.

At the time of his death, Jordan was about fifty years of age. He was the father of two daughters, Laura and Betsy. His wife had been dead many years. It was the talk about the place that he was very much in love with Cynthia but it was claimed she did not encourage his attentions. Since the coming of Jesse, she had been seen in his company many times, and it was evident, therefore, that if she ever had had any affection for Jordan, it was readily transferred to the handsome new coachman.

THE PUNISHMENT OF CYNTHIA

On the day following the murder, Master went to the laundry where she was confined, took with him two new raw hides, and questioned her closely concerning the murder, and she denied everything. He had her stripped to the waist and, having taken off his coat and rolled his sleeves above his elbow, he began whipping her. After each severe blow on her bare back, he would ask: "Why did you kill Jordan?" She denied to the last: "Master, I didn't do it." He whipped her until blood ran in streams down her back; and finally she dropped to the floor and fainted, and he left her there. The laundry girls, who were sewing upstairs, came down and revived her. She was confined to her bed for two weeks recovering from the terrible beating she had received. Cynthia was a queer girl. She made her home with Lawson and his wife, and was seldom seen in company with the other girls and boys of her age.

GHOSTS

As a rule, all of the youngsters on the place were afraid of the dark, for the ghosts were abroad then, and we were in mortal fear of meeting them. Cynthia, evidently, was not one of those who were afraid. She had no dread of meeting strange spirits, or anything more terrifying than herself. Every living soul on the place was more or less superstitious to the extent that they believed in ghosts; and every one had, or pretended to have seen one. These weird, grewsome stories were the general fireside tales on long winter evenings; and, if the teller happened to be Vann, Abe, or Henry, it was sure of a large audience. I heard Vann tell one story I shall always remember, and where he got hold of it was a mystery. He could not read, and it sounds as if it had been taken directly from a novel. As he told it, it ran as follows:

There were two lovers who had quarreled, and the young man in the case freely acknowledged his wrong and agreed to submit to any punishment that she chose to inflict. She required him to meet her at one of their frequent haunts along the river bank, where there were huge rocks, a high embankment and a sweeping current below. When she arrived, at nine o'clock the next morning, it was Sunday, and she found him sitting on their favorite rock, sad and humiliated, and apparently in a state of great suffering. He asked the nature of his death, that is if she really intended to carry out her awful program. Oh, yes, she was entirely unchanged, and stated briefly that she much preferred this method of disposing of him because she wanted to make it as easy and painless as possible. She asked if he was ready to die, and he said that he was. Then she told him to stand up and face the rapidly moving stream, while she tied his hands behind his back. Having done this, she bade him good by, then walked several paces up the hill behind him, and told him she would count three before she started to run down and push him off, so he would have time to say his prayers. She started down the hill side on a keen run, and when she had reached him, put out her hands to push him over the bank, but he quickly stepped aside and she plunged into the stream. She cried out: "Jack! Jack! Help me or I will drown."

"I can't do a thing, for my hands are tied."[27]

The startling influence on his hearers, of this story told by Vann, can easily be imagined. Every one believed it to be a true story, and thought they could see the poor girl struggling in the mad river below.

Vann was also a good singer. He used to lead the corn husking songs that were greatly enjoyed by all.

The spring from which water for all purposes was obtained, was a remarkable one. It bubbled under a small hill and a great mass of rocks. It had been carefully walled up, and was always clear and cold. A nice little house, with a good roof, stood over it and a good sized stream flowed from it. Grandmother's large flock of geese and ducks made merry around this stream. There was a solid stone floor in the spring house, and here she kept milk, cream, and butter, and such things necessary to be kept cool. It was shaded by a number of hickory nut trees which had grown very tall. The nuts from them were of the large flat variety, and delicious eating in season. The first heavy frost usually ripened them and, owing to the distance they had to fall, the outer shell would be broken and the nuts would be clean, bright rich color. I don't think I ever failed to get the first that fell.

Grandmother Hanna was a strict member of the church, and the oldest one on the place.[28] As a rule, the weekly prayer meetings on Friday nights were held at her cabin. To make room for the large crowd that usually attended, we boys were sent to bed so as to be out of the way.

Aron, who was about forty years of age, and an epileptic, had been attending the meetings regularly of late and declared he had experienced religion. As proof that he had the "Great Gift", he stated that he had gone to the grave yard, and all the most lonely and dismal places on the darkest of nights, knelt and prayed, according to custom. There was a great deal of interest manifested owing to the fact that there might be a new convert. On one Friday night, which was a perfect one, with a clear sky lighted by the brightest of moons, the crowd had gathered and the big room was packed to suffocation. We boys had stolen outside and remained outside until the meeting began. A hymn or two was sung, some one led in prayer. Then it was stated that Brother Aron would be admitted to full membership. There were several three-legged stools in the room, used by the boys around the fire place in the winter. When he was called upon to relate his experiences, he being short of stature, concluded to stand upon one of these stools, saying that he wanted to get up as high as he could to talk to the Lord. When he began talking, warming up to his subject, as it were, his enthusiasm got the better of him, the stool tottered under him, and he fell in an awful fit. The women screamed and every one ran from the room, leaving Brother Aron wrestling with the Lord and his fit. He soon came out of it, however, when the men ventured in and led him to his sister, Laura's cabin, in which he made his home. The meeting was finally resumed and went on without further interruption until a late hour.

SLAVE MARRIAGES

There was no objection by the masters to their slaves marrying on neighboring plantations. The rule was—and generally accepted—that if there were offspring from such a union, the children would belong to the master owning the mother. Stephen the head miller and carpenter, was married, and his wife and four fine children belonged to the McRidleys, three miles southwest of the Hoggatt place. My father, John McCline, for whom I was named, belonged to a man named Smith, who owned a grocery store at Silver Springs, Wilson county.[29] His store was a good sized frame building, set on the east side of the pike fifteen miles from the City of Nashville. Father hired his time from his master, as was the custom of many slaves; and, owning his own horse and covered wagon, was a huckster, making two trips a week to the city; and in this way made a fairly good living. I used to see him quite often when on my way after the cows, and he was so kind,—always had a present for me, some times it was a silver dime, a bit of candy, or a pocket knife.

VISITORS

There were many visitors, or house guests, during the summer. Those from the city remaining only a few days. There were two ladies, mother and daughter, from the North, judging from appearances, who remained with us a month. During their stay, Mrs. Hoggatt was extremely kind, seldom, if ever, using the raw hide. She carried it of course, but usually hidden in the folds of her dress. Her idea was doubtless to impress upon the minds of these innocent ladies from the North (where, she was certain, the feeling was bitter against the system) that the only real bad thing about slavery was the name—that the retention of the Blacks under a legitimate rule of enforced servitude was far better for them than freedom. For what would an ignorant people do with that they knew not of? What, indeed!

Miss Emma and Miss Delia invited two young chaps from the city. They were Master Prince and Master Wallace, aged about fourteen and twelve. The fact that they were sons of rich, influential parents from the city, assured that every courtesy was shown them. They were furnished with fine saddle horses and I, myself, on a third, was their servant. It was a real event in my life. I never enjoyed anything on the place so much as the long pleasant rides with those boys. We saw much of the beautiful country, for miles around, that was new to me. Taking an early start one morning, we rode to "The Hermitage", the magnificent home of President Andrew Jackson, some fifteen miles from the Clover Bottoms.[30] The house, the prettiest I have ever seen, as I remember was a one story building covering a great deal of ground. It stood in the middle of a large cedar forest and could not be seen from the pike. The entrance was through a gate with huge capped pillow posts, and a gravel drive, perhaps half a mile in length, wound round through the forest and up to the beautiful mansion. The tomb in which the great man lay, stood just to the right of the front door and was shaded by two large weeping willows. It was enclosed in white marble. A long inscription on the slab that covered it, was read by the young gentlemen, after which we mounted our horses and went away.

On our way back from "The Hermitage" to the covered bridge, a distance of about twelve miles, I noticed there were many sharp turns in the pike, which was heavily shaded on both sides with cedar and many other varieties of trees.

The high rail fences could scarcely be seen for the hemp weeds that grew so luxuriantly in this part of the state. We reached the bridge about eleven o'clock and here, on either side, it was rough and precipitous. The great rocks stood out so prominently that it seemed as if a mere touch would start them rolling down to the river below. There were many winding paths leading from the pike down to the stream which, here, was rather deep. The young gentlemen proposed that we swim our horses across instead of using the covered bridge. It was a great lark, though I was considerably frightened as I had never dared do anything like it before.

After passing the grain fields, we ran a race up to the White house, and for the second time, Master Prince reached the gate first.

On the last day of these young gentlemen's visit, we took the long lane, a dirt road running across the plantation from West to East, a distance of two miles, where it crosses the river. This road was used principally by the poor Whites, many of them living in the hill country on that side of the stream. Here the river is shallow, and the fact that the bottom was more or less rocky, made it easily fordable most of the year. The country is rough and rocky for quite a distance after leaving the river, when it becomes level and heavily timbered. The biggest and finest poplar trees I had ever seen grew here. We saw many squirrels, both the red and grey variety; and how they scampered about when we rode by them!

The young gentlemen left the following morning and my delightful holiday came to a prompt end, having lasted three weeks. They bade me good-bye, saying they would come again next year. Each gave me a silver dollar, and I was the happiest boy in the world. I ran to my grandmother to show my good fortune; and, as always when I brought a piece of money to her to keep for me, she would say, "Drop it in the chest, honey." This chest was the smaller of the two in the room, and was kept locked, and there was just play enough so that I could raise the big lid and drop in my two dollars. Judging from the rattling noise they made, there were a lot more to keep them company. Strange to say, I never saw the inside of that chest. Hitherto I had contributed many quarters and dimes, which went into it, and which, I suppose, she used to the best advantage.

GOOD FISHING

A strip of fine pasture land of about five hundred acres, lay east of the pike, and extended to the river. It was separated from the corn fields by a high rail fence. Here roamed the brood mares and their colts. Lying gracefully between two hills, was a good sized pond. Here the stock came to drink, and here we fished. It was the last Sunday in August that Brother Jeff and myself went fishing, after having secured a big can of worms, which we dug up back of the gin mill, we started for the pond, a half mile away. Arriving on the scene a little before nine, we proceeded to unravel our line from the long reed poles; and after baiting the hook and casting out, took seats under a large thorn tree. It was awfully hot, and we sat there a long time and didn't get a bite. Indeed, it looked as if we were not to have any luck. Finally I decided to shift my ground and going around to the south side, I cast off there. I sat perhaps ten minutes, when I noticed the cork on my line beginning to shake a little, and at last was sure I was getting a bite. Then it went under with a heavy jerk, when I rose quickly to my feet and drew out my line, and found a perch weighing about a pound on the hook, I was very happy and excited. Extricating him from the hook, I baited and threw it in again. In a few minutes there was another nibble, and with intense excitement, I waited for perhaps a minute or so, when the cork went down again, and when I drew up, I had another perch, but not quite as large as the first I had caught. After baiting my hook for the third try, I looked across the pond to see how Jeff was getting on, and was surprised to see him stretched on the ground under the thorn tree, his hat over his eyes, and hands clasped under his head. He was sound asleep. He had thrown his line way out, and his pole stuck in the soft mud at the edge of the bank. I waited a long time but didn't get another bite. Taking up my line and two fine fish, I started to the west end to try my luck there. Just as I was moving away, I noticed Jeff's pole fall into the water with a loud splash. I stood watching it. Every little while it would move with a quick jerk—surely something alive must be on the hook! "Jeff! Jeff!" I cried. "There goes your pole."

"Bring the canoe around with you, we will see what is the matter."

I got in and paddled around to where he stood waiting, and when he got in we moved slowly out to the pole which was still being dragged along by sudden jerks. Now, I thought all the time it must be a turtle because there were a lot of them in the pond. When he reached it, he picked up the pole, drew in, and to our great surprise, a long cat fish weighing nearly two pounds, was dandling on the hook. Well, we had had luck enough for one day, so tied up our boat and went home.

I had never been through the White House since it had been rebuilt. The family drove in to the city one day and Jeff took me through from top to bottom. It was beautiful in the extreme. Every room had its four poster silk curtained bed, completely furnished in every detail. Each room had its artistically arranged fire place; also the wide, spacious halls. What attracted my attention most, was the beautiful paper on the wall and staircase, clear up to the third floor. There were life-sized pictures of soldiers of the Revolution painted on it; and, to my boyish eyes, they looked to be alive and in action.[31] Then we went down into the big dining room, twenty by thirty feet in length. There were two large ornamented fire places, one at each end of the room. What a great house it was! I thought. So richly furnished, clean, cool, smelling so sweet. Then we strolled into the library. There was a large book case that stood at the south end of the room, which was filled with books. The heavy carpet on the floor felt nice to my bare feet as I walked on it. A great, heavy cloth covered table stood in the middle of the room, and many big easy chairs. I was greatly delighted with my visit in the new White House, and with the many beautiful things I saw in it.

A COMET MEANS WAR

When Jesse rode in to the city, he always brought some important news, generally discussed in Richard's cabin. Here the men would meet at night and talk over the events and progress of the Lincoln campaign. He stated that it was the general opinion in Nashville that he would be elected. It was thought, and generally believed, that if he stood by the principles of the Republican party and its platform, namely: "Free people, Free souls, and a Free press," there would be a civil war. I daresay there was not a man present who knew what all this meant—about principles and party platforms. Since the news of the hanging of John Brown had reached the Clover Bottoms, every man had hid his gun. The patrollers, however, continued their search for arms, night and day. The comet that made its appearance in the southeast a few weeks before, and the first I had ever seen, was now quite large, and had an enormous tail.[32] On a clear moonlight night the men were out looking at it, and in their simple way, were discussing its meaning. Abe was heard to remark: "That there was going to be a war." I wondered then, and even now, where he got the idea that a comet was a sign of war. And, to my great surprise, he began to point out certain stars, calling them queer names. The only ones I can remember now were the seven stars or Job's coffin.

PHILLIPS KILLS THE SLAVE AUSTIN

It was Dr. Hoggatt's intention to build a board fence, the length of the plantation, on both sides of the Lebanon pike, and thus remove the ugly stake and rider
rail fence that was an eye sore to the traveling public. The men worked at it only
when their time could be spared from the necessary work on the place. It was on
one of those quiet, cloudy days in October that five of the men, Austin being one
of the number, were engaged in building this fence on the east side pike [sic], and
about a mile from the house I was just coming out of the stable with Nell, as it
was four o'clock and time to go for the cows, when Phillips and Zuccorilla passed
the door with their shot guns on their shoulders. They went down on the pike
where the men were at work on the new fence. On reaching the scene, Phillips
unwrapped his big whip from his shoulders and laid it on the ground. Then he
took a piece of rope from his coat pocket, and called to Austin to "come over and
cross his hands, that he was going to give him a good whipping." Austin was digging a post hole and was using a long handled shovel for this purpose. He stopped,
looked across at the brute, Phillips, he was still holding the shovel in his hand, and
with his right hand on his hip, said:

"I aint done nothin to be whipped for and I aint going to be whipped unless
Master says so."

"Then you won't come over here and cross your hands?"

"No, sir."

Phillips dropped the rope he had in his hand, and with an oath, picked up his
shot gun, deliberately aimed and fired. Poor Austin fell on his face and died
instantly.

It seems that when he saw that Phillips was determined to shoot, he threw up
his left hand apparently to ward off the shot, and it was shot off at the wrist as
completely as if it had been cut by a sharp knife and hung by a little piece of flesh.
Buck shot had been used, entering his face and throat. Just after the shooting, the
stage was seen coming up the pike, and Phillips had the men remove the body
quickly back in the weeds where it could not be seen. He and Zuccorilla then shoul-
dered their guns and walked away. The remains of poor Austin were placed in a
wagon and hauled to his cabin. When his wife, Dilsey, began to scream and cry
Mistress sent word that if she didn't stop it she should come down with a raw hide
and wear her out. The next day was an extremely sad one, as we followed the remains of poor Austin to his final resting place.

A few days later we learned that when Phillips went to Master and reported the
killing, that he told him it was a bad time to kill a nigger because it was a question
of only a few days before election of Abraham Lincoln, and that he had better put
away his gun and whip. He did put them away, we never saw him with anything
more terrifying than a raw hide.[33]

WYATT—THE HOODOO

At the Clover Bottoms, like all other plantations in the South where there were so many superstitious and ignorant slaves, the herb doctor, the hoodoo, the conjuror, were to be found. The man of mystery bearing all these distinctions wrapped in one, was Wyatt. He was a man of medium height, light brown skin, and his hair and short, stubby whiskers were white. He lived alone in an old two-story house on the east side of the lane, and a half mile from the other cabins. His duties were to look after the jack, named General Jackson. He also had charge of feeding the hogs that were being fattened for winter killing. The boys and girls, and children in general, stood in vital fear of him. None of them dared to enter his house or even go near it. I took the cows to pasture in that direction occasionally, and don't remember ever to have seen him around or his doors or windows open. There was an air of mystery and gloom around his place that made me shiver with a feeling of dread and fear. It was said of him that his concoctions, made up of deadly poisons, were put up in bottles; and that these he sold to persons with instructions how to use them on their enemies. When it was necessary to remove an enemy by charm, the purchaser was requested to bury the bottle under his door-step early in the morning before he stirred abroad, and when he walked out and over the bottle something would happen to him.

Along in the month of January, 1861, Buck had been captured by three run-a-way hunters and delivered to the over-seer. They were paid their hundred and fifty dollars, the reward offered, and he was locked up. They stated they caught him in Wilson county, thirty miles away. Getting his trail with blood hounds, they followed him for ten days. When near a creek, the hounds in close pursuit, he was compelled to climb a sycamore tree to escape being torn to pieces. Owing to the fact that he had to wade streams frequently to prevent the dogs tracing him, his feet were badly frozen. With a ball and chain attached to one leg, he was kept locked up until his feet were entirely well, when he was sent South, to the sugar plantation in Louisiana. It was indeed a heavy blow to his wife and only son, Frank. We never heard of him after that.

Strange, what a difference there was on the place now that Mr. Lincoln had been elected to the presidency. The over-seer went about giving directions in the most kindly manner. Mistress, too, had put away her raw hide, and there was no cutting and slashing every one she met, as formerly. She seemed to have taken a special new interest in the people, and inquired daily if any were sick. The election was a fatal blow to the night prowling patrollers. The forty, or more, of them who had been organized by the rich planters throughout Davidson county, were disbanded.

Enjoying the splendid pay of fifty dollars per month for the nefarious job of apprehending run-a-way slaves, had been suddenly cut off, and their occupation gone. Their leisure moments were now confined to their former pursuits of hunting the fox and the rabbit by day, and the coon and o'possum by night. The woods were full of these little animals.

I had noticed in my numerous rides about the country, that these poor Whites lived chiefly in the woods, and seldom raised a crop; seeming to spend their time hunting and fishing. Dave Blankenship and his wife, who were in charge of the two toll gates for the Stewart's Ferry and Lebanon pikes, at Slipup, were the only ones I knew very well who seemed to have any spirit or energy. Their two boys, who were about my age, I knew well. I had many fights with them.

An annual event of unusual importance, that took place in the Clover Bottoms, attracted the attention of rich planters from many plantations. This was the horse and mule show occurring always on the first Sunday in May. Wyatt, with his great big General Jackson well groomed, slick, and in fine condition, took the lead, followed by twenty-five men each leading two brood mares followed by their colts. They were brought up on the land, and the Doctor with his great crowd of visitors, would be seated near the gates as they passed in review. As a rule there were a great many yearlings, fine young mules, that would be ready for the market soon, and they were much admired by the visitors.

For the first time in the history of the place, a part of the big corn fields on the east side of the pike, and along the river front, was planted in millet. As I had never seen it growing before heads, in a state of maturity, was a great curiosity to me [sic]. The golden headed straws were the most beautiful I had ever seen.

The bed ticks in nearly all the cabins were emptied once a year, washed, and refilled. Heretofore wheat straw had been used for this purpose, but now millet had been suggested by Mrs. Phillips as being cleaner and more durable.

How well I remember when I was so small grandmother had to put one in bed after it had been made up for the first time, on its great pile of clean sweet straw.

It was along in August that the men began cutting it, using sickles for the purpose. It was frightfully hot and, as usual, I had to carry the men's dinners to them as they were a mile or more from the house. At this time of the year, grandmother's bill of fare generally consisted of boiled potatoes, bacon, greens of some kind, and butter milk. The greens, potatoes and bacon, she would put into a large sized piggin; and the big pone of hot corn bread laid on top of it. The butter milk was put into a tin pail. When all was ready, I set the piggin on my head, and with the pail of milk in one hand, I would start off to the field. Naturally enough I always took the shortest route. And on this occasion of which I am speaking it led through the south woods pasture along a good hard dirt road, well shaded on both sides. I was going along this road with the men's dinner, when it became too hot for my head and I stopped to gather a few flat papaw leaves to put on my head under the piggin; when a big fox, the first I had ever seen, walked leisurely across the road in front of me. Though merely turning his head in passing, I was nevertheless considerably frightened. As there was not a single shade tree in that part of the field where the men were at work, I was glad to find them waiting under the black thorn trees along the pike. What a pleasure it was to me to see them eat, and listen to the stories they told about Lincoln, the new President. War was certain, they said, because several of the Southern States had seceded from the Union, and because Fort Sumter had been fired upon.[34]

CONFEDERATE TROOPS PASS ON THE PIKE

On my way back, I decided to take the pike; but had not proceeded far when I quickly changed my mind, for the hot dust burned my poor feet so that I was glad to climb the fence and take the same road back through the fields. I had not gone far when I chanced to look back down the fence, and noticed a great cloud of dust just this side of the covered bridge. I went back to the pike, climbed on the high rail fence and waited. As the dust receded, and as far as I could see, the pike was crowded with men dressed in fine new uniforms of grey.

The first to pass were three batteries drawn by six horses each. These were followed by men on horseback and hundreds on foot. Then came stages, carriages, covered wagons filled to overflowing with men, women and children. They all seemed happy, as they were singing as they passed along. I must have sat there more than an hour, in open-eyed wonder, without the vaguest idea of what it was all about.

The greatest excitement I had even witnessed amongst the people on the place occurred that night, when the men met at Richard's and discussed the question at issue. I learned that the men I had seen passing during the afternoon were three thousand in number, that they were Confederate soldiers, and they were Wilson county's contribution to the cause. There were many visitors at the White House, and I suppose they talked over the great and stirring event of the time. The passing of the Confederate soldiers along the pike on their way into Nashville, which had become the center and hot bed of secession, was now a common daily occurrence.[35] The very sight of them was of the greatest interest to me because they were young men, handsome, and so very enthusiastic.

How very strange it seemed to me that these young chaps, many of them doubtless not yet of age, marching to Nashville to enlist in the army and to become real soldiers, without the slightest idea of the horrors of war. The strenuous excitement of the time perhaps over-shadowed every consideration. Nor did they realize the danger and cost of the great undertaking. Many of them, the sons of rich planters, had left their beautiful and luxurious homes to share their patriotic zeal and love for their country.

In the meantime work on the place moved on in the even tenor of its way, regardless of the stirring events around us. The wheat crop, unusually large this year, was gathered and carefully stored in a large frame stable. There is nothing about corn that smells so sweet as the fodder when cured and tied into bundles. It was then hauled and carefully stacked near the stables. As no hay was harvested on the place, fodder was used in lieu thereof, and one bundle to the animal was considered a good feed.

PRICES BOOM

Owing to the great number of people that had gathered in the city, due princi-
pally to the prospective civil war, prices for all farm products had almost doubled.
Many big wagon loads of hams, bacon, shoulders, and other things were sent in.
Also wheat, corn and oats.

We boys, who hither to had gathered walnuts and hickory nuts in great quantities during the fall just for the fun and sport to be found in it, were surprised that
we could get a dollar a bushel for all we could gather and send to the city. There
was also a demand for coon and o'possum; the fact was that every man and boy
went hunting nights and Sundays. I shall never forget my experience with Jeff, one
night, when we decided to go o'possum hunting. It was late in November and there
had been a light shower during the afternoon, but it had partly cleared by night,
and the moon being well up, made it an admirable night for such sports. We had
a splendid dog, called "Pete", part shepherd, and various other mixtures, made up
the excellent qualities of a good o'possum dog. We concluded to go into the South
woods, for here was a great deal of heavy timber and blackberry bush; wild grapes
grew in abundance; of all of which this little animal is supremely fond. In hunting with a dog at night, it is always wise to keep as close to him as possible as there
is a tendency on his part to chase rabbits. To prevent this he must be scolded occasionally. We had followed him for about two hours and had got away down east
of the pond and not far from the river, when we heard him barking at a great rate.
This was a pretty good sign that he had treed something. He had disappeared only
a few minutes before, and supposed that we were following his course going East.
As we drew away, to our surprise the sound of his bark came from the West of us,
so turning sharply about, we headed in that direction. We climbed quite a little
hill, and on reaching the top, it seemed to be rather flat.

That Pete had treed something was evident from the frantic jumps he was making around the tree just ahead of us. Jeff, going to the left, was a little ways ahead
of me, and reached the scene first. Going to the right, and considerably out of
breath, I passed under a very large black oak tree, with its numerous branches
spread out from its trunk. It covered a good deal of ground. It had already shed
its usual quantity of leaves and they seemed to be knee deep under this tree, and
expecting to see the o'possum at any moment, I stepped right on the back of a big
black sow and about a dozen young pigs that had made themselves a nest there
for the night. I don't think I had ever been so frightened as I was when that sow
jumped up and made that peculiar sound like that of a surprised bear.

On reaching the tree where Jeff and Pete were waiting, I looked up and saw the
object of our hunt. He had sought refuge in a small hickory tree, and there he clung
in a small knot, looking very much like a bunch of mistletoe. I being the smaller,
Jeff helped me to climb the tree, and when I was almost in reaching distance, he
told me to give it a quick, violent, shake. I did so, and the o'possum dropped; and
by the time he touched the ground Pete had him back of the neck; and Jeff took

him by his long, smooth tail, and we took him home alive. We kept him a week, then killed him, dressed and sent him to Nashville and got a big silver dollar for him. To dress an o'possum is quite a task; he is very much like a pig, and the process of dressing him is very much the same. A kettle of boiling water, then take two or three shovels of wood ashes, drop him in, and the long, ugly red hair can readily be removed; when he has all the appearance of a well dressed pig.

UNION SOLDIERS APPEAR

It was now well along in the month of February, 1862, and, hearing that General Grant had attacked Fort Donelson, on the Cumberland river, and only sixty five miles from Nashville, we were having grave fears that the war would soon be at our very doors. One morning, a few days later, we could hear Commodore Foote's gun boats booming as they came down the river; and the following day, occupied Nashville, the Confederates offering little or no resistance. Their hasty leave from the city, to avoid being captured, was of the greatest disorder.[36] There seemed to be thousands of them—a few on horseback, and many afoot—running through the roads and fields, half dressed and bareheaded. The fact that they seemed so frightened and helpless left us under the impression that the yankee was an exceedingly dangerous foe.

A few days later there was an inch or so of snow on the ground but the sky was clear and bright. It was about eleven o'clock in the morning that some of the Union soldiers were seen passing along the pike. They moved with perfect evenness, like the waves on a lake stirred by a gentle breeze. Their muskets were bright and new, and fairly glistened against the sun. They wore cute little black hats, with one side of the brim turned up and fastened with a brass eagle. Their trousers and overcoats with capes attached, were of a rich blue color, and the big brass buttons on them were as bright as if they had just been polished. There were five thousand of them and, to our great surprise and astonishment, they turned into the south woods pasture, a mile from the house, and went into camp. Late in the afternoon they were followed by hundreds of covered wagons drawn by six mules each. The large open lot, south of the over-seer's house and farm hands quarters, with a great corn crib setting in the middle of it, was used for the 500 hogs to roam about in before killing time. Hundreds of young cattle, calves, and a large flock of sheep had been driven up into this field as a sort of precaution, as the yankees might be tempted to kill some of them.

The next day it was cold and rainy, and late in the afternoon we heard the crack of guns; and here the soldiers were, shooting down cattle, sheep, and hogs. Master and the over-seer went out, under their umbrellas, and begged them to stop, but they went right on, paying no attention to them. That night, the General in command, and his staff arrived, and Master invited him into his house; and here he made his headquarters. They remained on the place with us for six weeks, and the killing of stock was stopped. They were strong healthy, and handsome men;

and, up to that time had seen no actual fighting. On pleasant days they drilled a little in the afternoons when they would have what we called dress parade, it was a most beautiful sight I had ever seen. Here were hundreds of them, each keeping step with the other, and all moving as one, as if the whole body was one man instead of hundreds. They used up all the dead wood they could find in the woods, and then burned the rail fences.[37]

They were very kind and friendly toward us, giving us many good and useful things, such as clothing, blankets, etc. They paid the women well for work if done for them, and the money given in payment, they called "green backs", was new to us. The twenty-five cent piece, for instance, had five heads on each, and was paper, of course. The 50¢ was of light gold in color, and had ten heads. We were told that if we had any confederate money, which they called "shin plaster," we had better get rid of it as soon as possible as it was no use after they had taken possession. We learned also, with surprise, that every one of us were free—that is, all who agreed to follow the army and be of such use to it as it saw fit to put us. But, they said, it would not be proper for a married man to leave his family merely to free himself. That would be an act of greatest selfishness. Strong, young men not married, would be useful, and would doubtless, find employment as cooks, or servants for officers, and should get wages.

To our great surprise and astonishment, Mistress called all the men and women up to the house one morning and gave each a few dollars of confederate money. She did not, however, explain to them that since the yankees had all that part of the country, it was not worth the paper it was printed on.[38] Many of us, however, succeeded in making use of it by sending it way South of the Union lines, where it was exchanged for tea and coffee which could not now be bought in Nashville at any price. Two of the men, Abe and Henry, disappeared; and it was generally supposed by all that they had followed the Union army into Nashville. Abe was sadly missed, because he was a good blacksmith, whose place could not be filled very well.

FORAGING EXPEDITIONS

News came from the cotton plantation at Murfreesboro, that the crop was unusually heavy this year, and that more hands were needed to gather it. Two big carry-alls were got in readiness, and twenty young people were sent over from our place—seven girls and thirteen men. My brother Jeff, and Frank being among the number. The matter, of course, was discussed by the men at night, and they were of the decided opinion that the sole object in sending them to the Murfreesboro farm was a precautionary measure taken by the Master to prevent any more running away and going to the Yankees. He had told the Union soldiers when leaving the place, that though he owned slaves, he was nevertheless, a Union man. They may have gone away under that impression, but I doubt very much whether they believed the statement.

We learned that the plantations west of us, and more especially those in Wilson county, suffered terribly from foraging expeditions. These passed our place two or three times a week. It was late in June, and the first crop of fine water melons had been picked and hauled up to the house to be sent off to market next day. They were piled up on the lawn under a big elm tree, when Mistress, who was always on the lookout for Yankees, saw a company turn off the pike, into the lane, and march straight up to the house. She rang the servant's bell, and eight of us responded with alacrity. We were instructed to get those water melons in and out of sight as quickly as possible, because a lot of Union soldiers were approaching. There were about a hundred of them. They marched into the yard, stacked arms in the gravel driveway, and sat down on the grass. The officer in charge walked upon the porch, took off his hat, bowed to the ladies, then shook hands with Master, and was invited by him to a seat. He was a tall, fine looking young man, dressed in dark blue blouse, shoulder straps with one bar in them, bright brass buttons; and the trousers of a rich blue and with red stripes down the legs.[39] His long bright sword dangling at his side; and as he sat there on the porch, his legs crossed, his big hat and long gauntlet gloves laying carelessly by his side, he had the appearance of a man of authority. We never learned the object of his call. A lot of water melons were brought out for his men. Master and their Commander talked in a low voice as they strolled about the beautiful lawn. Then rejoining his men, they marched away.

A VISIT FROM GENERAL FORREST

It was late in August, one afternoon, that our place was visited by the rebel, General Forrest, and his cavalry of about three thousand men.[40] The General and his staff proceeded to the White House and announced that they would remain during the night. His men made their camp in a big field just west of the garden and extending along the pike, up to the toll gate. Only about half of them, however, wore the regular grey confederate uniform, while the other half were dressed in ordinary citizens clothes. Many of them had on linen dusters.

Phillips, who had been sent for, soon after their arrival, rushed out and called all the men, women, and boys together, and said that they were to give them supper. Fire was started under the three great kettles used for scalding in the killing season, and twenty-five hams put in each to boil. The women, in the meantime, were busy making and baking corn pone, corn dodgers, hoe cakes—bread in every conceivable shape, to feed these poor starving soldiers. Everything being ready, all the men and boys on the place with tubs, barrels, and baskets filled with ham and corn bread, marched forth to feed the hungry. Boards had been put up in the corners of the rail fence, as a sort of temporary table, and ten men, with sharp knives, did the carving, then the hungry hoard marched by in single file and each man was handed a good big piece of ham and corn bread. It was twelve o'clock that night when we got through feeding them. The next morning, it being pretty hot, they withdrew into the North woods, just across the pike.

A part of the army made a dash within five miles of Nashville, wounded one Union cavalry man, who made his escape, but succeeded in capturing two of his comrades, who they brought out with them.[41] What a striking difference in the appearance of the men in the two armies. These men of the Union army seemed healthy, had good complexions, and looked good in their uniforms.

Late in the afternoon, General Forrest, with his army, pulled out, and we supposed that he had declared to Master that he would capture, and then eat supper, in the City of Nashville. But, on leaving our place, he took the Stewart's Ferry pike thirty miles southwest of that city. Here, General Bragg, with the main body of his army was in force and strongly fortified, waiting for the Federals who were drilling in the open fields around Nashville. Scattered bands of the Federal cavalry could be seen daily, passing along the pike, and were frequent visitors at our place.

It was one afternoon, late in the month of August, that a squad of fifteen came galloping down the pike from Nashville. Five of them turned into the land and rode up to the house, while the other ten rode slowly down the pike towards the river. The five dismounted in the land opposite the house, stood their horses in the corners of the rail fences, then took the bridles off, put on those funny mouth feed bags, on each horse, containing shelled corn and oats; then the men opened up their haversacks and ate their lunch which consisted of bacon, hardtack, and coffee. Standing near, and looking out at these strange men, with open-eyed wonder of the average country boy, I wondered if they had ever killed anybody with those little sharp guns, called carbines, and the long swords which had carelessly laid aside on the ground [sic]. They wanted some drinking water, and asked me to get them a little. I ran to the house and getting a bucket full, returned with it, carrying it on my head, which greatly amused them. They filled their canteens, and two of them gave me ten cents, each, which was real yankee money. They stayed for an hour or so, and one of them, a stout light haired man, had his long heavy sword out, sharp and bright, and was chopping a rail as it lay on the fence, apparently amusing himself by testing the quality of the steel.

Booker was a big, stout, fellow, with a light brown skin, and the most powerful man I ever saw. He was the only man on the place who plaited his hair. He was seldom seen in company with any one, and seldom dressed up on Sundays as did the other men, nor did he go to church. As a rule he was around when the boys were out playing with marbles and, with a sharp pocket knife, was constantly whittling. His attitude, always striking and conspicuous, was to find a post, or a tree to lean against; and with his left foot crossed over his right, he would stand for hours at the time, talking to himself as the shavings made by his keen knife flew in every direction. One bright Sunday morning, I went to the spring for a pail of water for grandmother, and here he stood, leaning against one of the big hickory trees, his hat tilted over his left eye and with his usual silly smile, said: "Hello, son, are there any girls about here? I am going to church today with some of 'em, I reckon, because I expects to get married some of these day." The hearty laugh that followed this, the longest speech I had every heard him make, was amusing in the extreme. I suppose it was characteristic of the age in which I lived, and in families where there were boys, that the youngest suffered many things. At least it was so in our family, as I was unfortunately the youngest of four boys, it seemed to me that I was the butt of all painful circumstances. If grandmother wanted a bucket of water, or a basket of chips, which was often the case, when the three other big stout fellows were sitting around the fire, she would invariably call upon me to get it. Of course there was no objection on my part if there was a bribe in sight—a turn-over pie, a good sized piece of maple sugar, of which I was extremely fond, or a doughnut. But when none of these good things were in sight, or promised, I generally showed signs of rebellion. On such occasions grandmother usually resorted to force, to the amusement of the three conspirators.

One day she drew back with the intention of giving me a good cuff on the ear; and as I was somewhat of a sprinter in those days, I easily dodged the intended blow, but in doing so I fell flat on my back. Though not hurt, I felt as a matter of precaution it would be safer to lay there. In the attitude of the conqueror, she stood with her hands resting on her hips and looking down upon me, said in a loud voice, "Are you dead?"

"Yes'm", I replied.

"Then rise, sir."

In her youth, grandmother, doubtless was a very handsome woman. She was very light in complexion, and had very dark brown hair.[42] She was the mother of three children, two sons and a daughter, who was my mother.

The two most useful men on the place, Stephen and Richard, were her sons. Both were married. Uncle Richard having two children, a girl and a boy; and Uncle Stephen was the father of four, but his wife and children belonged to the McRidleys, and we saw very little of them.

The saw mill and grist mill, which stood on the river a mile and a half from the house, were run by water power, and were operated only during the winter and early spring months when there was plenty of water. The other grist mill with the gin mill combined, was nearer the house, and operated by horse power. Grinding for home consumption was done once a week, generally on Saturday. The manner of conveying wheat or corn to the mill was especially in the winter, a very dangerous one. A long sack, holding all of two bushels of shelled corn, would be placed upon the broad fat back of Nell, or some other safe and gentle mule, and Frank, or myself, placed upon the huge load and started off to the mill. Of the many trips I took seated on that great round, heavy sack, the mere touch of a tree, or a miss step of my mule, there would be a fall, and a great one which would be a shock even to "Humpty Dumpty."

It was in the beautiful month of September, 1863,[43] when all the fruits on the place, such as apples, peaches, and plums, were numerous and in the splendid state of maturity. We small boys were kept busy picking peaches and apples, bringing them to grandmother; and when we had brought in several bushels she would invite all the young women and young men to a paring bee. Then ten, or more, of the older women would be engaged in quartering the apples and pitting the peaches, and placing them on racks to put out in the sun to dry. This was grandmother's way of preserving large quantities of fruit for winter and early spring use.

UNCLE SILAS PREACHES ABOUT THE COMING WAR

As the coming Sunday was the fourth, when Uncle Silas would preach at the Methodist Church according to custom, every one was discussing the always enjoyed meeting. He was greatly respected and loved by everyone who knew him, and the church was always crammed when it was known that he was to preach.

On the Lord's day, which was a perfect one, the church was packed to its fullest capacity; when the grand old man arose from his seat with the Bible in his hands, and stepped up to the pulpit, it was so still in the church one could have heard a pin drop. In a calm but distinct voice he gave the familiar hymn "Rock of Ages", line upon line, which was sung by the entire congregation with spirit and enthusiasm. After a long and fervent prayer, he read from the 2nd Chapter of St. Luke, and selecting his text as the 30 and 31st verses: "For my eyes have seen the salvation which thou hast prepared before the face of all people." After describing the simple and lowly birth of our Saviour and the great events that would follow, he said: "We are now in the midst of a great crises, and we, as a people, ignorant and unprepared for it in every sense, must look to, and pray to our Lord and Saviour, Jesus Christ, for divine guidance."

"A great and terrible civil war is raging in the land, even at our very door, and many of us in one way and another, will be drawn into it. Many of us who know no other home than the cabin on the plantation, with kind and indulgent masters, will be scattered about the country and will never return."

"When you leave your homes, going into other states, take God with you, or you will be regarded as strangers in a new country, and you will need the Comforter."

"Freedom will come to you, and you will be thrown upon your own resources and held responsible for your conduct, by God and man. . . . Do not think that this new condition in your lives will end all the trials and tribulations that will confront you. In fact they have just begun and you must, God being your helper, work out your own salvation. When you are alone, talk with God, believing and trusting in Him when He says: "Come, let us reason together." . . . You who hear my voice this day, are a pastoral people, born on the plantations in the neighborhood of this church, you know little or nothing of any other kind of work save farm work, and I advise you, then, to remain on them as long as possible. . . . Many of you will drift away into the great cities. Avoid them as much as possible; but, once in them, first call at the church, and then work. Never allow yourselves to become idlers on the street, for, as such, your troubles will soon begin. In many cases wages will be offered you for labor and, doubtless, will be small. As you know nothing of its value, I advise you to accept what is offered and do your work as well as you know how, . . . as a rule, the man who hires you will be the better judge of your real worth and will reward you accordingly. Be honest, faithful, and trust-worthy. And may the Lord bless you, is my prayer forever. Amen."

This was the last I saw of the grand old man, who left his pulpit with the tears streaming down his cheeks.

II.

DURING THE WAR

I JOIN THE UNION ARMY

It was one clear, cold day in the last part of December, I went for the cows feeding the south woods [*sic*] along the pike, just west of the lake. Many soldiers were passing, going in to Nashville. And, as my interest and curiosity about them was as keen as ever, I directed Nell up to a board fence along the pike, and I sat there on her fat back, seeing them pass. It was a regiment of infantry, or, perhaps two of them; and there seemed to be so many that as they marched in fours, they filled the pike. They were extremely kind, and greeted me with the usual: "Hello, Buddy—Hello, Bud." I sat there on Nell's back fully ten minutes and, as she paid no attention to them, I thought she had gone to sleep. The regiment was followed by a very large covered ambulance, drawn by four fine horses. Just then it got opposite to where I stood. A tall handsome soldier, wearing one of those cute little caps slightly tilted over his right eye, knapsack on his back, his long musket on his shoulder, stepped out of the ranks, walked up to me, and said: "Come on, Johnny, and go with us up North, and we will set you free."

I looked at him, smiled, and with much surprise wondered how he knew my name. Without a word I slid from Nell's back, climbed over the fence near where poor Austin had been killed, got hold of the rear end of the big ambulance as it passed, and was off with the Yankees. Nell, having waked up and realizing her freedom, turned, and with the reigns dangling on her neck, started on a keen run over a slight hill back of which nestled the lake. With her head well in the air, turning this way and that, she ran out of sight; but for some unaccountable reason she turned, came back half way to the pike, snorted, turned again toward the lake, and was gone. The whip with which I had driven Nell and the cows, I carried along with me. What I was to do with it, I had not the slightest idea.

As we reached the land leading up to the White House, I could see plainly, and for the last time, Mistress Hoggatt, her two nieces, the Doctor, and the house girls, standing on the lawn, looking at us Union soldiers pass, for I was one of them, indeed, and in action. What a jolly lot of fellows—they were laughing and talking all the time.

When we reached the toll gate at Slipup, I became frightened and anxious, for I was afraid of the Blankenships, and the two boys who knew me well, for I felt sure they would tell Master, and try to interfere with my plans. Sure enough, just as we marched past the porch, there sat the two young rascals, and, seeing me holding on to the boot of the ambulance, jumped from their seats, walked up by the side of me, and taunted me by saying: "Where are you going? You are running away and we are going to tell your master." They finally turned and ran back, leaving me there frightened and uncomfortably wet with perspiration.

The sun had set clear and his golden streak, and long shadows were fast disappearing along the hillside country, as we began to approach the country strange and unfamiliar to me, twilight, and the big stars came out, promising a clear, cold, and frosty night. The soldiers were quieter now as we trod along under the cover and darkness of the night. As I marched along amid my strange and unusual surroundings, the thought occurred to me, "What am I doing? What have I done?" Tears came into my eyes, and I began to think of dear old grandmother and my home—the only home I had ever known. I was aroused from my sad, boyish, reflections by the halt of the army, for there was a long bridge just ahead of us and the regiment had to pass first. It seemed to me to be slow in doing so.

When the little army had all got safely over, there was a sharp turn to the right; and, after following what seemed to be a dirt road, for half an hour, we reached the camp in a wide field. The ambulance was driven to a slight hill, a little ways from a big tent, and stopped. The driver, a little short, thin man, got down from his little seat in front, and noticed me unhitching a tug of the near wheel horse; and seeing me in the dark for the first time, said "Hallo, who are you?"

"I am Johnny," I said.

"Oh, you are the little chap we picked up back in the country?"

"Yes," I replied.

"All right, John we will take care of you."

When the horses were unhitched, they were brought back two on each side of the tongue and facing each other, and tied by a halter. Then the hames taken off. Then he went to the rear end of the ambulance and unstrapped the long, heavy feed trough, with long pins in each end under the bottom which just fitted in two holes on the tongue, so that the horses couldn't tip it over. He then pulled from under his seat, a sack of corn and oats, mixed, measured out four half pecks, and poured it into the trough. The horses having been cared for, he led the way to the big wigwam-shaped tent. He opened the flap door and we walked in. Ten more men were seated around the comfortable fire built in the middle of the tent. They all greeted him with: "Hallo, Chat, where did you get the boy?"

"We picked him up in the country."

When he told them my name was "Johnny", they all laughed and shook hands with me. I learned soon after that they called the rebels "Johnny."

A long wide, smooth board, with legs under it, was placed to one side. This served as a table, and two big bright pans, one with bacon and the other containing a mixture of potatoes and other vegetables, plenty of hard tack, and strong coffee, were on the long table, and we all sat on the ground and ate supper. How strange it all seemed to me! I didn't eat much because nothing tasted right. Had these been corn bread, sweet potatoes, boiled bacon, and fresh buttermilk, I could have eaten with a relish. But these yankee preparations were too much for me. The dishes too, were new to me, with tin plates and cups, knives, forks, and spoons which closed up like a pocket knife.

After supper some of them lit their pipes, some played cards, while others told stories. I sat and looked at them with wonder and astonishment for about an hour, when I heard many horns blowing outside, which they called taps, or bed time.

While in the camp and by the dim camp fire, I had got a look at my adopted friend, the driver of the ambulance, whose full name, was Chat Baker.[1] The regiment I had joined was the Thirteenth Michigan Volunteers.[2] As I have already stated, he was a thin man, of average height, short, full whiskers, and slightly grey. Shortly after the sounding of taps he gave me a great heavy blanket and, to the amusement of all in the tent, made me lie on the edge of it and showed me how to roll up in it.

Although they were extremely kind to me, yet all seemed so very strange, I could not help crying myself to sleep. I was awakened next morning by many bugles sounding reveille; and when I rolled out of my warm blanket, a good fire was glowing, lighting up the dark tent. Chat, and myself, went out together and attended to the horses, and when we returned the breakfast was ready. He washed his face and hands in a tin basin, set on a stationary stool, and then I washed. He gave me a comb and one of those folding looking glasses, and after I had combed my hair, I looked like a real Yankee soldier.

The sun rise on this, my first morning in camp, was not a cheerful one, for there was a long streak of black cloud before it which took an hour or more to get over. The most impressive sight which greeted me on leaving my bunk was, what seemed to me, a world of tents. Clean and white, they seemed to cover the earth for miles around; and, as far as the eye could trace. As the morning hours passed, many soldiers began to shave themselves. There seemed to be thousands of them.

To the right of the big wigwam tent, where I had spent the night, and not far away, stood eleven covered wagons in a row. Each had six splendid mules standing at the tongue feeding. The eleven men who had spent the night in the tent, were the teamsters. The regiment was made up of ten companies, each having its own individual wagon. The eleventh wagon was the medicine wagon, containing four large chests in which were carried surgical instruments, medicine, and so on. To the left of the wagons, and a little further away, were two big square tents, the first being the Doctor's tent, and the other the Colonel's headquarters.

Along about eleven o'clock, the sun came out nice and warm. I was sitting on a big rock in front of our tent, watching the soldiers cleaning their guns, as they

Col. Michael Shoemaker of the Thirteenth Michigan Infantry in 1863. Courtesy of the Michigan Library and Historical Center.

laughed and talked, when I happened to look up toward the headquarters and saw a little black fellow in a soldier's uniform. I was both surprised and delighted. He was coming in my direction and I straightened up at once. He carried a long tin bucket in his hand, and was on his way to the spring for water. I quickly joined him and we lost no time in introducing ourselves. He had been picked up by the regiment somewhere in Kentucky, and had been with it several months. He invited me up to the Colonel's tent, and after carrying in his pail of water, he came out with his marbles, and we played. This was my first day in camp, and I was perfectly happy. The way we played the game of "seven-up" with marbles, was entirely new to the soldiers, and they gathered in crowds around up to see the excitement.

A wide strip of smooth ground in front of the Colonel's headquarters, was the parade ground, and every afternoon, between two and three, the entire regiment would be called out by the sound of the bugle and they would have what they called "dress parade." During the few months he had been with the regiment Aron had acquired considerable knowledge of army life, which consisted mostly of long marches and drills in camp. He knew all the captains and lieutenants and commanders of companies by name, and many of the private soldiers. The Colonel of the Regiment, a little short, dark haired man, with burnside whiskers, was named Shumaker, and was of German parentage. Lieutenant-Colonel Culver was a tall man, rather quiet, but a very pleasant gentleman. Major Palmer was a college pro-

Col. Joshua B. Culver of the Thir-
teenth Michigan Infantry, ca.
1863. Courtesy of the Michigan
Library and Historical Center.

fessor, highly educated; and, being a Democrat in politics, usually led the discussions.[3] Dr. Pratt, the regimental surgeon, was a tall, dark complexioned man, with
long dark hair and whiskers and the keenest of eyes. He was exceedingly cross,
crabbed, and impatient. Judging from his manner of speaking to the sick or com-
plaining soldiers who came to his tent for treatment.

MULETEER IN COMPANY "C."

I had been in camp now about ten days, and having outlived my awful home-
sickness and being somewhat familiar with camp life, felt myself ready for any kind
of duty or amusement. So one morning I reported to Aron, "My superior officer",
and to my surprise he had gotten hold of two old, rusty muskets; and handing me
one of them, we took up our position on a nice smooth piece of ground a little
ways behind the Colonel's tent. Then taking the guns and setting them aside, he
stood up straight in front of me, hands flat against his legs, heels together and toes

Dr. Foster Pratt of the Thirteenth Michigan Infantry, ca. 1863. Courtesy of the Michigan Library and Historical Center.

out. While it all seemed easy, I was extremely awkward. But, nothing daunted, he would take hold of me, give me a violent shake, and, laughing good naturedly the while, we would try it all over again. After several tries, and seeing that I was getting the idea into my thick head, he stood back a little from me, and with arms akimbo, he took a good long look at me. As my attitude seemed to satisfy him, he picked up the guns, handing me one of them, and showed me how to hold it. He then proceeded to go through the drill, telling me to do just like he did. Finally, when he saw that I was taking an interest in my new duties, he gave the order to ground arms; and, standing as I was, I let my gun fall flat on the ground. He roared in laughter. After an hour or two of military training, we broke ranks, and I was told to report every morning at 10 o'clock which I never failed to do. Being exceedingly clumsy, I found it very difficult to right about face, for it required a neat turn on the heel, a thing Aron could do with perfect ease.

There was another movement where skill and quick action was needed. This was the fixing and unfixing of bayonets. I was left-handed and tried to do the trick in that way, but he stopped me and said we could not fight rebels in that manner. So I got accustomed to using my right hand for the first time in my life.

It was on a pleasant afternoon, that I was called into Captain Yerkes' tent. He was in command of Company "C", and I was told by him that I had been assigned to his Company. Dick had charge of the Company's wagons, and I was told to report to him. Before leaving his tent, the Captain gave me a handsome suit of clothes, consisting of cap, coat, and trousers, two all-wool shirts, two pairs of socks, and overcoat and knapsack. I was the happiest boy in the world, and the Captain, I thought, was one of the nicest of men. He was tall, and rather stout, perhaps a little past forty, with dark brown hair and full beard closely cropped and slightly sprinkled with gray. Though always correct, he seemed to be a little slow of speech, having the appearance of a quite religious gentleman. Always scrupulous in his uniform, he expected and demanded the same of the men of his Company; and before they went for drill or dress parade, were drawn up in line and carefully inspected by him.

Though I was accustomed to mules, there was a lot to learn in the care and handling of a team of six of them. Dick was an Englishman, short, stout, and with sandy hair and small blue eyes. He was, I should think, twenty-five or thirty years

A quartermaster's wagon, Belle Plain, Virginia. Courtesy of the Massachusetts Commandery Military Order of the Loyal Legion and the U.S. Army Military History Institute.

of age, liked whiskey, and when he could get it, drank to excess. He was a good teamster though, always kind to me.[4] Of the thirteen teams in the regiment, ours was one of the best, and had the best care. The six matched only in their work, not in color. The wheelers, Kitty and Tuff, were heavy dark brown mules, while the middle pair, Pete and Rhoda, were nearly the same in color, but lighter in weight. The leaders, Jimmie and Jenny, were much smaller, very smart and active, and were of an ashy gray color. Although we had one of those long black whips, we never, to my knowledge, had occasion to use it with anywhere the violence as was often the case with other teamsters.

Two days after I had become Dick's helper, we had orders to break camp. Early that morning we hitched up and drove around in the middle of the Company's parade grounds, and commenced loading, first putting in the Company's tents, closely rolled with the poles and stakes inside of them.

Along about nine o'clock, the bugle was sounded, and all the Companies wheeled into line, and when the Colonel and adjutant mounted their horses, and with Jenkins[5] and his band of five snare drums and bass, began to beat time, the command was given to march, and the regiment was off. It was an hour later, when Jordan, the quartermaster, ordered the teams to pull out. Every teamster mounted his near wheeler, and with whip and jerk line in hand, was ready to move. Chat Baker, with the four horse ambulance, was close in the rear of the regiment, and the medicine wagon in charge of Jess Starkweather came next, with all the other teams strung out behind.

"Crack team" of the 1st Division, 6th A.S., near Hazel Run, Virginia. Courtesy of the Massachusetts Commandery Military Order of the Loyal Legion and the U.S. Army Military History Institute.

An hour or so after we were out on the pike, Dick put me in the saddle, on Kitty's back, and gave me my first lesson in driving a team of mules, and I was happy.

The sun rose clear, cold and bright, but along about eleven o'clock, it clouded and got very cold. There were other regiments moving with ours and, with the great number of wagons following, made an enormous train, stretching for miles along the pike. While the pike was dry and in perfect condition, the movement was exceedingly slow. We reached La Verne,[6] a railway station ten miles from Nashville, about two o'clock; and, after crossing the tracks, stopped an hour for dinner. Dick and I unhitched our team, as did all the others, and following a dirt road leading south through the woods for a quarter of a mile, found a nice little rock-bedded creek where we watered our mules. Going back to camp, we fed them, and after starting a fire of fence rails and dead pine picked up in the woods around us, we all joined in the cooking of our dinners. There was plenty of hardtack, bacon and coffee; and the great big coffee pot, holding enough coffee for twenty men, was boiling and ready by the time the bacon was cooked. They were a lot of jolly fellows, laughing and telling stories as they ate.

The quartermaster rode up and gave orders to move. We had not gone far when the pike began to wind about through a strip of hilly country, heavily wooded on either side of the pike. We were evidently in the enemy's country for we could hear very distinctly the booming of cannon. Grenades were distributed along the train, one or two to each wagon. The movement was dreadfully slow due possibly to the general apprehension that the army was far ahead and was likely to have a brush with the rebels at any time. The sun came out again but it was still very cold. A little before dark, we got up to the regiment which had gone into camp in a level strip of woods a little ways to the left of the pike. It was a beautiful sight to see the great rows of fires already built by the soldiers while waiting for tents which we quickly unloaded. The night was clear, and the moon as bright as it could be, but bitter cold. As all of the wagons had heavy canvass covers, it was very comfortable, with plenty of good warm blankets, to sleep in them.

MURFREESBORO

After loading the next morning, the slow tiresome movement began about nine o'clock. All was quiet now as we moved along the pike. We were in fine farming country now, and as the great cotton fields, stretching for miles on either side of the pike, splendid houses, built as usual, a good ways from the pike, looked comfortably prosperous [sic]. Hundreds of people, White and Colored, lined up along the road to see the Yankees for the first time in their lives, pass through their country.

Between four and five in the afternoon, we approached the first line of the great battle field. Here and there on either side of us, could be seen many disabled cannon, and not a few dead horses. Much of the heavy fighting seemed to have taken place on the left side of the pike which was a level strip of country, but heavily timbered.

Here, the carnage had been the greatest, for great big, pine trees had been uprooted and many cannon balls had passed through the thick trunks,[7] leaving holes as neat and smooth as if they had been bored.

The regiment went into camp some distance to the right and after the wagons had been unloaded, the stock was quartered a half mile to the south in a nice bit of grassy pasture. To reach it we had to follow the dirt road that lead [sic][8] through a strip of woods and the main part of the battle field. The sun was setting, and it was very cold. I had seen very few dead men in my lifetime and, naturally, was afraid of them. Of all the horrors that ever greeted a boy's eyes, here were the worst of them. Thousands of soldiers, killed where they stood—no breast works—and here they lay in heaps, ready for burial. They were fine specimens of manhood, shot in every conceivable manner—hands, arms, and legs literally blown off; and where the blood had oozed from their wounds, it had frozen. There was no mistaking the fact—this was real war—and coming upon the scene so suddenly made a lasting impression on my young mind.[9]

To the East of the low fields where our wagon train was camped, stood the long row of hospital tents, where thousands of the severely wounded were being treated. They were admirably situated along a sloping hill, extending East to West, somewhat protected from the cold north-east winds. A large mess tent, where meals for the wounded were prepared, was only a little ways from our tent, and thousands of men nurses, were constantly going and coming, trying in every possible way to make the poor helpless fellows comfortable.

Jordan, the quartermaster, came after supper, and told us he thought we would have to move on the next day, and that we had better not put up our big wigwam tent, which of course meant that we would have to go to bed early as it was too cold to sit by the camp fire. Dick disappeared immediately after supper, and I had to spend the night alone in the wagon. It proved to be one of the most uncomfortable nights I had ever experienced. Disturbed as I was in my mind from the awful sights I had seen while crossing the battle field, it was quite natural that I be unable to sleep. The long rows of hospital tents were so situated that every loud or unusual sound would be echoed right down to where I lay. Among the badly wounded soldiers brought in, was a handsome Confederate officer who had been struck by a piece of exploded shell, making a bad wound in the side of his head. He grew worse during the night, became delirious, and would cry out in a loud voice: "Take me away, these damned Yankees are killing me!" He died the next day.

I was sick at heart. There had been so much excitement during the past few days that I had not time to think of grandmother and the grand old home. Now, I wished with all my heart that I was back in the big four-poster bed with one of my brothers to keep me warm. The scene I had witnessed during the day, and more especially the weird and terrible noises of the night, had taken away all my desire to become a brave Yankee soldier.

The next morning Dick made his appearance very early in the morning, without any statement or apology as to how he had spent the night.

Several long, deep trenches, had been dug along the slope south of our train, and here, the thousands of dead were being buried. Many men, with heavy wagons, drawn by two to four big mules, were engaged in hauling the dead soldiers to their graves. After breakfast, for which I had little appetite, the order came to move up to where the regiment was encamped, a half mile to the north. The location was a beautiful one, being high and dry, gradually sloping to the East, with plenty of wood and water close at hand.

As the railroad, in many places between Murfreesboro and Nashville, had been torn up and the bridges destroyed by the rebels, there was no way to get provisions for the troops except by wagon train. The next morning all the wagons were ordered to pull out for Nashville. I was happy and glad to get away from the dreadful sight of the past few days. Dick and I had to make all necessary arrangement for the long trip of thirty miles. A big, wide slab of bacon, a box of hardtack, and plenty of coffee. Our mules were fresh, and in good condition and, like ourselves, anxious for the trip. A sack of corn and oats, two bales of hay, and we were ready for any emergency. When we reached the pike, we found hundreds of wagons from other regiments, had pulled out ahead of us, making an enormous train which stretched for miles along the pike. The day was clear and cold, and after climbing an occasional hill, over which the pike ran, we could trot along very easily. Troops were camped every few miles along the way, which afforded precaution to the train against possible rebel attacks. We reached the City of Nashville about five o'clock in the evening, without a single accident or mishap, and camped for the night just outside the city limits.

The place selected was an open field where corn had been planted, but carefully gathered, so that not even a stalk was left standing. Nearer the pike stood a large brick house, which had been totally destroyed by fire, but the walls and huge chimneys still stood intact; and a high rail fence encircled the field, and there was no wood anywhere in sight. We carried a lot of those rails, which were of cedar, and made an excellent fire. Selecting the largest room, which doubtless had been the parlor, we built a great fire and prepared our supper. There were eleven of us to sit down. The meal being the usual bacon, coffee, and hardtack. Just as we were pouring the coffee, Dave Shulters, who had charge of Company K's wagon, rushed in carrying in one hand on a plate, a fine roll of nice yellow butter, and in the other a can of milk. This was indeed a luxury. I had been in the army a little over a month, and during that time had not tasted, or even seen any butter or milk. What an improvement it was over the tin cup of strong coffee!

The supper over, those who smoked lit their pipes, and story telling began. Dave, as we all called him, was a short, thick-set man, dark complexioned, with black hair and whiskers, and small but very keen eyes. First, he told how he had made a raid on a dairy near a large farm house which we had passed on our way in, and not far from where we camped. After unhitching his team, he had walked back to this house which, like all southern houses, had its long wide porch with a row of negro cabins in the rear, and a dairy. As there are always in these dairy buildings many wide shelves on which pans of milk, butter, and occasionally a few eggs, canned fruits, etc., were placed—the moon was just rising and no one in sight. He slipped into the little house and helped himself. Dave was the funniest man I had ever known; he had a squeaky voice, and a squawky laugh. He was about thirty years old, and had been a sailor, serving in the United States Navy. He had been to China, Japan, and many other foreign countries. The next morning, we got an early start, and by nine o'clock the long train pulled into Nashville. As it was the first city I had ever visited, there were many curious things that attracted my attention. As we crossed the railway tracks a good many times, I had a chance, for the first time, to see a very great steam engine, which moved with such ease and power as it came puffing along the railroad, I was afraid of it.

There were several large stores standing on the side of Cherry street, that had been used by the Government as store houses, and here, after a long wait, our wagons were loaded with supplies of various kinds. Into our wagon went a hogshead of sugar, a lot of coffee. Others were loaded with supplies of various kinds—ammunition, bacon, hard tack, and bales of clothing.

Leaving the city late in the afternoon, we reached our camp of the night before a little before dark, and there spent the night.

It has always been a wonder and surprise to me why Nashville was not more strenuously defended by the Confederates. Situated as it was on the North bank of the Cumberland river, a wide and navigable stream, with many railroads connecting it with every southern state, should have made it a great central base for military supplies. Why the Confederates did not concentrate here and put forth more desperate efforts to hold so important a post, instead of Murfreesboro, is a mystery. It was extremely fortunate for Nashville, and more especially so for its people, that it escaped the disastrous calamity of a long siege, as suffered by so many of its sister cities further south. When the Federals took possession of the City, apparently without firing a gun, the Confederates quickly evacuated, and the people went right on in their daily pursuits, as if nothing unusual had happened.[10] There was no destruction by the Union soldiers, so apparent in other places, and yet, there was the house where we had camped two nights outside the city, which had been destroyed by fire, which surely was by accident.

Getting an early start the next morning, and leaving with some regret our comfortable four walls camp of two nights, we were fortunate in being the head of the immense train leaving Nashville that morning for Murfreesboro. It was February—cloudy, cold and snowy. Being heavily loaded, the trip had to be a slow and tedious one. Owing to the fact that much heavy traffic had passed over the pike, badly cutting it out in places, made it necessary to turn out occasionally into the fields, making a new roadway, with heavy pulling for the teams. I had by this time become quite accustomed to driving our splendid team of six mules, and could now handle them easily, even on a difficult road. While in Nashville, Dick bought me a good pair of gloves, and I was very comfortable indeed, and no longer suffered with cold hands. When my feet got cold, I would stop, and he would climb into the wagon, and I would walk or run along until my feet got warm again. We reached La Vergne about five o'clock, and, turning into the woods a short distance from the pike, we went into camp for the night.

The weather being clear and bright next day, we got an early start, leaving La Vergne about seven in the morning, and reached the camp about four o'clock in the afternoon, without accident. It was a great surprise to us to see the many improvements that had been made during our absence. Logs had been cut and foundations laid under all the tents, making it very nice and comfortable. A wide space, smooth and clean, for drilling purposes, had been cleared, and all the tents stood in a row facing it. To the South, where the teams were parked, a well had been dug, a windlass made, and two big, iron buckets hung in it, making water plentiful and near at hand. With our teams cared for, and having had supper, I went to see my friend, Aron, who, with Osborn, the cook,[11] occupied a small tent back of the Colonel's. I found him well and glad to see me. I was glad to learn from him that we were to remain there all winter, and that many new recruits had been enlisted and would join the regiment soon. Next day Aron and myself took a long walk over the great battle field situated a mile or more south of the camp. Everywhere through the heavy timbered country we saw the awful destruction caused by cannon fire—great trees uprooted and exploded shells scattered everywhere. And dead had all been gathered up and buried. The spot selected for this purpose was a beautiful piece of land sloping to the southwest and heavily sodded. Thousands of dead soldiers were buried there. Each had his name, also the name of his regiment and company, written on a piece of smooth board, which stood at the head of his grave.

We then paid a visit to the long row of hospital tents. Thousands of wounded soldiers, heads bandaged, arms in slings, and many on crutches, were stirring about in the warm sunshine. There were long rows of cots, nice and clean, extending away up the hill side, almost as far as the eye could track, and many of them still occupied by the more desperately wounded soldiers unable to go out. Many doctors and nurses, in clean, white caps and aprons, were busily engaged waiting on them. The long operating tent stood just to the south. There were many doctors, and long tables where legs and arms were taken off. We started to go in, but the doctor met us at the door, and said: "No, boys. Not today."

We made our way back to the camp, reaching it just in time for dinner. In view of the fact that we were to be in camp for a long time, the Quartermaster thought that the teamsters mess, consisting of thirteen men, ought to have a cook. He supplied this demand. James Moran, a little short, stockily built Irishman, was detailed from Company F, to be our cook. Jimmy, as we all called him, was about forty years old, or earlier in life; and in some unaccountable way, had the misfortune to break his right arm just above the elbow, making it difficult and rather painful to handle the heavy muskets. So he was glad of the change from soldierly activities to that of the teamster's cook.

Salt pork was an entirely new dish to me. Nothing of the kind was in use on the plantation. With us it was smoked meats of various kinds. As the salt pork was regularly used in the army, Jimmy often gave it to us fried or baked with beans; and, when cabbage could be had, boiled with it. It was a good dish. He accompanied us on the second trip to Nashville, and after giving us a good supper, disappeared immediately. He had walked into the City, a distance of more than a mile, and returned about eleven o'clock gloriously drunk. How he ever found the way back to the camp, was a mystery to us all. He was born in Cork, and told us many funny Irish stories, only one of which I can now recall. It was this:

He was crossing the street one day, and met an American. Jimmy stopped and asked him, why the Queen of England was called Victoria. The poor American hadn't the slightest idea. "Why," said Jimmy, "it is her name."

After our long walk over the battle field and the visit to the trenches where many soldiers were buried, and then to the hospital where we saw hundreds suffering from terrible wounds, my enthusiasm began to cool. I became very much discouraged, and did not think I would care to become a soldier. One pleasant afternoon, after our usual drill, I laid before Aron my gloomy state of mind. I told him that I had had enough of war. "Why", he said.

"Oh", said I, "I don't want to be a soldier if I have to kill people."

"Look here, John, are you an American citizen?"

"I don't know, I reckon so."

"Why, of course you are", he said. "Now then, being an American citizen, your first duty is to your God, and your country; and you may have to lay down your life in defense of it. What do you suppose we have been drilling for?"

"Oh, just for the fun of it", I said.

"Well, we ain't. Now, Colonel Shumaker says there is no more honorable death than to die for one's country. You ran away from slavery because you wanted to be free. You were tired of being whipped by a mean old mistress and over-seer. Well, I did the same thing. Colonel says further, we are fighting for two reasons. First, to save the Union; and secondly, to free the slaves. While we are just boys and not big enough to enlist, we are helping by doing what we can to free ourselves. This war may go on until we have grown up—we don't know—then we can be soldiers and help fight the Johnnies. You say you don't want to kill anybody. Let me tell you something, John, when you get on the battle field with your regiment, and when the order is given to fire on the enemy, you don't know, and none of your regiment knows whether they have killed any rebels, because there is so much smoke you can't see. About the only time you can tell when you kill a man, is when you are doing picket duty. At such time you must be cool, take good aim, and get your man if you can."

SHILOH

"Now, I will tell you how the regiment fought the rebels at the battle of Shiloh. They were strongly fortified along a ridge in a big wheat field, and our regiment, with a lot of others, had to fight them in the open. They had to lie down on the ground to load their guns, for protection against the awful rebels fire; then rising on one knee, and fire. It was in April, an awfully hot day, and pretty soon our men were ordered to get ready to charge. So they loaded their guns, fixed their bayonets, and the whole line, nearly a mile long started on a keen run, yelling at the top of their voices when they ran; and when they had reached the rebel's works, they fired, and you ought to have seen the 'Johnnies' run out of their breastworks."[12]

With much interest, I asked why they yell when they charge? "Oh," he said, "it gives you courage and you forget yourself and all about being afraid."

It was in the latter part of March, and having been in the army now nearly four months and having had many and various experiences, I began to realize, after my long conversation with Aron, that I owed something in the way of duty to the government that protected me. It clothed and fed me, and had freed me from the terrible lash, so mercilessly inflicted. Though a mere boy, I could do little in helping the great military system. Yet the little I could do would be some help, and I should do it as well as I knew how. Aron's remarkable influence had made a deep and lasting impression upon me; and, feeling greatly encouraged, I made up my mind to do my duty as I saw it.

Thirty-five new recruits had reached the regiment—fine healthy, young fellows, who were being drilled daily, to the amusement of everybody, who laughed heartily at the stupidity and awkwardness of them.

TULLAHOMA

Along in April, orders were issued to move, and our objective was Tullahoma, forty miles south, as it was reported the rebels were gathering in that quarter. It was cold and cloudy when we left our old camp, and hadn't gone far when it began to rain. The regiment halted and every man put on his tarpaulin, a rubber covering, being a square piece of oilcloth, having a hole in the middle of it, through which the men stuck their heads, affording splendid protection as it covered the body to the knees. We camped just before dark in a strip of woods just outside the little town of McMinnville. A slow, drizzling rain fell all night, making it the most uncomfortable night I ever spent. Strange to say, the men didn't seem to mind it, they took it good naturedly and seemed as jolly as ever. It was still raining next morning when we moved out, but toward mid day the rain stopped. We reached Tullahoma about four o'clock in the afternoon, and as we marched through the streets of the little town the sun shone bright and warm. With banners unfurled and band playing, the whole population turned out, entirely filling the streets, to see us pass. We went into camp in an open pasture just north of the town, and not far from the river, which we had to cross to reach it. A large farm house stood a short distance to the East of us, and was occupied by White people. A great plantation lay north of it, and many slaves were at work planting the season's crop. We learned that the man who owned the place was named "Law," and that he and his two sons were in the Confederate army.

We learned also that we were the first of the Union troops seen in that part of Tennessee.

Many had gone from the place to join the Confederates. Some had been killed in the great battle at Murfreesboro. A battery Battalion was encamped near our regiment, and its daily drills greatly interested me as heretofore I had seen little of this most important branch of the army. I took a good look at the big cannon balls and shells that had done such terrible and deadly work on the battle field around Murfreesboro. The ease and quickness with which the men handled them, made it seem to me that they were very light, but when I lifted one of them, I found it quite different.

One night, it being unusually warm, I concluded to sleep under the wagon instead of inside; and, so taking a nice clean lot of hay, spread it out underneath the wagon, and with my blanket on top this made a very soft and comfortable bed. I lay down, and was sound asleep when I was suddenly awakened by something pushing at my back. I arose, and quickly discovered a big hog rooting around, trying to find something to eat. I was awfully frightened, and when it discovered me, it ran away.

During my ten days stay in this beautiful strip of country we engaged in many very successful foraging expeditions, bringing in corn, vegetables, a few chickens, and some fodder.

We were ordered to move again, and taking a route further to the east, returned to Murfreesboro. A number of bushwhacking bunches of rebels were encountered on our trip coming back, but we quickly scattered them, without any serious results of our men in pursuit. On reaching our destination, after two days march, a new camp site was selected about two miles north of our old one. It was a large open field, with a long hill sloping gradually to the west, and a strip of heavy timber land lay just to the north of the camp. Learning that we were to remain here for some time I was happy. As we were only three miles from Murfreesboro, hucksters and peddlers soon found us out and came into camp every day, in wagons and carts loaded with vegetables, fresh bread and pies. These things were scarce, and the poor soldiers were glad to get them at any price. The price charged by the vendors being ten cents a loaf for bread, and twenty-five cents a piece for pies. These things, real luxuries to the soldiers, were not included, nor could they be carried in his large stock by the sutler who was attached to the regiment. Amongst the articles chiefly used, and which could be bought from the sutler at an enormous price, be it remembered, were various kinds of liquor, tobacco, and jack knives.

Up to this time, no music was furnished the regiment, but fife and snare drums. Lora C. Jenks, a sergeant of Company "F", did what he could, with a patriotic spirit to cheer and enliven the monotonous moments, with an assistant fifer, five small drums, and a bass. All the other regiments in the brigade had brass bands, and splendid music was furnished by them. So Jeremiah E. Glines, of Company "F", who had enlisted as a musician, was detailed to organize a band. Instruments were ordered, and when they arrived in due course of time, they were received with interest and admiration by every one in the regiment. He was allowed the pick of the men in the regiment, and selected fourteen to blow the big and little horns. Practice at once began, and all seemed to take a great interest in their new duties. It being summer weather, they practiced day and night. Within a few weeks they were playing tunes, and when it began to play for guard muster every morning, and dress parade in the afternoon, the regiment, for the first time in its existence, was up to the times with other regiments, and was happy. How well I remember those tunes to this day. Not their names, of course, but their high spirited sound which would echo all through and around the camp.

Of the many men in the regiment with whom I had become personally acquainted during the first months I had been in the service, there was none, it seemed to me, so imbued with and enthusiastic in their duties as Jenks. He saw to it that his invincible army of drummers did not oversleep of mornings; and, down in the edge of the strip of woods, regularly every morning, sounded reveille. He was a tall, thin man, with short wiry whiskers, and an inveterate chewer of tobacco, the juice of which oozed from the side of his mouth as he vigorously blew his fife. The bandmen having qualified and become able to furnish all the necessary music, Jenks and his little squad, was disbanded, and the men transferred back to their various companies. Though commissioned as sergeant in his Company, he did little or no service. His occupation was gone, and he took it hard, and regretted it as a severe blow to his honor.

Just beyond this strip of timber land situated to the North of the camp, there had been a clearing, evidently for the purpose of planting. This was a bit higher than the ground on which the camp stood, and any one moving about up there could be seen distinctly from the regimental grounds. Here, late in the afternoon, generally between four and five o'clock, when the regiment was resting from its drills, sham battles, and so on, our old friend Jenks would march up and down, keeping time with his beloved fife in his right hand, carrying himself in a most perfect military attitude. Having made several trips up and down, apparently working up the spirit of the "Seventh", he would then put his fife to his lips and would play his favorite tunes with the same pride and energy as when he had furnished all the music for the regiment. One day, as I sat in the shadow of our wagon, watching him for a long time, he seemed to be so worn out from his many rounds that he threw himself down on the ground in a heap, his hat off and his hands folded clasping his knees, his head resting on them. It was an attitude of utter dejection. I was sure he was suffering and I pitied him with all my heart and soul. Why he was not made a member of the newly organized band, I never learned. Both Glines and he belonged to the same Company, and a great injustice had been done him, it seemed to me.

As the railroad between Murfreesboro and Nashville had been repaired, the bridges, destroyed by the rebels, rebuilt, provisions were now being shipped direct to Murfreesboro by train, the distance to the town being only three miles from the camp, the hauling of supplies by wagon train was easily made in one day. We were often delayed, owing to the difficulty in loading so many wagons.

COL. SHUMAKER RESIGNS

It was a great surprise, and generally regretted by every one in the regiment when news went the rounds of the camp that Colonel Shumaker had resigned. No particular reason, as far as I could learn, was given why he was leaving the service.[13] It was said, however, and generally believed, that the step taken by him was because of failing health. He looked to be a good deal past forty, which in the opinion of the soldiers in that day, was old for a man in active service. I knew the regiment had been in many battles and had seen a great deal of the war before either Aron or myself had joined it. In a sharp engagement with the rebels at Tyree, Tennessee, on September 7, 1862, he was taken prisoner, and exchanged at Richmond, Virginia, September 27, 1862.[14] How well I remember the little keen eyed man, with rather a large head, dark hair sprinkled with gray, heavy mustache, and burnside whiskers, the style of that day. The style of combing the hair at that time seemed odd and peculiar to me, for it was parted behind as well as in front.

Colonel Culver was a tall, slender man, of neat appearance. Although extremely kind in his manner toward every one, there was that about him which made one feel that his authority must be respected.

It was late in June, 1863, when orders were issued to move again. Though the weather was frightfully hot, every soldier seemed anxious for a change. This was chiefly noticeable among the new recruits who had lately joined the regiment. When we moved out early one morning, utterly disregarding the terrible heat, their haversacks were stuffed and overflowing with useless things. But after hard marching for miles, a halt was called for a few minutes rest. The "green horns" as they called them then, began to unload shirts, paper collars, razors, shaving cups, books, writing paper, in fact everything that seemed to be weighty was quickly cast aside. The poor fellows, inexperienced and seeing real military service for the first time, (some of them said they had enlisted just for the fun of the thing), were now quite ready to quit. Many of them collapsed completely and had to be taken into the ambulance.

However, after several days hard marching, we reached the Tennessee river, a few miles west of Florence, Alabama. There were some sharp skirmishes with the enemy.[15] We camped for the night to await the laying of the pontoon bridge before crossing the great wide stream. There were several regiments and a battalion of artillery. These passed over first, and then came the long wagon train, heavily loaded with ammunition and provisions. This was my first experience in crossing a bridge of this kind, and I was very much frightened, and so were the mules for they hugged and crowded each other all the way over.

As it was necessary to drive very slowly, Dick put me in the saddle, and he walked ahead of the team, and so reached the other bank in safety. It was dreadfully slow and tedious work, as only two teams were allowed on the bridge at the same time, and

Wagon train crossing a pontoon bridge over the Germanna Ford, Rapidan River. Courtesy of the Massachusetts Commandery Military Order of the Loyal Legion and the U.S. Army Military History Institute.

one must be well over before the other began to cross. As the banks were rather steep and rough, it was really interesting to see our splendid little six mules, every one of which was as true as steel, pull with all their strength up these long high banks.

Strange to say, during the half year I had been with Dick, not a single accident had happened to Dick, myself, or to any of our fine mules. They were always sleek, and in good condition. We never swapped mules, as many of the teamsters did. Jesse Starkweather's team was the biggest and the finest in the regiment, but it was bulky, and when on rough roads would get stuck in the mud and would have to be drawn out by the team behind. Dave Shulters, our funny old Dave, was constantly trading, and every week or so would be showing off a new mule.

Leaving Florence after a couple days rest, we reached Tuscumbia, where we remained for a week. As bushwhacker bunches were numerous again, a battalion of cavalry was sent to our aid to clean the country of the Union enemy. We left Tuscumbia early in the morning, and glad indeed I was when we learned we would not have to cross the river over that dreadful pontoon bridge. We were to follow the main road, going east, which ran close to the river bank, awfully rough and rocky. Late one afternoon we reached the low flat country along its course, densely wooded on the opposite side, so that nothing distinctly could be seen. On our side it was quite different. It being rocky and hilly, with an occasional clear spot, so that the troops and trains were exposed to view. A company of rebels had concealed themselves in the dense forest, close to the stream, and opened fire on us. It was immediately returned by our train guard. There were no casualties amongst the men, but seven mules were killed. We were told by the quartermaster on reaching these exposed spaces, to drive quickly so as to avoid being caught by flying bullets. Jesse Starkweather some how did not heed the warning, and his off mule was shot through the neck and killed.

The next day we reached a low shallow place in the stream, which we forded, and camped for the night.

Two long, hot days march brought us into the beautiful little city of Huntsville. As I never kept track of the days of the week, I was surprised when Dick told me it was Saturday. First, the troops marched through the crowded city, bands playing and flags flying. The people seemed to enjoy it immensely, regarding us as their friends instead of as conquerors of their country. I never saw so many pretty mulatto girls as we found in this little southern city.

The regiment was camped in a beautiful strip of woods, just outside the town, and the poor tired soldiers spent the day sleeping in the shade. Aron came down to where the teams were parked, and proposed a game of marbles. It had been months since we had engaged in this, our favorite sport. A hard, dry spot was selected under a big spreading oak tree, and here we spent the entire afternoon playing.

At night we went to church for the first time since we had been in the service. The sermon was preached by a tall, White man and many soldiers from the regiment attended. I was surprised to find that the custom here was the same as that at my home, the White people occupying the front seats and the colored people the back seats. Seeing us dressed in complete uniforms, we were of great curiosity to them, and after leaving the church, they crowded about us and plied us with many questions—where we came from, how long we had been in the service, and how we were treated, and so on. We left the pretty little Alabama town next morning, taking with us many pleasant memories of it and its people.

Going North again, we passed through some of the most beautiful farming country we had seen in the state. Late in the afternoon we reached the heavy timber again, and camped for the night.

About eleven o'clock the next day, we reached the state line, marked by two huge rocks, one on either side of the road—Alabama on one side, and Tennessee on the other. We were back in my native state again, and camped opposite Fayetteville, a little town situated on a small stream called Elk river. It was late in July, and here we rested for ten days.

LOOKOUT MOUNTAIN

Leaving here and entering Lookout Valley, there were many sharp fights with the rebels, who we kept on the move ahead of us.[16] We were now approaching the Cumberland Mountains, which could be seen in the distance. They were the first mountains I had ever seen, and were a great curiosity to me. Reaching the Town of Dayton one morning about nine o'clock, without opposition by the enemy, we marched through it in triumph, and arrived at the foot of the Cumberland Mountains late in the afternoon, and camped for the night. It is a most beautiful bit of country, with low, flat meadows, extending from north to south along the base of the mountains. A stream of cool, clear water, perhaps ten feet wide, flowed directly from under the mountains. It was the most delicious drinking water we had tasted.

We were awakened by Horace Easton, the regimental bugler, at five o'clock the next morning, sounding the reveille. Orders were issued by the quartermaster that, owing to the precipitous conditions of the mountains, only half of the original load could be hauled at a time, the other half to be left and we would return for it. Two companies of the regiment were left behind to guard the great quantities of supplies and ammunition; and, about nine o'clock, Dick and myself, with our splendid little team of six, had the lead. I being the lighter of the two, was placed in the saddle on Kitty's back. Our mules were in high spirits and eager for the climb. Dick walked on first one side and then the other, seeing that everything was all right. The road was rough and rutty in many places, and was getting very steep so that we could go only about the length of the team when we had to stop for a rest. During those short intervals I would dismount, and Dick and I would pet and talk to our little team, encouraging them all we could. They seemed to appreciate it.

Men of the regiment were thickly scattered on either side of the long wagon train, and were of great service, for they could watch the hind wheels and when I started, as many as could, would lift and push, and up we would go for a few feet further, stop and rest. It was the last days of July and awfully hot, and along about eleven o'clock, a very refreshing shower came, lasting perhaps a quarter of an hour. This was bad for parts of the long winding road that had a clay surface, making it difficult for the mules to keep on their feet because of continuous slipping.

There was a halt for dinner, which was very welcome. Only three miles of the uphill journey had been covered. While the troops and teams were resting, Aron and I took a walk through the heavy timber in the mountains, where we found many paths, leading to springs, with wooden troughs arranged so that the water could be carried a good ways down the mountain side. The largest chestnut trees I had ever seen were literally weighted down with nuts; but, unfortunately, they were not yet ripe. The little village of Dayton, which we passed through the day before, could still be seen, slumbering in the valley below. How beautiful and quiet it seemed to be way down there in the little town, having the appearance of the Sabbath day.

The bugle sounded, and we hurried back to the command, and were soon tugging away up the mountain again. It was getting so steep now it looked as though we were going straight up in the air, and long ropes tied on each side of the wagons and grabbed by many soldiers, aided the mules a good deal in the heavy pull up the great mountain. Whether there were other roads leading through and across the great chain of mountains, I never learned. It was a fact that this road however, over which we climbed with such difficulty, was an old and frequented one, made plainly visible by its rough usage by heavy traffic that had previously passed over it.

Along about four o'clock in the afternoon, we reached a portion of the road which seemed to have been cut through the solid rock, for there were great walls of smooth rock standing on each side, perhaps twenty feet high, for a distance of more than a hundred feet in front of us. The troops and train were completely hidden from our view while passing through this great gulch. Being in the enemy's country, and to avoid possible surprise or attacks from guerilla bands—said to be numerous in these parts—troops were sent ahead to cover the country on both sides. As the road between these massive walls was so narrow the soldiers could not use their long ropes and the only aid rendered by them was pushing the wagons from behind. This helped considerably as it enabled the teams to get an easier start, and when they once got going they would go until we stopped them for another rest. We reached the top of the great mountain between eight and nine o'clock at night, and found that the long string of troops which had been marching ahead of us all day, had gone into camp in a fine level strip of woods to the left of the main road, and camp fires were burning brightly everywhere. There was no moon but the stars were all out, shining brightly. I was surprised to find it so much cooler way up there on the mountain top than it was in the valley below.

After we had parked our wagons, fed and watered the teams, and while we ate our suppers, Ruggles, the quartermaster, announced, to our great surprise and astonishment, that we were to unload at once, hitch up, and spend the night in going down to the valley for the remainder of our load. It was about eleven o'clock before we got started. As I had driven all the way up, covering the entire distance of ten miles in the saddle, Dick suggested that he drive the team down. We locked both hind wheels, and we carried only a sack of mixed corn and oats and a bale of hay. When Dick had got started on the downward trip, I rolled up in my blanket and tried to sleep, using the sack of corn as a pillow. Just as I would begin to doze the wheels would jolt over a big rock in the road, and I would find myself on the other side of the wagon bed. It was the roughest and most disagreeable night I had yet experienced. I believe I did sleep a little, because I was wakened occasionally when I would sit up and look out under the canvas covering. Troops were scattered all along the route and had built fires, making the long trip down less lonely and tiresome. We reached our former camp in the valley just as the sun was rising, and were greeted by many shouts from the men left behind. While we cared for our teams, they loaded the wagons. We spent the day sleeping and giving our teams a much needed rest.

Next morning we got an early start, and finding it much cooler after the shower of the previous day, we made splendid progress and reached our destination at the top of the mountain an hour earlier than the night before. Nothing of importance had occurred during our absence and when taps were sounded at the usual hour of nine, all was quiet and peaceful. Getting an early start, the descent down the east side of the mountain was begun. This part of the road was in much better condition and less precipitous. Reaching a fine farming district in the valley below along about noon, we went into camp for the day.

As there were many fine fields of green corn and sweet potatoes, we lost no time in helping ourselves to these delicious things. We reached the Tennessee river next day, and the pontoon bridge having been laid, the perilous crossing began. Here, the river is a good quarter of a mile wide, very deep, and awfully swift, so that the frail river bridge fairly rocked under the heavy traffic passing over it.

There was another long, tedious wait, owing to the great number of troops to pass over first. After these, several batteries of heavy artillery had gone across, and the train started. To avoid the high clay embankment extending all along the great river front, the engineers had made a temporary road with a gradual curve to the right, to reach the river. I was in the saddle again, and although one hind wheel was locked, my leaders were frantic with excitement, and not until Dick stepped in front of them were they quieted.

We were going along all right when a remarkable thing happened. There was a sharp turn to the left, and my left hind wheel went over and caught on the narrow edge of the bridge; and, feeling the heavy jolt of the tongue, I looked back and seeing the danger I was in, I gave Kitty a sharp kick in her fat sides and brought it up into place again. I had never been so frightened. And, if that wheel had ever touched the water some two feet below the bridge, myself and the team, and all, would have been drowned.

After safely crossing the big stream, we pitched our tents on a light clay hill, not far from the river, remaining there for many days. It was one of the most wretched of camps, raining every day, not a farm house anywhere in sight and wood exceedingly scarce. Water for all purposes was taken from the river, and it was the exact color of the clay soil on which we camped. Many soldiers were made sick from drinking it, and several died, as might be expected in a camp which was so extremely unhealthy. The rain finally ceased, and the sky cleared.

Before crossing the river, we had passed a deserted cabin a half mile from the river, which could be plainly seen from our camp. A company of rebels had taken possession of it as a precaution against the continuous rain, and perhaps to keep an eye on our movements. A cavalry man was seen to ride up at top speed, from a strip of woods to the West, dismount and go in; and in a few minutes, he came out and quickly mounting his gray horse, rode off in the direction from which he had come.

The commander of the battery, camped just below us, was watching their movements through his field glasses, and being sure that there were a dozen or more in the lonely hut, had one of the small guns drawn up by a few of the men; and, taking good aim, opened fire on it. One shot was sufficient. The entire building seemed to rise up, and then fall in a complete heap. Several of the rebels ran out, waving their hats at us, and then disappeared in a bit of woods north of the old shack. Whether any of them were killed or not, I did not know.

Breaking up our camp the next morning, we marched South through the valley toward Lookout mountain, which we reached after a long, hot day's march, and camped for night. Chattanooga being our next objective, an early start was made. The road ran southeasterly through the mountains, following the course of the river which could be seen to our left, between steep embankments. The railroad ran close to it but no trains could be seen in motion. It was not quite dark, and the road very rough. We had just rounded a sharp turn in the narrow ridge when a tire on the left hind wheel came off and several spokes were broken. Of course we had to stop, and the long train behind as well. The quartermaster rode up and suggested that we unhitch the team and with the aid of teamsters and train guards, we succeeded, by many heavy lifts and shoves, to get the wagon out of the road so that others could pass. We were told that we would have to spend the night there, and that another wheel would be sent us next day. While I removed the harness, Dick made a close search for a path, or road, down the steep hill, to see if we could get the team down to water. It was impossible, he said, to find anything in the way of a road or path, owing to the intense darkness, so we concluded to get out big tin buckets and carry water for the thirsty mules.

After many trips and hard scrambling up the mountain side, giving each mule all he wanted, we kindled a fire and had our supper. We sat around and talked for an hour or so; then Dick proposed that we go in swimming, a welcome suggestion, to which I readily agreed. Getting out a clean shirt, and taking along our empty buckets, we proceeded through the heavy foliage, down the steep decline, and, crossing the railroad track we quickly undressed and plunged in. It now being September, it was a bit chilly, but the water was warm. Returning to our wagon after a most refreshing dip in the Tennessee river, we retired for the night. As many troops were camped a little distance back of us, we had no fear of being captured by the enemy.

CHATTANOOGA

Along about nine o'clock next morning, Ben Wade, with Company "F's" wagon, drove up with a brand new wheel to take the place of our broken one. We soon had it on, and started off for the city, five miles below. The morning was clear and bright, and we had not gone far along the continually winding road, when the little city in the valley below appeared in full view. At that distance, say four miles, the buildings looked small and crowded. The long straight macadamized streets running through the city, and the occasional church spires, could be plainly seen. A long strip of country lying between the city and the mountains, was dotted here and there with long rows of tents, and many soldiers moved about. We came to a very large and imposing frame house, standing on the left side of the road. The owners, or occupants, had departed, taking with them everything that was movable, and even the "iron-bound buckets that hung in the well." We drove into the city, hot and dusty, and were surprised to learn from the troops that they had entered the town without the least opposition from the enemy and that not a gun was fired. The large population of women, children, and old men, seeing the "Yankees" for the first time, so crowded the streets that the cavalry had to gallop along with swords drawn and force them back so that the troops and train could pass. Our quartermaster found for the ten wagons of the regiment, a suitable spot for a coral, it being in a large vacant lot just back of a big four-story frame hotel, now vacant.

Louis Gordon, of Company "F", the regimental blacksmith, had established his shop in a shed near by, and was kept very busy for many days for the feet of the mules had to be reshod. Though the nights were cool it was warm enough during the day, and there was nothing of importance to do but to rest and enjoy ourselves. We had two whole days of this delightful inaction, when we learned that Bragg and Longstreet with their immense force, were strongly fortified along the Chickamauga Creek in the woods two miles west of the town.

On the morning of September 16th the regiment moved out and went into camp in an open field just north of the strip of woods in which the great battle was raging.[17]

In the afternoon of the same day many troops passed our train camp, and among them was a cavalry troop, having a splendid brass band. It was a great curiosity to me to see the members of the band sitting astride their horse and playing such beautiful tunes at the same time. A few minutes later, General Rosecrans, Commander of our force, rode by with his escort. I had heard much of the great little man, but this was the first opportunity of seeing him.[18]

During the day I had walked about and saw much of the busy little city and its buildings. Walking down as far as the river, I saw many steam boats, the first I had ever seen. None of them were in motion, all seemed to be tied up. Several I noticed were loaded with cotton, others were loaded with various kinds of freight. Many peddlers were stationed along the bank, selling fruit, etc. My long walk about the town and the many excitements during the day had tired me somewhat and I was going to bed, when the quartermaster rode in from the front and said provisions were needed and must go out right away. We looked around, and examined every wagon, but no teamster could be found.

"What is your wagon loaded with, John?"

"Bacon, coffee, and hardtack", I told him.

"Well", said he, "Hitch up as quickly as possible and get out there."

It was quite dark, but I soon got the team hitched up and was on the move. When I arrived, several other teams were waiting, lined up back of the row of tents, and helped to unload the wagon.[19]

After standing for several days, the mules were inclined to be frisky and anxious to go. Realizing this fact, I had the presence of mind to lock the left hind wheel. I was just climbing into the saddle when our men in the long line of trenches, fronting the enemy, opened fire. It was so sudden and unexpected that both myself and mules were awfully frightened. The men helping to unload said: "Don't be scared, Johnny, we are just putting the Rebels to bed." My team wanted to run, but I managed with some difficulty to keep it down to a slow trot. Reaching the camp in safety, I unhitched, watered and fed my team and went to bed. I looked around, and called, but none of the teamsters had put in an appearance. I didn't go to sleep for a long time; and, for the first time since I left Murfreesboro, I had a bad spell of the blues. First, the regiment was out there on the battle field and, perhaps, was being cut to pieces by the enemy, and I wanted to be with it. All were so kind to me. Many of them I knew by name. I think I cried myself to sleep.

When I awoke next morning, Dick was feeding the teams and, the others were busy, and all looked guilty. The quartermaster appeared on the scene, and told them what I had done; also, that if there was another occurrence of shirking on their posts, like that of the night before, they would be court martialed.

The battle began while we were eating breakfast, cannon roared, smoke from the awful fighting field, could be seen rising slowly in the distance. In the afternoon slightly wounded soldiers, heads bandaged, arms in slings, began straggling into town. Then the ambulances, loaded with the more desperately wounded, came stringing in. All reported that our forces were greatly out numbered and that a setback was probable.[20] The glaring facts were apparent when, late in the evening, the entire force was driven from the field, sustaining heavy losses, and were practically shut up in the town. Our regiment, the last in the field, suffered heavily, losing a hundred and seven men, killed, wounded, and missing.[21] Colonel Culver was injured by a shell bursting over his head, deafening him so that he could not hear. Captain Clark D. Fox, of Company "I", was killed in action. How well I remember him! He was of medium height, light, sandy hair and whiskers, and was one of the nicest men I knew. Francis Murray (we called him Frank) of my Company, received terrible wounds from which he died on September 21st. He was the handsome young soldier who, nine months before, said to me as I sat there on old Nell's fat back: "Come on, Johnny, and go with us up North, and we will set you free." The regiment met its fate when it charged across Mill Creek. Here, the enemy was strongly fortified, and as our lines approached, a deadly fire was turned upon them; and here, many dead and mortally wounded were picked up.

A few days later, General Grant came with reinforcements, and, as Bragg had moved his army to Lookout Mountain, there was nothing to do but surround it and cut him off. Three divisions of Grant's army came up from the Northeast side of the mountain and, while the enemy were being attacked on that side, the pontoon bridge was hastily thrown across the river and troops of our division passed over and were soon seen scaling up the mountain side, climbing slowly, but fighting as they went. It was a dull, cloudy day, and along about noon snow began falling.[22]

When the mountain peak was reached by our forces, it was completely enveloped in clouds—but that seemed to make no difference to them, for, once they had gotten a footing on the top, the Rebels fled to the westward in great disorder.

It was still snowing later in the afternoon, when two thousand Rebels that had been captured during the day's fighting, were brought in to the city. As they were the first I had seen in such great number during my ten months of service, I took a good look at them. It was a most pathetic sight, and in my heart I pitied them. Poor and thin, many without coats, hats, or shoes, plodding dejectedly along down the rough, winding mountain road. The mountain, and country around the town, had been thoroughly cleared of the enemy, our regiment moved to Missionary Ridge and established winter quarters. It was an ideal spot, being in a bit of heavy timber, and protected by the high hills from the cold northeast winds.

Colonel Culver found it necessary to leave the regiment for a time, on account of illness; and, to my great surprise and sorrow, took Aron with him. We spent pretty near all of the night before his departure together, and he told me the Colonel lived in a little town of Paw Paw, Michigan, and that he had promised to send him to school; and that when he had learned to read and write, he would write to me and tell me all about the North and freedom.

For many days after my little friend had gone, I was gloomy and sad, for he was such a comfort to me. Always cheerful and happy, quick to catch the spirit of the most difficult problems, his loss to me was very keenly felt. As I knew nothing of the time required to fit him sufficiently to educate himself so he could write letters to me, the only thing I thought, was to wait, and rely upon his promise. I felt confident he would be faithful and do what he said.

As it seemed to be a settled fact that we were to spend the entire winter here, the officers and men decided to make the camp as comfortable as possible. Men, detailed from the companies, were organized into squads; and, with sharp axes and long crosscut saws, went into the woods near by; and, selecting, straight, smooth pine, oak, white wood trees, the teams were kept busy hauling logs and wood into the camp. Although it was December, and the camp occasionally greeted by light snow storms, the men seemed to enjoy it and amused themselves in various ways. When the great piles of logs were hauled in they were used for foundations of the tents, bunks built above ground in them, making them cozy and comfortable.

A good sized chapel was also built, where our chaplin conducted services twice a week. Here also Glines and his band found a comfortable place to practice in.

After completing the work in and about the camp to the satisfaction of the officers and men, the government called upon us to assist in constructing several forts, as the City of Chattanooga, which it intended to hold, was practically defenseless in case of attack.[23] As logs, very long and very big had to be hauled a good distance from the camp, we removed the beds from the wagons, long coupling poles were put in so that the logs could be handled with ease.

RECRUITS

Along in January (1864) recruiting officers came around, and more than a hundred, Dick being one of them, reenlisted for another three years, or until the close of the war. As an inducement to encourage reenlisting, those whose terms of service would expire from time to time, a furlough of thirty days would be granted them by the Government. Many of those who accepted the Government's offer, were termed veterans, returned to their homes in various parts of the State of Michigan and had a jolly good time during their short stay.

It was one fine day in January while we were at breakfast, that it was suggested we go on a foraging expedition. As a good deal of is [sic] had on a trip of this kind, all agreed, and we proceeded to saddle our mules. Dick suggested that we use our leaders, Jimmie and Jenny, as they were easy and more active in the saddle. I had just mounted Jenny when my brother, Jeff, astride a big bay horse, and in company with a number of other soldiers, rode up. Why, I was taken so completely by surprise I could scarcely believe my eyes! We quickly dismounted and went into each other's arms. Oh, I was so glad to see him! He stood off and looked at me, and said I had grown a little. I told him what regiment I was in and he said:

"Oh, yes, I have heard of the 'fighting thirteenth.' I am with the Sixth Ohio Battery, have been with it six months. Having heard that you had gone and supposing you had joined the army, I ran away from the Murfreesboro plantation to look you up and bring you home."

"Do you know, Jeff I have been in this regiment over a year and haven't been sick a day! How is grandmother and all the people?"

"I have heard from no one since I left, but a few days before I left she and the boys were very well. Old Master died a month after you left. Miss Emma Gentry married a Mr. Brogan, and lives in Lebanon, Miss. Miss Delia lives with them. It became so lonely that Mrs. Hoggatt has also moved there. She took all the beautiful furniture, and not a soul lives in the grand old house, and it has become a rat hole. It is too bad.[24] Now, when you return from your foraging trip come up to my camp and we will have another chat. Good bye—don't forget."

And thus we parted. Returning from our trip late in the afternoon, having got hold of a few chickens, potatoes, and a cabbage or two, we felt very well satisfied with our day's sport. Immediately after caring for the team, I hastened up to Jeff's camp with the happy expectation of seeing him again. Imagine my keen disappointment when on reaching the spot, I found their entire battalion had gone. Where? I had not the slightest means of knowing. Not a tent, nor anything visible that would indicate a camp, or anything of the sort. Oh, but I was miserable! Days, weeks, and months passed, yet I never heard of or saw anything of him. It seemed I would never get over this dreadful disappointment. I did not see him again for fifteen years, when we met in Indianapolis, Indiana.

HOSPITALS

As the woods near the camp had been pretty thoroughly cleared of timber suitable for building purposes, it was necessary to go about three miles further west, where a better class of timber was obtainable. The distance to the river being much shorter, we hauled the great logs there instead of to the town. Great rafts were made of them and they were floated down. Judging from the Government's activities in and about the city where they were completing several forts, it was evident that its intention was to hold Chattanooga and make it a permanent military base for supplies of every description. This was plainly noticeable in General Sherman's vigorous campaign against the Confederates in Georgia. Hospital buildings, where wounded and sick soldiers could be treated more conveniently and successfully than in the ordinary tents, were being erected. The army medical corp, decided that Lookout Mountain should be used for this purpose. In its palmy days, when slavery was in flower, it was one of the South's most famous resorts. There were several very large hotels which undertook the difficult task of caring for the wealthy and fashionable southerners followed by a large retinue of servants. These hotels stood on the most beautiful part of the mountain, five miles from the City of Chattanooga, and about a mile and a half west of Mount Lookout. The buildings, in fairly good repair, were still standing when the union army took possession. They were immediately utilized as hospitals, but they did not supply the great demand, and many other buildings had to be put up.

The discovery had in some way been made known that there were many mechanics, carpenters, and brick masons amongst the Michigan regiment; and so the Thirteenth and Twenty-first, were detailed to build and construct a lot of new hospital buildings. Although these regiments had been in many battles and suffered heavily from the military strain placed upon them, and their ranks had been painfully thinned, this summer's respite from military activities in the field would give them a chance to recuperate and swell their ranks with the recruits that were slowly coming in. It was along in May when our regiment moved up. The camp selected was a beautiful one, a level, thinly wooded spot, with many high chestnut trees standing about.

The top of the great mountain formed a sort of table-land somewhat in the circle of a horseshoe, extending five miles from the East at the point overlooking the Tennessee river, and five miles to the West was Lake George, a very pretty lake. The

Confederates had built several forts. The one at the point proved to be rather disastrous to the Union troops camping in the valley below, for the Confederates would occasionally drop a shell down among them.

Judging from the elaborate preparations everywhere, a long siege was expected, and they were ready to meet the issue. They were very much surprised when reinforcements arrived and surrounded the mountain on every side, came up like ants along the narrow paths leading to the top, and the Rebels, panic stricken, fled in every direction. As before stated, thousands of them were taken prisoners and marched down the mountain road in a blinding snow storm. After a siege of nearly three months, Chattanooga was safe at last from any further attacks from the confederates. It was now July, and many splendid hospital buildings, some two and three stories high, had been put up and occupied. There were a great many women nurses, the first I had seen, in attendance on the sick and wounded.

These buildings had been erected perhaps a half mile from the point affording the splendid view of the river valley, a site five miles below. As usual Fourth of July exercises were engaged in, there being a banquet held in one of the buildings which was attended by many of the officers. Lieutenant Colonel Palmer of our regiment, was one of the speakers.

Of the many good carpenters in our regiment, John C. Colton, Company "D", I remember well. He was a splendid fellow and liked by every one. He met with a serious accident which caused his death. With one of those great, sharp broad axes, he was hewing a big log one day, when in some unaccountable way, the axe slipped and cut a large ugly gash in just about the cap of his right knee; he limped about on it for several days, and for some reason it refused to heal. Doctor Pratt and his assistant surgeon thought best to amputate it. It being a very warm afternoon, the operation was carefully performed in one of the large open tents. As this was the first leg I had seen taken off, it was greatly interesting to me. The instruments used by the doctors were of various length and sizes, and had a peculiar attraction for me. A woman nurse, dressed entirely in white, stood over Colton's head holding a large sponge over his mouth and he seemed to be sleeping soundly. He lived only about ten days after the operation. The entire regiment, led by the band, attended his funeral and he was buried with full military honors.[25]

In no camp, during my time in the service, were there so many pleasant and varied attractions. One could go about wherever he liked with such perfect freedom, and without the least danger or fear of being captured or fired upon by sharpshooters. Huckleberry bushes, the largest and most delicious I have ever eaten, grew everywhere in abundance. Several of us went down into the south valley one hot day, some five miles from camp, and just as we got down to the face, we discovered another of those wonderful mountain springs, almost as cold as ice, and bubbling up beneath the great mass of rock covering it. We learned that this spring was the boundary line dividing the states of Tennessee and Georgia. It seemed to be a prosperous farming district, judging from the many large houses, great fields of wheat, corn and cotton could be seen in every direction, on our way back, I being ahead, turned out to the right on the mountain path into the heavy undergrowth, and, not paying much attention where I was walking, came suddenly on one of those long blue racer snakes [sic]. The snake being as much surprised and frightened as myself, he started off up the mountain side at a great rate of speed, and I in hot pursuit with a large stick I picked up. But it was quite impossible to keep up with him. He was the first of his species I had ever seen. As he ran, he stood up, and was almost as tall as myself. He ran into a hole, under a big oak tree, where, I suppose he made his home.

A half mile further up the mountain, we turned into a path leading to the right, and here discovered a long clean flat table rock, thirty by ten feet, and just above it was a great raft of rock and over this ran a good sized stream of cool water. We all sat down admiring the beautiful scene, and then six of us dropped off and had a most delightful shower bath.

Returning to the camp about four o'clock in the afternoon, we found most of the regiment engaged in the exciting game of base ball, with the long thin body of Captain Yerkes behind the bat.

I was surprised and pained to learn that orders had been issued by the quartermaster that all of the regiment teams, except two were to be turned over to the Government, and the teamsters to be assigned back to their companies. Our splendid little team of six mules, was so gentle and well behaved, that I had driven for a year and a half, and loved as if they were my own, would be taken away and I was quite sure I would never see them again. The next morning Dick and I hitched them up for the last time; and, about nine o'clock, nine teams, with the quartermaster riding on horseback—we started down the long winding mountain road to the government coral [sic].[26] Arriving about noon, we found the corral consisted of a ten acre lot, surrounded by a high board fence, and in this enclosure were hundreds of horses and mules, of all ages, sizes and conditions. Here we unhitched and turned them loose in the big lot, leaving them to their fate, whatever it was to be. Dick, with the other teamsters, disappeared into the city, and asked me to go along, but I told them "No", that I would go back to the camp.

Sad and disheartened, I was glad to be alone, but I felt the loss of the team keenly. It was extremely hot and I took the road to the right, leading to the mountain, as this was a shorter route by a mile or so; and, on reaching the open country, I came suddenly upon a camp of colored troops. These were the first I had ever seen and, naturally, greatly interested me. There were three regiments of infantry; and, as their headquarters were close to the road, I stopped to investigate.

Going up a light rise where stood several large square tents, I stopped, and was cordially invited to enter. There were four or five in the great tent, and to my great surprise, some were reading, and others writing. All were neatly dressed and looked so nice in their uniforms—their shoes even were polished. This was a custom that did not prevail in my regiment—none seemed to take pride in polishing their shoes. They were very kind and asked me many questions about myself. They told me the names of their regiment, and of their colonels. I can't quite remember their names. I told them of my regiment, of its many engagements, before and since I had joined. They asked if I would not like to be with them—enlist and be a real soldier.[27] Yes, I told them, but I didn't think I was quite old enough; also, having been with the Thirteenth a year and a half, I hated to leave it.

I then walked out where they were drilling. I was actually surprised to see how well they did it. So clean in their uniforms. The regiment had its own splendid band. A very large tent was used for chapel, also the school room where they were taught by their Chaplin to read and write. Feeling very much impressed with what I had seen and heard, I bade them good bye and started for camp, reaching it a little after five o'clock. It was much cooler than in the valley below. I immediately reported to Captain Yerkes, who I found comfortably seated in his tent reading a newspaper. He told me that I was to be his boy now, and to report to Enos Larkin, his mess cook, in the rear of his tent. I had known him for a long time, but only by his Christian name. He was a short, thick set man, light complexioned, sandy hair and slightly bald. I found him to be pleasant and agreeable. He said, when I entered his little dog tent, as they were called in those days: "Well, John, we are to be pals now, and look after the Captain and Lieutenant Flint." We then proceeded to put up a tent by the side of his, which was for me. This done, we rigged up a neat bunk to sleep in, and then I brought my blankets and knapsack, and was comfortably settled in my new quarters.

My work was to bring in the wood and water, which was easy, and he did the cooking. I had, also, to look after the officers' boots, which I kept clean and polished to perfection.

Larkin was a splendid cook. He had gotten hold of a Dutch oven, like the one used by grandmother, and made the most delicious light bread and biscuit. One fine morning I took a walk, a half mile or so through the woods just north of the camp and, noticing a dark bay horse, rather thin, feeding on the fine blue grass, a little way ahead of me, I walked slowly up to him coaxing and talking to him, and was surprised to find him so gentle, I could pet him and shew the flies off him. He had a nice long tail and mane and, taking hold by his forelock, I led him into camp. Captain Yerkes came out and said "Hello, John. Where did you get the horse?"

"I found him over in the North woods," I replied.

By this time a dozen or more men had gathered, and the Captain called for a rope, and when it came, a yankee halter was quickly made and put on the new horse. Having carefully looked him and finding no blemishes or the U S which was branded on all government stock, Captain said: "I will take him in as contraband, and use him while we are here." Though he had no shoes on, it was evident from the two or three white spots on his back that he had been ridden. I was told by the Captain to take him over where the ambulances and medicine wagon stood and have him cared for until we had made other arrangements. A few days later a small shed stable was built a little ways back of the tents, and "Toby", as the Captain had named him was over to his corral. In connection with other simple duties, I was to take care of him. I wouldn't be so lonely now as I had been since the mules had gone. Toby proved to be an excellent saddle horse, good style of head, an easy canter, and the fast running walk peculiar to the average Southern saddle horse.

With a good curry comb and brush, I kept him looking nice, which pleased the Captain. On days when Captain Yerkes was not using him, I would turn him out to graze in the fine grass he liked so well.

Late one evening as was my custom, when I went for him, I found him further away than usual; and, as I had taken no halter or bridle, I mounted him and he started on a keen run toward the camp. By lying down on his neck and clinging to his long mane, I managed to stay on his back until he reached the shed, where he stopped. I had a narrow escape of being thrown, and thereafter took a bridle with me and thus prevented Toby playing another trick on me.

In order to give the men a chance for target practice, each individual Company was sent out to a camp a mile or so in the woods to the northwest, to remain two weeks at the time. When Company "C" was ordered out, a most delightful camp was selected, situated on the slight, heavy timbered slope, using the deserted huts left by the Rebels; and by using our tents as roofs, they were made very comfortable.

One day while wandering about, I strolled into one of these huts some distance away, and not occupied by any members of the Company. I was kicking the leaves and stones about and found an old blue back spelling book and a letter. As I could not read either, I carried them to Larkin, who read the letter to me, which he said was addressed to "Tom Allen", giving the name of his Company and regiment, which I can not remember. It had been sent by his sweetheart, from Bridgeport, Alabama. She signed her name as "Millie." It was a long love letter, and her last words were: "Good by [sic], dear Tom, and if we should never meet again in this world, I hope we will meet in heaven where there will be no wars. Ever your loving, Millie."

Larkin passed it around, and all the Company read and laughed over it. During our two weeks stay there, Larkin taught me the alphabet so that I could say it by heart, forward and backward.

We returned to our original camp, and for ten days I was making splendid progress with my spelling book—got so far advanced I could spell words of one syllable—when orders came that we were to move. The startling news went the rounds of the camp that the Rebels were again invading Tennessee.

It was late in August, and an ideal day. We started immediately after dinner, and was interesting to see the men taking down tents, rolling their blankets in them and then tying the ends so it could be carried over the shoulder. About two o'clock in the afternoon, the bugle sounded and the regiment lined up. Our objective point, we learned, was Franklin, Tennessee, and we were to proceed with all haste to intercept the Confederates who were expected to cross the river at that point and attack the city of Nashville.[28]

To our surprise and amusement we were mounted in wagons drawn by six mules, with board seats so arranged that twenty men could be hauled in each wagon. Our leaving one of the most delightful of camps was sad in the extreme.

The wives of some of the officers had been visiting them for a month or more. We left them in tears. They were a sad forlorn group as they stood on the edge of the mountain and wept as the regiment moved down the winding road.

As the pikes were in excellent condition, the journey of nearly a hundred miles was made in three days. The route taken was through some of the finest cotton raising country I had ever seen. The cotton was in full bloom, and the rows—perfectly straight—seemed to stretch for miles across the great fields.

Arriving at Franklin late one afternoon, we abandoned the wagons and went into camp on a beautiful strip of lawn not far from the railroad station. During our stay of two days in the pretty little town, we were of great interest to the people who crowded about, anxious to learn all that they could of the dreadful Yankees, as they called them.

Up to this time we had seen nothing of the approaching enemy.

An amusing incident, worth recording occurred just before reaching Franklin. Among the many new recruits who had joined the regiment in its summer camp on Lookout Mountain, was one, Joseph Sinclair. He had enlisted for one year, as substitute for James Story. He was a reckless, dare devil and always ready for anything going. The command had halted for a brief spell on a slight rise along the pike, and several fine shoats were noticed grazing in the corner of the fence opposite our wagon. "Oh, boys", Joe exclaimed, "here is a chance to get some fresh meat for supper." And all, with one accord, said: "Yes, Joe, get him!" He fixed his bayonet and alighted from his seat in the wagon, and creeping up cautiously, with the intention of running him through back of the right shoulder, he made a quick dart; but the pig was quicker, and got away without a scratch. Joe's stab was such a vigorous one that he went headlong, gun and all, into a heap, to the intense amusement of all in the wagon.

On the afternoon of the third day of our stay in Franklin, orders were issued to move. The wagons were abandoned, and we marched out of the little village, keeping step with Glines' brass band which played its liveliest tunes. It was an ideal day for marching—clear, cool, and the air bracing. The course taken was northeast of the town, along a rough hilly country road. Late in the afternoon we camped in an open field, in the center of which stood a very large farm house, the owners, or occupants having deserted it some time before our arrival. The colonel and many of his officers made it their headquarters. In the rear of the big house, and not far from it, stood hundreds of bee hives, arranged on long flat tables, with ample space between so that a person could pass along and examine each hive separately. As many bees were still flying about and the men had a fear of being stung by them, they wondered how they were to get some of the honey which they were certain could be had for the taking. The hives were closed boxes, except a little slit at the bottom where the bees went in and out, and the only way to get the honey was to tip them over. After a few minutes discussion amongst themselves as to the means of solving so difficult a problem, a tall soldier of Company "I" ran up, grabbed a hive, threw it over his shoulder and ran with it. The bees, of course, came out and blew back to their house. While we all looked on amazed, others followed suit; and many hives were moved and cleaned out.

After supper, orders were issued to move to the river, some three miles north of our camp, where there was a ford and where we expected to meet General Forrest and forces.[29] We left the camp intact, taking nothing but our arms and ammunition. Though the weather was extremely chilly, the moon shone clear and bright as day. The road wandered through the woods and brought us to a narrow creek about ten feet wide. As there was no bridge, we had to ford it. The water was very cold and by the time we reached the river front a few rods further north, our feet and legs were pretty cold.

Marching up to the bank where the enemy was expected to cross, there was a long strip of level clear ground, covered with nice green grass. Here the regiment drew up in line, loaded and stacked arms. There were to be no fires built, no loud talking or unnecessary noise of any kind. Should Forrest attempt to cross here during the night, we were to give him a surprise.

To the left of our camp, and extending along the river front for a mile or more, was a dense thicket of cane brake, so dense in fact that it was almost impossible for man or beast to go through it. Many of those selected to do picket service in this thicket, were quite a number of men, new recruits, who had seen no service outside the camp. They were instructed by the officers to halt everything approaching them; and whoever it was, to fire if it did not stop. The remainder of our troops, wrapped in their blankets, laid down close to their guns, for a quiet and much needed rest. We had been lying there perhaps half an hour, and many of the soldiers were sound asleep, when several shots were heard in the cane brake.

"Fall in! Fall in!" The command was given by the officers and every man was on his feet. Then ordered to take arms. The men were stationed at the ford, a little to the right of us and stood, guns in their hands, looking eagerly across the rapidly running stream, but saw nothing. Standing at attention for a good half hour, expecting every minute to see the enemy wade the narrow stream, they were finally ordered to stack arms again and retire. Many times during the clear, cold, night we had these interruptions, but no enemy appeared. We were indeed glad to see day break clear, bright and warm. Along about seven o'clock the bugles sounded and the pickets came in. On investigation it was found that there were many cattle, hogs and horses feeding in the thicket where the new recruits were doing picket duty during the night. There were two dead horses, three cows, and one hog. Acting on the strict orders given to halt every thing and anything, approaching them and to fire when the order was not obeyed, the brave young gallants were certain they had got some of the enemy. After an hour or so spent reconnoitering for a mile or more up and down the river without any apparent sign of the enemy, we were ordered back to camp.

As I remember, it was Sunday, clear, bright and beautiful, I think I never was so hungry in all my life, as I was that morning, as doubtless was the case with every soldier in the line. The little creek we had forded the night before, and which had so thoroughly chilled us, had been roughly bridged, thus enabling us to cross more comfortably. Reaching the camp about eleven o'clock, there was no time lost in preparing our simple breakfast of bacon, hardtack and coffee, which had never tasted so good.

We were glad to learn that the beautiful day was to be spent quietly in camp.

Returning to Franklin late in the afternoon of the next day, we resumed our old camping grounds near the depot, where we remained quietly for two whole days. Then orders came that a long march was to be made northward in the direction of Clarksville; where, it was said the enemy was concentrating. Early on the morning of September 20th, 1864, we broke camp and, with colors flying and bands playing, we left the pretty little town where our brief stay had been so pleasant. The weather which was delightfully clear and cool for marching, and the roads being in excellent condition, by noon when we halted for dinner it was stated by the officers, that we had covered a little over ten miles. We were now passing through some of Tennessee's finest farming districts, where cotton, tobacco, and sweet potatoes flourished in amazing quantities.

Reaching one of the numerous plantations with its great house, as usual, a good quarter of a mile from the main road we halted, stacked arms in the middle of the road, and every soldier ran in the direction of the house in pursuit of water and many other good things like milk, butter, chickens and the finest of sweet potatoes. These were just being dug and gathered up. After an hour's rest and a delightful dinner, the bugle sounded, and we proceeded on our march. Along about five o'clock in the afternoon we reached the Cumberland river, and camped for the night.

Arriving at Clarksville the next day at noon, we found the hilly little town very quiet, and no Rebels anywhere in sight. We learned, however, that quite a large force had been in that vicinity a few days before, and had moved in the direction of Dyersburg.

Leaving Clarksville early the following morning, we struck their trail and, on reaching the Tennessee river late in the afternoon, we camped for the night, as a pontoon bridge had to be laid before we could cross the great stream. Fortunately there was another big sweet potato patch near our camp, but the owners had not begun to dig them yet; and, as we just had to have them, we dug them ourselves, the men using their bayonets, and sharp pointed sticks, for the purpose, which worked admirably.

Approaching a pontoon bridge which had been laid by the engineers the day previous, about nine o'clock in the morning, we could see troops and long provision trains already crossing ahead of us. All the heavy equipment necessary to an army of five thousand men, having crossed without a single accident. Our regiment was the last to cross over. We were ordered to remain near the river as a sort of precaution, or protection guard for the engineers, until the bridge had been carefully taken up and loaded in a wagon used for the purpose. When the loading of the pontoons had been completed, they moved out ahead of us, and our regiment brought up the rear. It was an admirable day for marching, and all the men were in the best of spirits.

We had been prowling through the country now about ten days, foraging all sorts of nice country produce, but as yet seen no signs of him. Following the splendid road which led through a strip of heavily timbered country, we reached the splendid farming districts again and halted for dinner. As had been the custom on these long marches, the regiment halted and stacked arms in the middle of the road. A large two-story frame house stood a little way back from the road, and in front of it several White women appeared. At the back of the house was a large stable enclosed by a high rail fence, and within this enclosure stood several stacks of fine new mown hay, and two of our wagons were engaged in loading some of it. There were many fine chickens running about the yard and, as they were property of the enemy, there was no reason other than to appropriate them. There was a lot of fun in catching them, and when we camped at night, the air was fragrant with chicken stew. Several soldiers of Company "I" made a rush for the front door, going in to see what they could find in the way of eatables. On reaching the door, they were met by a woman with a shot gun in her hands; and, furiously angry, she shrieked: "You can't come in here, you thieving Yankees." Lieutenant Clark rushed up, grabbed the barrel of the gun; she pulled the trigger and it went off into the air. He immediately confiscated the gun, and told her, any more performances like that and she would be taken into custody. The house was then searched for arms, but none were found. After two long, weary days of marching we returned to Franklin and camped there a few days.

Early in the morning of the third day, which was October 10th, we were ordered to take the railway for Dalton, Georgia. A long train of freight cars was drawn up and we climbed into them. There was not enough room inside for all the members of our Company, so Larkin and several others, including myself, climbed to the top which was provided with an iron rail all around it, so there was no danger of falling off. It was my first ride on a railway train and I was the happiest of boys. The train moved very slowly at first, and there were many stops at night. Finally our long train got into motion again at a good rate of speed, and did not stop until we had reached Nashville the next morning. Getting tired and sleepy from the long ride, I had taken off my knapsack and was using it for a pillow when the train pulled into Nashville. When we reached Dalton in the afternoon I was very much surprised to find that my knapsack was gone. In some unaccountable way it had while I was asleep, worked its way from under my head and off the train. I was very sorry because it contained not only our precious coffee pot and frying pan, both of which were strapped to the outside, but two clean shirts, a pair of socks, and also my beloved blue back speller. The next day I walked back along the track a mile or so, hoping to find it, but never did.

Some three miles west of the little town, and in a big heavily timbered country, our camp was established. As we were to remain here for some time to give the men a chance to vote for Mr. Lincoln who was running for a second term, especial pains were taken to make the camp a comfortable one. Our Company "C" was camped on a long level spot a short distance from the railroad along which trains were constantly passing.

The men of the company had cleared a spot, a sort of parade grounds, with their tents in perfectly straight lines facing it. Captain Yerkes' and Lieutenant Flint's tents stood at the east end of the nicely arranged grounds; while Larkin and myself had ours just back of it. We had been in camp about ten days when it began to rain. It was a slow drizzle, lasting for many days and making the camp a despondent and gloomy one for the men. There was nothing for them to do but sit in their tents and play cards.

THE ELECTION IN 1864

On November 8, 1864, the day of the Presidential election, the sun came up bright and warm, to the joy and delight of the men. The candidates were, President Lincoln on the Republican ticket, and General McClellan heading the Democratic ticket. The voting at camp was spirited and lively, but the majority of the regimental vote went to Mr. Lincoln.[30] It was the morning of the tenth, two days after the election, that news came announcing the election of Mr. Lincoln. He had carried the country by a very large majority. There was great rejoicing throughout the camp.

One afternoon, a few days later, Captain Yerkes called me into his camp and told me he had been promoted to the position of Major and that we would move in a few days to the Colonel's headquarters. Owing to the absence of Major Culver, Captain Eaton would act in his place,[31] and from that day on, I would receive eight dollars a month in wages. He handed me eight paper dollars. To say that I was surprised, happy, and astonished, is to put it mildly. I had been in the army now a little over a year and three months, and during all that time I had never dreamed of wages. Hitherto I knew nothing of the months, their lengths, or their names, only as I was told them by Larkin. It came and went with me, in the course of things. But now that I was on the government pay roll, I seemed to wake up, and felt a keen interest in time as it passed.[32]

The next day being fine and warm, Captain Yerkes mounted "Toby" and rode away. Lieutenant Flint being the Officer of the Day, was sitting in front of the tent reading the newspaper. I went to him and asked permission to go to the Colonel's headquarters. Yes. I could go, he said, but to be back in three quarters of an hour.

There were two big square tents on the hill, a little way to the northeast of the regiment, in a clump of pines. The headquarters mess consisted of Major Eaton, Lieutenant Dunlap, his adjutant,[33] Doctor Pratt, and Owen, his assistant surgeon. William W. Ward, a German, was the cook, and Bradley Brown, a colored boy, some five or six years older than myself, had charge of the Major's horse and did other work around the quarters. My visit to the headquarters that morning was to see "Bart", as we called him, and to tell him of my good fortune and how I was to get eight dollars every month. He told me he was getting ten dollars a month, and to convince me he pulled out his roll of bills and stated that he was paid on the tenth of each month. He went in to his tent and brought out a pack of cards, which were the worse for dirt and usage, and suggested we play seven-up, or "old dutch" as it was then called. As he was a much better player than I, he would give me two points to start with, and we would play for fifty cents a game. This plan being satisfactory to both, we took our seats behind a big pine tree, and the fascinating game was on. There was little, if any, conversation between us during the intense excitement, of the game, and strange to say, I was lucky from the start. After playing for nearly two hours, I found I had won every one of his ten dollars, his whole month's wages. Rising, I told him I must go back to my Company. I wish the reader could have seen the proud, eager spirit with which I ran down the hill with my eighteen big paper dollars in my pocket.

Reaching our tent, I noticed that Lieutenant Flint still sat where I had left him. I was on my way to Larkin's in the rear, when the Lieutenant called me back. I began to feel guilty and frightened.

"John, where have you been?"

"Up at headquarters," I replied.

"I told you that you could stay there three-quarters of an hour and you have been gone over two hours. What have you been doing?"

Now, I knew, for some reason or other, that it would never do to tell him what I had been doing, so hung my head and said nothing. I could see plainly now that he was terribly angry, for his thin white lips fairly trembled. As before stated, there was a big pine tree standing just to the right of the tent door. Without moving from his seat, he said with a keen snap and rising inflection of voice: "Stand up close to that tree with your back to it, and take your hands out of your pockets." Strange, my fear of him had entirely disappeared, and I became angry myself, for I regarded Captain Yerkes only as my superior officer, and no one else, so as I was lolling against the tree and my hands still in my pockets, he sprang from his tent stool and called: "Sergeant! Report at once with three guards and a rope." The little squad marched up, saluted, and he gave the order: "Tie that boy, with his hands behind him, to that tree." They stacked arms and proceeded with their work. Sergeant Clark,[34] who was my friend and who did most of the tying—while his back was turned to the Lieutenant—whispered to me: "John, this is a darned shame, but we won't tie you tight." This, of course, gave me more courage. Although he was officer of the day, I had not the slightest fear of the Lieutenant. I carried in my pocket my new mess knife which I had bought only a few days before.[35] Owing to the slackness of the rope with which I was tied, I was able to get my hand in my pocket, take out the knife and open the blade with my teeth; and, cutting myself loose, I cut the rope into several pieces and deliberately laid them down in front of the Lieutenant. He jumped from his seat again, more angry than ever, and called the guard and gave them orders that I should be taken to the guard house, there to be kept in close confinement; and that I was to having nothing to eat or drink until he gave the order. So, with two guards behind me, and Clark ahead, I was marched up to the comfortable, little square, log building temporarily used for this purpose. I was surprised to find six other jolly chaps confined in the little house for minor offenses; and I had a good time playing cards with them. When dinner time came, Bart having heard of my arrest and confinement, brought in a big plate of pork, beans, and bread, which I was glad to get.

Along about four o'clock in the afternoon, the Lieutenant came up in person; and, calling me out, asked if I thought I could behave myself. "Yes, sir", I replied. And, he leading the way, we returned to the Captain's tent.

Larkin and I laughed and joked over this for many days. Whether Captain Yerkes ever heard of my disgrace, I never learned. Certainly he never mentioned it to me.

If my memory serves me right, it was on Tuesday, November 13th, that orders went the rounds of the camp we were to move the following day and that we were to turn our faces towards Savannah.[36] Our regiment was attached to the First Brigade Second Division, of the 14th Army Corps.

Early in the morning of November 14th, the sun came up bright, and when the bugle sounded, the regiment moved out of our old camping ground, in military style, the band playing one of its merriest tunes. On leaving camp, we marched to the railway track, a little to the North, and when the regiment reached it, it was halted and stacked arms. Then orders were given to tear up the tracks.[37] Picks, hammers, and crowbars were brought up by four mule teams, and when the spikes had been loosened, every man taking hold, it was raised tipped over. The ties were then torn up and placed around a tree and the long iron rails placed on top of them, and a big fire built under them. When the rails were red hot in the middle, one end of them would be chained to the tree and the mule team hitched to the other, and they would be bent around it, thus making them entirely useless.

For three fine, beautiful days we followed the track and tore it up as we went along. Camping at night along the track, we used the ties for wood, and they made splendid fires. On the fourth day of our march, we reached the Chattanooga river,[38] having torn up and destroyed twelve miles of the enemy's important railroad. Here we were ordered to leave the railroad and to take the dirt road leading across the river in to Atlanta, some ten miles to the South.

Reaching the top of a hill where the Rebels had built a fort to protect the bridge over the river below, the command was halted for a few minutes, and stacked arms in the middle of the road. The view from the hill overlooking the river below, winding its way carefully to the southwest, through a fine strip of level farming country, was beautiful in the extreme. It was Saturday, and the sun was setting, throwing its golden rays over miles of the fine valley as far as the eye could trace.

The command marched down, crossed the wooden bridge, some forty feet long, and was halted again. Our regiment was ordered to remain here for the night, and went into camp. It was to stay until all troops and the train had passed over, and then we were to destroy it.

It was twelve o'clock Sunday night before the last of the straggling army had passed over the little stream. The bridge was then blown up and the great mass of heavy beams rose and fell into the stream.

It being a fine sunny afternoon, Bart, three others, and myself, walked up the hill to the little fort we had saved, bent on a spirit of mischief and to see what the "Johnnys" had left in their hasty retreat. Here we found a small cannon mounted on two wheels, of perhaps five inch caliber, with its deadly muzzle turned toward the bridge below. Whether it was loaded or not, we did not know, or care. Anyway, we all got hold of it, rolled it out of the fort, and turning it loose down the steep hill, it turned many somersaults down the hill, and plunged into the river. When we broke camp and started on our midnight march to Atlanta, the sky was completely overcast, and the air quite chilly. It was awfully dark and the march was a silent, dreary one as we seemed to be feeling our way along the lonely road.

ATLANTA

Reaching Atlanta just at dawn, we marched through the streets of the once great Southern City and, in an open field went into camp for an hour or so, and prepared breakfast. What a tired and hungry lot of men we were! I was very much surprised to find a great city in complete ruins. The advance guard had burned it to the ground—not a single building had been left standing.

A little ways north of the town, where many railway tracks met and what I suppose had once been the depot, there stood a long, low shed, a hundred by fifty feet wide. This shed was filled to the roof with provisions, enough to ration a large army for months. There were hundreds of barrels of flour, hogsheads of brown sugar, sacks of coffee; and on the other side were piled up like cord wood, great heavy slabs of bacon.

The sky cleared about eleven o'clock, and it was nice and warm. There was a radical change in the Captain's mess which pleased me very much. Owing to the absence of Colonel Culver, Major Eaton would act as Colonel; and Captain Yerkes, the senior captain in the regiment, would act as Major. He would, therefore, transfer himself and me to the regimental headquarters which, as arranged, would include Major Eaton, Captain Yerkes, Chaplin Ellis, Dr. Pratt, his assistant Dr. Owens,[39] and Lieutenant Dunbar as Adjutant. William W. Ward was the cook, and a grand one. He could speak German as well as English, and was therefore able to talk with Thomas Bissinger, who had charge of the horses and could speak no English at all. But he was splendid in the charge of horses. Bart and myself would be together; and our duties were to look after the two big square tents, put up and take them down, carry the wood and water, then keep the six officers' boots clean. Oh, I was so glad of the change! For it would take me away from Lieutenant Flint who was now acting as Captain of the Company, and whom I did not like. But I did hate to leave dear old Larkin who had been so kind to me.

ATLANTA TO THE SEA

Along about ten o'clock, the whole army had orders to move. Going by way of
the big store house mentioned above, every soldier was told to go in and help himself. All having gone in and taken what he could conveniently carry, the great store
house with its valuable contents, was set on fire and burned to the ground.[40] A few
miles south of the once great city we halted for dinner. The roads were in good
condition, and the farm country through which we passed, was beautiful in the
extreme. As two great army corps, under General Sherman, the Twentieth and the
Fourteenth, were to live on the country, it was planned that the corps should operate in a radius of ten miles apart, the Twentieth to sweep the country to the South.
All cattle, horses and mules were to be captured and taken along with the army.[41]
Where was the enemy? We had heard that Johnston and his army, fifty thousand
strong, were somewhere ahead of us. As yet we had seen no sign of them.[42] Two
days of pleasant but unsuccessful marching brought us into the pretty little town
of Milledgeville.

It being a fine sunny day, the entire population, consisting principally of old men,
women and children, crowded the streets to witness the triumphant march of the
Yankees, with colors flying and bands playing. Arriving late in the day, it was decided
by the officers in command, to remain over until the following morning. Many Confederate government buildings were established here, among them was one where all
the government paper money was made. The buildings, of course, were thoroughly
demolished by the soldiers. Our pockets were crammed with the crisp new confederate five, ten, and twenty dollar bills, which in value were not worth the paper they
were written on. There was much fun and amusement by the soldiers running down
and catching chickens which were running about the yards of almost every house we
came to.[43] When passing a house that seemed to be prosperous in appearance, many
soldiers would rush from the ranks, and into it, and the many women and children
usually crowded at the front door, would scream and run into the house thinking the
soldiers were after them. They were soon assured, however, that the real object of
invasion was to find some thing to eat.

Milledgeville, is an admirably situated little town, occupying a low flat, agricultural strip of country, chiefly devoted to the cultivation of peanuts. Much of the
crop had just been gathered and spread out on long sheds to dry. Naturally enough
we helped ourselves to them. Strange to say, the owners looked on in dumb silence,
making little or no protest to the soldiers who, unmolested, took and carried away
everything in the way of eatables.

Our regiment had an ideal camp, being an open field with gradual slope toward
the southwest, through which a small creek of clear water flowed near at hand, and
sufficed for the men and animals. A small farm house which had been hastily va-
cated by the owners, was occupied by the headquarters during the night, so Bart
and I did not have to put up the tents. A closet of the little house was found to be
locked, and was pried open and of the things of no particular value to the officers

was a soldier's red coat and cap, and an old flint-lock musket, of the George Washington period and type. These the officers took along as souvenirs.

Just before sundown a colored man rode up to the headquarters on a fine mule. He was very talkative, and the officers questioned him closely as to the master, or owner, of himself and mule. He stated that his Master's name was Watson, that he was very rich, owned a big plantation five miles to the North. His master, he said, was a Colonel with the Confederate army, and at the present was with Johnston's army somewhere in North Carolina. There was no saddle on the mule, but there was a splendid felt pad, for use, probably under heavy army saddles. It was the first I had ever seen. Doctor Pratt took it, and told the man he might go, so, mounting his fine mule, he rode away to his home.

Breaking camp early the next morning, we resumed our delightful march towards Savannah. After two days of straight marching, we reached the little village of Sandersville, chiefly noted for vicious dogs. Several soldiers having been bitten by them, orders were issued to shoot all in sight; and from that time, there was no further trouble. As we were now reaching the low, flat, swampy country, the roads were getting bad, and our progress was necessarily slow.

SHERMAN

For the first time during our ten days march out of Atlanta, we had General Sherman with our brigade for nearly two days.[44] His magnificent appearance on horseback, was a real sensation to many of the men in our regiment who had never seen the grand old man. His attitude on horseback was most striking. He seemed to be a very tall man; when seen mounted on his big bay horse with one white hind leg. He rode perfectly erect in his saddle and seemed to be looking directly ahead of him.

One day just after crossing a creek, we halted for a short rest. It was an unusually warm day and the General and his entire staff had dismounted and were seated on the grass under a big oak tree. The General had taken off his coat and was talking with members of his staff. I came along, on the way to the creek to fill my canteen, when he called to me, and said:

"Here, boy, I have seen you a good many times. What regiment do you belong to?"

I was taken completely by surprise, but stepped up, came to attention, took off my cap, and said: "I belong to the fighting Thirteenth."

"Oh, you do, do you. How old are you?"

"I don't know, sir."

"Well, you are nearly big enough to carry a gun."

"Yes, sir. I do carry one once in a while, when a tired soldier drops behind."

"That's right", he said, "help all you can."

I then saluted and passed on.

General Fitzpatrick,[45] in command of a Division of Cavalry, of about five thousand men, was our advance guard, and with the engineer corps, kept the roads in repair ahead of us. It was a tremendous job, for many times a bed of corduroy road had to be laid before the heavy artillery and other traffic could pass. Strange to say, the main road, low and flat, ran through a dense forest, so thick on either side that it was almost impossible for a man to pass. For many days the march was exceedingly slow and difficult, and the great army, stretched for miles along the road, seldom made more that five or six miles a day. It was a very noisy march, too, as hundreds of head of cattle, gathered by the men daily for the purpose, were driven along in the rear of the army and slaughtered at night for its use. There was plenty of fresh meat, to be sure, but there were times when no flour or bread of any kind was to be had. As there were plenty of potatoes, both sweet and Irish, we got on fairly well. Many roosters, captured and carried along by the soldiers, strapped to the knapsack, afforded much amusement and excitement when in camp for a day as many cock fights were brought off. Owing to the swampy condition of the country, there were heavy fogs every morning, and the sun could scarcely be seen before ten o'clock.

SAVANNAH

We were now nearing Savannah, our objective point. We passed several heavy wooden mortars stationed in a clear place along the road by the Rebels, and which had been hastily abandoned. Late in the afternoon we reached the canal, a stream of dark water flowing gradually toward the City of Savannah, five miles to the southwest. A bridge had been hastily constructed and our brigade crossed and, climbing a slight knoll, marched into a long line of breastworks in an open field. Another large field, to the North of us, was a patch of rice planted and flooded under several inches of water. A low, flat strip of country, perhaps a mile wide, where stood much heavy timber and underbrush which had been previously cut down by the Rebels, and here it lay in every conceivable sort of mass, and the area flooded to prevent attack. A mile to the West, directly in front of us, the Rebel General Hardee, with fifteen thousand men, were camped behind strong fortified positions, ready for any emergency.[46] Just back of our line of breastworks, stood an empty two-story frame house. As no tents were allowed to be set up, many officers and men rushed into it, with the expectation of making themselves very comfortable for the night. Along about eight o'clock, when all had eaten and were perhaps enjoying their story telling, or playing cards, the enemy turned loose its battery of ten guns on it, tearing it to pieces and making it a complete wreck. The men ran out, yelling and laughing, treating the matter as if it was a huge joke. Fortunately none were seriously hurt.

Our battery of six guns, situated a little to the right of us, did not reply. The rebels however kept up a terrific fusillade for an hour or so, when all was quiet again. The bean and rice field through which our breast works extended from north to south, was fringed with a heavy pine forest and dense undergrowth, making it so dark and almost impassable. Situated and concealed in the tops of these great pine trees, were many Rebel sharpshooters. Along about ten o'clock next morning when the heavy fog had left and the sun was clear and bright, and the soldiers beginning to move about, the hidden enemy opened fire. Some twenty-five men were wounded more or less seriously. Then orders were issued that no one was to show his head outside of his dugout until the enemy could be located. Wood and water, taken from the canal back of us, was to be secured after dark, or at our own risk. In the afternoon, between two and three, the Rebel battery in all its terrible fury opened fire on us again. Ours, of six heavy guns, mounted by a company of Germans, responded vigorously until the enemy, by direct shot, threw a post hold and dismounted one of the guns, taking off a wheel, but no one was hurt. Strange to say, though the long bombardment lasted nearly three hours, no one was killed or injured.

Lieutenant Flint and myself had been down to the canal, when the heavy shelling began, and were on our way back to the trenches, and just as we crossed a narrow ditch, a big shell exploded right over our heads; he threw himself flat on the ground and yelled to me: "Lie down, John, quick!" I did so, and lay there, not daring to move, until he did. The great herd of cattle, captured and driven along and corralled just across the canal in the woods back of us, were terribly frightened by shells exploding so close to them. They stampeded and the men in charge had a hard time getting them together afterwards. They were slaughtered daily and issued to the army, and were the only rations we could get. It was stated that the only way to dislodge the enemy was to build a road and flank him.

A corps of engineers were sent into the forest, a half mile to the North, cutting tough pine boughs and undergrowth, eight feet in length. Then making a bundle of them, they were securely bound at each end with heavy wires, and laid close together so a good road was constructed so that the heavy artillery could be readily and easily moved. This hastily built road, a mile in length, laid directly, and within a few hundred yards of the enemy's position, and the charge was to be made some time during the following day.

Just as the sun began to break its way through the heavy fog, the sharp shooters, as usual opened their deadly fire on our works.

Bart, two other soldiers and myself, were on our way to the canal for water. The spent bullets began to whistle around us. We were walking in a line, one behind the other, and just as one of the soldiers reached the farther bank of a ditch over which we were passing a bullet struck him between the shoulders. He was not dangerously hurt, and on our return to the camp, it was easily extracted by the doctors. Late that afternoon orders were issued that the entire force would move on the enemy's works the following morning. Between eight and nine that night, when the stars came out clear and bright, the Rebels began their pastime, bombarding our works, but there was no reply from our batteries. They shot over us all the time, doing no damage whatever. It was an amazing sight to me to lie on my back in my dugout and see the great shells bursting high up in the air.

Early the next morning, no fires were built, and the entire force moved quietly out of the works and proceeded to the new road a half mile north. On reaching it a halt was ordered, guns loaded and bayonets fixed, then the march continued slowly along the new road. As this road had been made through that part of the forest where the sharp shooters were most active and annoying, our movements were very cautious. We expected every moment to be fired upon by the hidden enemy. It took perhaps an hour to go through and reach the clearing where the Rebels works were situated. Just as we were nearing our objective point, a squad of cavalry under command of General Kilpatrick, dashed up and reported that the "Johnnies had fled, leaving most of their heavy artillery."[47] Of course, there was much cheering, as we ran into the deserted fortification. They were admirably built, being made of heavy cotton sacks filled with sand, and laid up in a systematic way, like a brick wall. After a short rest and a thorough examination of the enemy's works, their big guns and quantities of ammunition, we were ordered to march into the City of Savannah, five miles to the south of us. There was a splendid dirt road, dotted on either side by immense residences. Reaching the depot, in which stood many railway tracks, about two o'clock one sunny afternoon, the command halted, broke ranks, and looting began in earnest. There was a mad rush into the stores and houses, and where the doors were closed they were quickly forced open.

There were many trains, freight and passenger, with dead engines attached to them, standing about the depot. A little ways from the depot there stood an old dry, disused cistern. Several soldiers had been told by an old colored man, evidently an employee about the depot, that he had seen two or three White men go into it with small bags, and he supposed they were hiding treasure of some sort. A man looked around, secured a ladder, went down and thoroughly explored the dark recesses of the cistern, but found nothing of value.

On leaving the Rebel's works in the morning, we noticed that many of the soldiers had sacks, they had emptied the sand, and carried them along. Bart, Larkin, and myself, did likewise, and later on found them mighty useful.

The three of us agreed to stay together; and, on leaving the Depot, we came to a wide wooden bridge, perhaps a hundred feet long. Many men, women and children were passing over it; but notwithstanding this fact, two soldiers, both drunk, had gotten hold of an old Rebel hat, stuck it up on a pole on the left side of the bridge which they had to themselves, and were shooting at it.

Passing through many narrow and hilly streets, we entered the northwest part of the city, where stood many beautiful residences, all having high ornamental fences in front, with bells attached to the gates, which visitors had to ring before they could enter the house. Leaving this part of the city, we followed the street that lead to the river; we passed the jail, and to the left of it, was a large slave pen in front of which stood a high wooden platform with an auction block in the middle of it. Reaching the river, there was a steep incline, wide and nicely paved, clear down to the big wide stream.

There were many fruit peddlers, men, and women, stationed about. Here, I bought and ate my first banana, which I thought tasted very much like the persimmon, with which I was familiar. A great number of steam boats stood along the docks. Whether they were waiting for orders, or had been taken over by the government, I did not know.

Going along the stream to the left, we came to the great rice mill, which we entered and thoroughly explored. There were long, high platforms back of it, and on these stood hogsheads, half filled with clean, white rice, which we immediately appropriated, putting as much into our sacks as we could carry five miles back to camp.

Coming up from the rice mill, we entered a big gate that led into a good sized yard, in the middle of which stood a nice little two-story brick house. Several soldiers were chasing chickens, of which there were quite a number, about; and, dropping my half sack of rice, I joined in the chase, succeeding in capturing a big red rooster just as he was running into the chicken house. Just then a provost guard, a mounted cavalryman, with his saber drawn, rode into the yard and said: "Boys, get to camp. No more looting." The sun was just sinking in the West when we started to camp, very well satisfied with the day's sport. Reaching camp about eight o'clock, tired and worn out, we hastily provided a little supper and went to our bunks.

Next morning we had orders to move, going toward the city, and when within three miles of it a camp was selected in a pretty strip of pine woods where we were told we would remain for some time. Men were detailed from the regiment to clear a nice wide space, and when this was done, the tents were put up in and around it; a big well was dug, and there was plenty of water to be had close at hand.

Alligators were reported to be numerous in the low banks about us, and we were told to beware of them. The finest long moss I had ever seen grew on the trees everywhere in the woods. It was perfectly clean and owing to its extraordinary length, we used it and found it excellent for bedding. Being soft and nice, it was like lying on feathers. For five days in our new camp there was not a hardtack, or bread of any kind to be had in the entire army. There was plenty of fresh beef, and rice and these made up our sustenance until steamboats could get up the river.[48]

It was January 15, 1865, we got the news that torpedoes which had been planted in the river by the Rebels, making it dangerous, and obstructing the passage of steamers, had been removed and that boats were now coming in with provisions. This news was received with shouts of gladness by all the men. A few days later, a long supply train, heavily loaded with ammunition, provisions and mail reached the camp.

There were many sacks of mail for the men and hundreds of Christmas packages sent them by friends and relatives from home. My old friend, Larkin, had received quite a large box containing many good things, various kinds of cake, and two mince pies. He called me over to his tent to sample them. They were fine and the first I had ever eaten. There was also a picture of his wife, a tall, slender woman, with light hair.

Of the many pretty things that had been sent as presents, or bought there was nothing that attracted my attention so much as a number of very large, fine silver watches. They were the double, heavy case watches, with splendid movement.

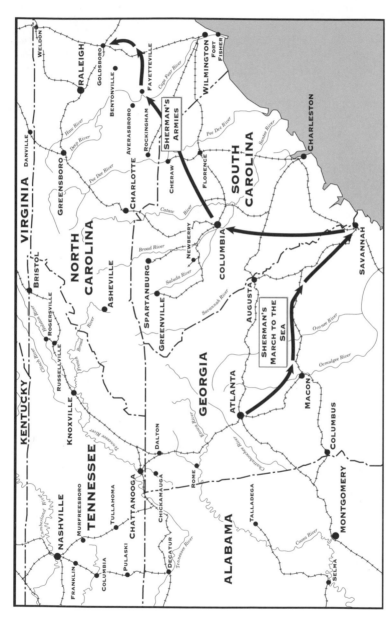

General Sherman's Carolinas campaign.

Where they were made, I never learned, but it was told they cost fifty dollars apiece. I learned also that they could be bought on time through the Express Company.

There were many trips to the city during our stay of five weeks, and many of us spent all our money before we left.

Orders were finally issued to break camp, and that our new line of march would be through South Carolina. Reaching the state line the second day out, we were surprised to find the country so poor compared with Georgia. Sweet potatoes were very scarce and very small. Great quantities of sorghum were raised—in fact every farm would have a field of it somewhere on his place, and very little of it had as yet been cut. The rebel army, said to have passed ahead of us, cut up and chewed the sorghum, as we could plainly see by the signs along the roadway and in the corner of the fences.

For many days before we reached Columbia no cattle were seen and for that reason our meat supply was running low. We learned that the farmers were driving them away into the dense pine forest so as to save them from the yankee invaders. We were some two days march in the state when we came in contact with a new kind of soil, described as quicksand. It was many times dangerous for heavy wagons or artillery to leave the main road, for fear of coming in contact with these treacherous quicksand stops that were so deceiving in appearance. Many is the time I have seen a team of six fine mules moving gracefully along a grassy slope, and all of a sudden the wheels would sink in up to the hubs, and then stick fast. With a dozen or more men with priers, and a few hours hard work, we would be ready to move on again.

In addition to the poor condition of the roads and scarcity of provisions, the march of the army was still further retarded by thousands of fugitive slaves that followed it daily, as their leaving the plantations would tend to weaken the Southern cause, General Sherman rather encouraged them to leave. But there were times when many of them were on the point of starvation, and at such times many of them were told they would have to shift for themselves. How they managed to get anything at all, was a mystery to all of us.[49] The country through which we had passed was exceedingly poor and, where there were chickens, they seldom escaped the attention of the soldiers who were on the alert continually.

Three days of continuous marching brought us to the North Carolina state line; and, on reaching the pretty little town of Charlotte we found plenty of stored provisions left by the enemy in their houses. Many thousand bales of cotton were also captured. These were immediately destroyed.[50]

There were many forts, thoroughly equipped with great guns, and plenty of ammunition, but the rebels seemed to have considered a retreat as the first thing of importance. One big warehouse was discovered which contained many barrels of flour, sugar, and coffee, which was a great blessing to the men who had had no coffee for months. The many stores in the town were thoroughly looted by the Union soldiers before they left late in the afternoon. Camping for the night on a slope north of the town, camp fires were quickly built and many varieties of things were being cooked for supper—fresh pork, chicken and beef were in evidence, all of which had been taken from the enemy's country, and for that reason more greatly enjoyed.

Breaking camp early one morning, we proceeded west, with Raleigh, the capital of the state, our objective. After crossing many streams, many of which had been bridged, we reached the city on our third day's march. It was in March, and signs of beautiful spring were everywhere manifest. Going into camp north of the town, we remained there for two days, then leaving this camp, we followed the Bentonville road east of the city of Raleigh.[51] The road lead through some fine farming country. Along about eleven o'clock sharp firing was heard in a strip of woods just ahead of us. Johnston's entire army was strenuously fortified in this strip of woods and was anxiously awaiting our arrival. The First Division of the Fourteenth Corps was in advance, taking its course along the edge of a dense wide strip within a quarter of a mile of the enemy who were well protected behind breastworks and could not be seen. Evidently a great surprise awaited General Sherman and his badly scattered army, for he sent out orders to the advance guard to brush them away.

Neither the General or any of his army were aware, or had knowledge that Johnston and his entire army of fifty thousand men were well fortified in the woods east of us.[52] As before stated, the First Division being in the advance marched into the woods and massed in front of the enemy. Here, it had orders to prepare to charge. The bugle sounded and the entire command plunged into the thick undergrowth with a great yell. The enemy fire was direct and deadly, and our charge severely repulsed. The force was rallied and another attempt was made, but failed miserably. The Second Division having just arrived, was ordered to the right and, when in position, charged and finally succeeded in breaking through the enemy's works and taking a lot of prisoners. Between three and four in the afternoon the entire Rebel army had disappeared.

Our regiment, the Thirteenth, suffered heavy losses in the day's battle. Among those who fell in action, whom I knew so well, was Major Eaton, instantly killed in the first charge on the enemy.[53] David Shulters, one of my best friends, was also killed.

Later in the afternoon, after the wounded had been gathered up and placed in a long row of hospital tents, Bart and myself visited the hospitals to see those whom we knew. One of the first badly wounded, lying on a cot to the left, was Lieutenant Flint. He had been shot through the head. It was March 20th, and fortunately, the weather was fine and in a few days the wounded men were moved to Goldsboro where they were provided with more comfortable quarters. Ten days later, all those able to travel, including Lieutenant Flint, were sent home on furlough. Our camp near Goldsboro located near a beautiful strip of woods just east of the pretty little town, was ideal in every respect. There was plenty of wood and water at hand. Here we lay for six weeks watching Johnston and his army, practically hemmed in on all sides. It was here on April 15th, one of those fine days in Spring, when the sad news of the assassination of President Lincoln reached us. Only a few of our regiment had ever seen the great, good man, and they spoke of him in terms of the greatest love and respect. Only a few days later, news reached us that Johnston and his entire army had surrendered.[54] The news was received with the wildest enthusiasm by every soldier in the camp.

Orders went the rounds of the camp for the men to dispose of all ammunition, except ten rounds, in any manner they saw fit. So they loaded their guns and fired into the air. Now the Twentieth Army Corps camped three miles South of us, heard the awful racket and, supposing we were having a general engagement with Johnston, came at double quick in order to reinforce us. We met them a mile from camp and there was great rejoicing when we told them the good news.

Taking the road to the North, and after three eventful days marching over splendid roads in fine spring weather, we reached the small town of Danville, Virginia. Here we halted and rested for one day to give us a chance to do a bit of foraging. There was little in the way of provisions to be found, as the Rebel army which a few days before had preceded us, had taken about everything in sight. Starting early next morning, we reached the farming region where wheat fields stretched for miles. As seen from the main road, it was evident that the Yankees had never been in this part of Virginia before, for the very large population was afraid of them. Our visits to fine plantations and their big well stocked smoke houses were rewarded with the best of cured meats—hams and bacon. These were certainly great luxuries, for meat of any kind had been scarce for a week.

Two days of steady marching brought us to the great city of Richmond, the Confederate Capital. I don't think I ever saw so many people line up in the streets as we marched through. Other troops, of course, had preceded us; and though the great mass of people were not demonstrative, there appeared no hostility toward us. Some two hours were required to march through the great city, when we were ordered to camp three miles north of the city and close to the James river. The water was clear and beautiful, and here we camped for two weeks. For the first time during my more than two years in the army, whiskey was issued in small quantities to the men. We had been in camp about two days when the peddlers began to stroll in. While only a few of the men seemed to have money, yet they were glad to pay for a few dainties, such as pies and cakes.

It was one pleasant morning about eleven o'clock, when a Rebel officer in full uniform, accompanied by his son, also in uniform, drove a one horse wagon into the camp loaded with every conceivable good thing to eat. Under the front seat of the little wagon, a large platter contained a splendid roast pig; in the seat of the wagon sat a huge jar of spiced peaches. There were also fifty or a hundred pies stacked up like cord wood. Driving within a few feet of the Colonel's tent, he stopped, and the men, like ants, gathered around the little wagon so thick it could scarcely be seen. Those who had little or no money at all began asking the price of things. The little wagon and its Confederate owners had been standing some ten minutes and little of its precious cargo had been sold for cash, when some soldiers grabbed the pies and ran. Every one present grabbed something, and in less than a minute there was nothing left in the wagon but the jar of spiced peaches. The Rebel owners yelled lustily for protection, and the Colonel and officers ran out to see what the trouble was, but not a soldier could be found. They ran into the woods, scattered like sheep. It was generally considered that if the owners had left their uniforms off there would have been no trouble.[55]

Having had much pleasure and excitement in the city, and in the camp along the beautiful James river, for three seemingly short weeks, orders were issued for us to proceed to Washington, a distance of a hundred and twenty-five miles.

Every one was happy when we started on the march to the National Capital. Frequently the roads were fine and the weather perfect, so that we averaged twenty-five miles a day, covering the entire distance in five days. Never had I done such fast continuous marching during my time with the regiment, and I was always glad when night came so that I could lie down to sleep. Few of our regiment had ever been to Washington, hence the eager desire of all to see the great city. When the bugle sounded at five o'clock, every soldier would rush from his bunk and get busy with his breakfast. Coming from one of the best appointed farms I had seen in the State of Tennessee, or in any other southern states through which I had passed during the two years I had been with the Federal forces, it was quite natural that I should be a close and quick observer while marching through Virginia. I had always heard that this was the empire state of the South, and as we marched along, it seemed in every way possible that it was. Most of the severe and hard fought battles of the Civil War occurred in Virginia. Judging too, from the vast number of Confederate prisoners I saw in Richmond, strong, healthy, and apparently well fed men, it seemed to me that they had been carefully selected for service in this state.

It was early in the month of May, 1865, when we left Richmond, on our way to the National Capital. Crossing the James River early one morning, our course due northward, we had reached the fine farming section. I was struck by a peculiar dark red color of the soil, and said to myself, "It is poor land." Though we had passed many fine fields of corn and tobacco, there was no cotton, which I thought strange.

On the second day of our march, the command halted for dinner and, stacking arms at the side of the road, the soldiers scattered in search of water. As no running stream was to be seen anywhere near, a rush was made toward a fine two-story brick, standing in the center of a beautiful lawn. Just back of the house stood the well, very deep, and containing clear, cool water. I did not like it very well because it had a flat sweetish taste which was new to me. On inquiry I learned that there was alkali in it.

I had noticed that the farm houses in Virginia were not so far from the road as was the custom in many of the Southern States. Then, back of the fine mansion stood, as usual, two rows of servants quarters, very neat in appearance and looking as if they had recently been whitewashed. As the halt would last a couple of hours, Bart and myself concluded to walk up to the grand old place and make ourselves acquainted, for there seemed to be so many colored people about. Taking with us two canteens to be filled, we made our way to the back of the house and came in contact with three fine looking colored men, the butler and his two dining room assistants. The two waiters were neatly dressed in suits of brown cut-a-way coat and brass buttons, knee trousers, ruffled white shirt, light blue stockings and low shoes. The butler's suit was of the same style, but black, and with red stockings. During our half hour's visit quite a crowd of men, women and children gathered around us. We were told that the place belonged to Colonel Wheeler, and that he and his son were in the hardware business in Richmond. There were seventy-five slaves and a thousand acres of land around the house. The Wheeler family consisted of four in number—father, mother, son and daughter. Colonel Wheeler had seen service in the Confederate army, and was wounded in the Battle of the Wilderness. He was with Lee's army when it surrendered to General Grant at Appomattox. They were very nice to their slaves, never had a white over-seer, and never whipped or sold them. And, what was more remarkable about the Wheelers, they were paying wages to all grown-up of the slaves on the place. I was surprised to learn also that none had run away to join the Yankees. Evidently slavery in Virginia was quite different from that in Tennessee, where the bull whip in the hands of brutal overseers was usual.

On our march through Georgia and the Carolinas, we were compelled to live on the country, by means of foraging, which was highly amusing to the average soldier. Every brigade and regimental commander had at least one man detached to forage for his colonel's headquarters mess. They usually went in companies of five or six, mounted and well armed; and, as a rule, far in advance of the main army. It was sometimes necessary to do a little skirmishing before they got possession of a big plantation. These men were known throughout the country as "Sherman's Bummers", and were greatly feared by the populace. On our march through Virginia no foraging at all was allowed, the army being well supplied with all necessary provisions. The "bummers" however kept busy, coming every night with the fine hams and chickens.[56]

Passing through Gordonsville early on our third day's march, we saw no sign of armed invasion anywhere, and even were surprised to learn that no Federal troops had ever visited that region before.

Reaching the great City of Washington about eleven o'clock on the morning of the 15th of May, 1865, we were received with a hearty welcome. The streets were densely crowded and our march through the city slow and difficult. Our camp, three miles east of the city, was a beautiful spot in a strip of woods—a clean grassy spot, slightly level, and sloping to the South, with a fine spring of clear water, and plenty of wood. Here we were allowed to rest and clean up, and get ready for the grand review to take place ten days later. As this was to be the last great event in the history of the regiment, brand new uniforms for all the men were issued.

The regiment numbered six hundred, including officers and men, and the next day there was a dress parade in the afternoon, and it was splendid in every detail. When on the next day after that, the paymaster put in his appearance for the first time in three months, there was great rejoicing. Crowds of peddlers, with every conceivable sort of articles for sale, infested the camp. An ice cream peddler came every day, driving a good horse and a covered wagon containing a portable house, which he could quickly set up, and into which he would place his two great freezers of delicious ice cream and boxes of blackberries. He never missed a day during our six weeks in camp; and, selling at the stiff rate of twenty-five cents a dish, he must have made a small fortune. He usually sold out in two or three hours after reaching the camp. Bart and myself were good customers, buying at least four times a week. Vegetable and confectionery dealers also did a good business with the men. A good deal of bootlegging was carried on in the camp. This was done by Irish women chiefly, selling to the men the poorest of whiskey at a dollar a pint. This illicit traffic went on for some time and became such a nuisance that the officers finally put a stop to it.

The spring from which we carried water for all purposes, was situated in a gulch east of the camp, which ran in a sort of zigzag fashion, north from the spring. Clean, close cropped grass grew all along its edges. Here, hundreds of men were gambling at chuck-a-luck. Those who acted as bankers had a piece of oil cloth with red figures upon it and spread out on the ground. They would call to the men going and coming to take a chance. Men from other regiments as well as our own, were thus engaged in a game entirely new to me. Had the game been marbles, in a ring of five, instead of leather box with five dice in it, I should have been glad to take a shot with any one, for I considered myself an expert at this game, and was always ready and anxious to tackle any one so inclined. I learned from Bart, and others, that a good deal of money changed hands at the chuck-a-luck game.[57] I heard that Horace Easton, the bugler, won $12.00, which I thought was a great fortune.

Getting permission from Ward, the cook, Bart and myself took a walk into the great city. It was frightfully hot, but that of course we were used to. We started early, right after breakfast, and had a good look at the city. The streets were very much crowded, as they were when we marched through a few days before. Going along one of the many streets, my attention was attracted to the long open street cars, the first I had ever seen. Each car was drawn by a pair of horses, or mules, dreadfully poor, and apparently worn out. Many of the cars were heavily loaded with passengers; and though the driver used his whip with great energy and freedom, the speed was little greater than a man's walk.

Passing along the crowded side walks, we came to a block of small clothing stores conducted by Jew merchants. Into one of them Bart and I were dragged bodily by the man at the door, and left in front of another behind the counter. He said we must buy something. I bought a pair of suspenders, and Bart bought a pair of trousers. These being wrapped up and paid for, and there being no possible chance of selling us anything more, we were roughly pushed out, as we had been pulled in.

The day for the grand review had arrived. Led by the band, the regiment appeared at its best. Leaving the camp at one o'clock, and reaching the road lead into the city a little past two o'clock [sic]. There was a short halt to give the men a chance to rest a few minutes. Although it was terribly hot, the streets were literally packed with people and though there were mounted cavalrymen with their swords drawn, it seemed almost impossible to keep the streets clear so the army could pass. Owing to the great mass of troops, the march was slow and tedious. When we reached the White House, late in the afternoon, President Johnson, and members of the cabinet, were out on the lawn, and we had a good look at the heads of our government. Although I was but a boy, not over fifteen years old, they allowed me to march with the Company. My one idea at the time was to see the President, and here my ambition was realized. President Johnson was a small, clean shaven man, with a large head and bushy hair.

This is my last vivid impression of the war.

Hot, tired and hungry, we arrived at the camp about six o'clock in the evening, and had supper, which, all declared, had never tasted better.

The war was over and arrangements were in line for disbanding the army. We remained in the camp in Washington, for two or three weeks after this event. Then the whole regiment was entrained and sent to St. Louis; and from there, going part of the way by boat, we were sent to Cincinnati. We had been paid off in Louisville, and from Cincinnati the men were sent, in batches, to their homes in Michigan.

III

AFTER THE WAR

When we were finally mustered out at Cincinnati, Colonel Culver, colonel of the regiment to whose service I had been attached at the regimental mess and who liked me, had arranged to take me and Bart, together with another colored man, named Osborne, with him to his home in Paw Paw, Michigan.[1] The Colonel and the other officers all rode in a passenger train, and the men of the regiment, including myself, were shipped in cattle cars. The trip was a very unpleasant one; and while on the way I met with an accident, as the train was about to start, jamming my leg on the platform, so badly that I was deprived of the use of it for some time afterwards.

When we got to Lawton, Colonel Culver sent me to the house of Dr. Bathrick. I stayed there until my knee was very much better; and by that time Dr. Bathrick had asked the Colonel to let me stay with him and his family. Dr. Bathrick, in addition to being a doctor of medicine was a liberal Baptist minister of the gospel. They were very kind to me. I stayed with them all winter, taking care of the horses and the cow. The next spring (1866) I went with Dr. Bathrick's son, Freeman, to Battle Creek, Michigan. He studied there during the summer. After that, I moved to the farm of a Mr. Servitas Bathrick, (one of the Doctor's brothers) near Battle Creek, and spent the winter with him, when the farm was sold. Early in 1867 I lived with a colored man, named Clay, at Paw Paw, doing odd jobs. A man named Matt Longwell, who was in the drug and grocery business, took a fancy to me, and employed me at a salary of $16.00 a month. Mr. Longwell was one of the best men in Paw Paw; and I stayed with him for seven years.[2] I always got along well with Mr. Longwell, and he was very kind with me. He wanted me to stay with him, but in 1874, word was going around in this part of the country that Chicago, since the great fire, had gotten out of its depression and was now being rebuilt at a great rate. Every one was going there to help in the reconstruction of this great city; and I, with others, got the fever.

So, on May 31, 1871,[3] with $32.00 in my pocket, I went by train to Chicago, which was only a hundred miles away, arriving in Chicago that night about six o'clock. I shall never forget the desolation of Chicago as I first saw it on that occasion—miles of ruins, charred buildings. Probably there had been a great deal of rebuilding done, but in the poorer parts where I went, the confusion was terrible.[4]

After having had supper in a restaurant, I stepped out on the sidewalk. I walked for hours, and finally, perhaps just about nine o'clock, (it seemed I was going West), I reached a big vacant spot where there had been a circus. The big elephant, "Jumbo" that was in that circus had died, and there lay the big carcass. This was not far from Sherman Street. I crossed the street, after leaving the corner just below where the dead elephant lay. Crossing Canal street, I came to the Sherman Hotel on the corner of Canal and Madison; and on reaching the entrance to the Hotel dining room, which was about four steps up, there stood John Hill, one of the waiters, on duty. They were short of waiters because it being then June, everybody went off to Saratoga, and other resorts, and the waiters had followed them out of the hotel. Most of the wealthy people were living in the hotels, and naturally, the waiters followed them to the big summer resorts in the East; and this made the hotels short of help, and that is how I managed to get into the hotel. I had never waited table, but was just off the farm. But this John Hill said to me, "You come here in the morning between nine and ten o'clock, and we will put you to work." He told me where to go to find a room, and I walked for hours. I finally found some men in front of a barber shop. The barber shop was conducted by colored people, and they had just closed the shop and were standing in front of it talking. They called to me, and I went over to them. I was so tired, I felt as if I had been walking for a week. I asked them where I could get a room, and they directed me to a rooming house, a six story building, and full from top to bottom. The landlady had just found room for two other colored men, in the attic, and she slept up there. She had made a pallet on the floor, with a mattress for the two men, and she put down another for me. I could look up through the roof, a sort of skylight, and see the stars outside. These two talked a good deal. I was very much interested in what they were saying. One of them had gotten a job at $25.00 a month. The other one seemed to have been from Haiti, and was telling about the beautiful country where there all colored people [sic], the king was colored, that they had conquered the nation living there, and the whole island was now in possession of the colored people living there.

Next morning I got up and went down stairs, paid the landlady fifty cents for my pallet bed. She told me to be a good boy, and to come and see her when I got work. This was between five and six o'clock in the morning, and when I stepped out on the street, it was literally crowded with people going to work. All seemed to be going in the direction leading from the lake. So I stepped out and followed the crowd. I had no idea where I was going; but about eleven o'clock I found myself in front of the Sherman Hotel. I was looking for this hotel, and there was the name in big letters, but I couldn't read it. I was standing right in front of the hotel I was looking for.

I went to work; and after about ten days was able to carry a tray. They gave me just one man to wait on until I learned to serve, and ten days later I was able to take an order, give it to the kitchen to be filled, and serve the man at the table. I worked there from June to November 18th, when the hotel gave up this property and went into a larger building. It was now called the Madison hotel and situated on the lake, and there in this Madison Hotel, I spent the winter. Now, in the latter part of November, that hotel was finally swallowed up by the new Sherman and Palmer House. The hotel was in the course of construction, but the dining room was completed and could be used. About twenty of the waiters from the Madison Hotel were transferred to the Palmer House. I worked as waiter in the Palmer House until about 1876. I remember that, among other wealthy guests, Mr. Marshall Field was staying there at the hotel.[5]

About this time I felt a desire to get in touch with my brother who, as described in these memoirs, I had seen for a few minutes during the war. So, I got a friend of mine to write to my former Mistress, Mrs. Hoggatt, asking her to let me know about my family and former companions on the plantation, my main object being to find my brother Jeff. She wrote me that I would find him in Indianapolis, Indiana, where she understood he was working at the Grand Hotel. So I wrote Jeff where I was working, and he replied, asking me to come to him because he was sick. So I gave up my job at the Palmer House and went to Indianapolis. I had left

Sherman Hotel in Chicago, ca. 1880s. Courtesy of the Chicago Historical Society.

Chicago with $75.00. I took my brother's place in the Grand Hotel and he went to the seashore. I spent the summer there.

In the fall my brother came back, and proposed that we go to see our people in the South. So we returned to Nashville where we visited quite a number of our kin folks. We found my two older brothers, Dick and Armstead, working farms on rented land about eight miles west of Nashville.[6]

My brother, Jeff, during the years he had been looking for me, had attended school, and taught in colored schools, in the South; and he wanted me to go to school then. There was a school for the education of colored people, near Nashville, called the "Nashville Institute."[7] The fee being nine dollars a month for board and room. I furnished myself with books, and with this capital, I went to school. I stayed there all winter, from about September to the first of May, occupying a separate room with my brother, and being fed pretty well. They taught us reading, writing, spelling, and arithmetic. And during this winter there, I made enough progress so that in May, when I quit the Institute, they considered that I knew enough to teach in a common school where the colored children were given an elementary education. Hearing that they needed a teacher at the little town of Hartsville, about forty-five miles from Nashville, I walked all the way there. The church building was used as a school room, and I taught about thirty-five chil-

Palmer House Hotel in Chicago. ca. 1871. Courtesy of the Chicago Historical Society.

dren. These children I taught the rudiments of spelling and reading. I stayed there until December, being paid $25.00 a month, and lived with some colored people named Dunahue.[8] However, at the close of the term in December, the funds had run out and I was forced to give up the school. So I went back to Nashville, with the money I had saved from my school teaching, and continued my education at the Nashville Institute, staying there until May of the following year (1877). During this second stay at the institute I had studied arithmetic, grammar, and United States history.

Early in 1878 I had decided to get hotel employment again, in view of the fact that the teacher's pay in the schools was very poor, so I went to St. Louis. I had been there only a few days when I got a job at the Lindell Hotel, which was a new hotel, and one of the best in the city. I started in as a waiter, because when the head waiter, a little Irishman named John Colbert, heard that I had worked in the hotels in Chicago and Indianapolis, he was sure I knew my business. I worked there for two years as waiter, and then they put me in charge of the hat rack.[9] In the old hotels, the hatrack man was a man of some importance, because it was not con-

Lindell Hotel in St. Louis, Missouri, ca. 1874. Courtesy of the Missouri Historical Society.

sidered proper to have hat checks, and the man at the rack must have a good memory for faces and hats. I took much pride in seeing that the proper hat was returned to the right man every time. I remained on this job for nine years. During these nine years, while in this position, I did my best to improve my mind during my off hours. In the lobby of the hotel was a news stand, run by a Jew. He had me go every morning to the printing offices of the Globe Democrat, and the Republic, the two leading newspapers. I would get about a hundred papers from one, and fifty from the other, and bring them to the hotel where the newspapers were sold. I would take a portion of them to the hatrack stand, and, as a rule sold a great many of them. I was paid two dollars a week for carrying the papers and selling them at the hat rack. I had plenty of opportunity to read these papers. The news stand men, also sold paper backed novels and kept a supply of all the best novels of that day. Mrs. M. E. Braddon, an English woman, was one of the leading writers of that time, and I read most of her books;[10] also various others which were for sale at the newspaper stand.

These were very lively times in St. Louis. The city was growing rapidly, and every body was prosperous and making money. The hotel was always well patronized.

During the last years of my life in St. Louis, I contracted malaria, also a very bad cough. After this cough had lasted for some time the doctor told me I had better go away from that climate, and that probably the thing for me to do was to go to Colorado. So in 1890 I pulled up stakes in St. Louis, and went to Colorado Springs. When I arrived there, I went into partnership with an old acquaintance of mine, named Charlie Collins. I had about a thousand dollars in cash when I reached Colorado Springs, but Collins got the most of it during two years. At the end of that time I went into the employ of Mr. Hagerman, the date being June 28, 1892.

Appendix I

Thirteenth Michigan Volunteers

(This partial roster includes only the soldiers to whom McCline refers in the narrative.)

BAKER, CHESTER (veteran), Mattawan. Enlisted in company K, Thirteenth Infantry, March 15, 1862, at Mattawan for three years, age forty-one. Mustered in April 12, 1862. Reenlisted March 19, 1864. Mustered in April 29, 1864. Mustered out at Louisville, Ky. July 25, 1865.

BISSINGER, THOMAS. Enlisted in company G, Thirteenth Infantry, January 21, 1864, at Kalamazoo for three years, age forty-five. Mustered in January 21, 1864. Mustered out at Louisville, Ky., July 25, 1865.

CHIRGWIN, RICHARD J. (veteran), Kent County. Enlisted in company C, Thirteenth Infantry, Nov. 8, 1861, at Cannonsburg for three years, age eighteen. Mustered in January 17, 1862. Reenlisted January 18, 1864, at Chattanooga, Tenn. Mustered in January 28, 1864. Mustered out at Louisville, Ky., July 25, 1865.

COLTON, JOHN C. Enlisted in company D, Thirteenth Infantry, October 17, 1863, at Jackson for three years, age thirty-seven. Mustered in October 17, 1863. Joined regiment at Chattanooga, Tenn., February 1864. Died of disease at Lookout Mountain, Tenn., September 7, 1864. Buried in National Cemetery, Chattanooga, Tenn.

CULVER, JOSHUA B., Paw Paw. Entered service in Thirteenth Infantry as first lieutenant and adjutant. Mustered in January 17, 1862. Discharged to accept promotion October 15, 1862. Commissioned major July 4, 1862. Mustered in October 16, 1862. Discharged to accept promotion April 6, 1863. Commissioned lieutenant colonel February 26, 1863. Mustered in April 7, 1863. Discharged to accept promotion June 12, 1863. Commissioned colonel May 26, 1863. Mustered in June 13, 1863. Commanding brigade July 23, 1864. Discharged at expiration of term of service February 23, 1865. Recommissioned colonel April 11, 1865. Mustered in April 24, 1865. Mustered out at Louisville, Ky., July 25, 1865.

DUNBAR, G. EDWIN, Decatur. Enlisted in company C, Thirteenth Infantry, as sergeant Oct. 9, 1861, at Decatur for three years, age twenty-one. Mustered in January 17, 1862. Discharged to accept promotion May 20, 1862. Commissioned second lieutenant May 15, 1862. Mustered in May 21, 1862. Discharged to accept promotion October 31, 1862. Commissioned first lieutenant and quartermaster Aug. 18, 1862. Mustered in Nov. 1, 1862. Captain and assistant quartermaster January 4, 1864. Major and quartermaster October 1, 1864, to August 1, 1865. Brevet lieutenant colonel March 13, 1865, for gallant and meritorious service during the campaign in Georgia and the Carolinas. Mustered out November 22, 1865.

EASTON, HORACE G. (veteran), Prairieville. Enlisted in company A, Thirteenth Infantry, November 4, 1861, at Prairieville for three years, age twenty. Mustered in January 17, 1862. Reenlisted January 18, 1864, at Chattanooga, Tenn. Mustered in January 28, 1864. Corporal December 1862. Regimental bugler March 1863. Mustered out at Louisville, Ky., July 25, 1865.

EATON, WILLARD G., Otsego. Entered service in company I, Thirteenth Infantry, as first lieutenant, age forty. Commissioned October 3, 1861. Mustered in January 17, 1862. Discharged to accept promotion December 5, 1862. Commissioned captain October 20, 1862. Mustered in December 5, 1862. Discharged to accept promotion June 12, 1863. Commissioned major May 26, 1863. Mustered in June 13, 1863. Commissioned colonel February 23, 1865. Killed in action at Bentonville, N.C., March 19, 1865.

FLINT, CHARLES C., JR., Three Rivers. Enlisted in company K, Thirteenth Infantry, as sergeant, December 1, 1861, at Kalamazoo for three years, age twenty-two. Mustered in January 17, 1862. Sergeant major November 2, 1862. Discharged to accept promotion April 16, 1863. Commissioned second lieutenant, company K, March 5, 1863. Mustered in April 7, 1863. Commissioned first lieutenant, company C, March 19, 1864. Mustered in March 19, 1864. Commissioned captain May 12, 1865. Discharged May 15, 1865, on account of wounds received in action at Bentonville, N.C., March 19, 1865.

FOX, CLARK D., Otsego. Enlisted in company I, Thirteenth Infantry, as sergeant, October 16, 1861, at Otsego for three years, age thirty. Mustered in January 17, 1862, first sergeant. Sergeant major May 31, 1862. Commissioned first lieutenant, company I, October 20, 1862. Mustered in December 6, 1862. Discharged to accept promotion June 30, 1863. Commissioned captain June 13, 1863. Mustered in July 1, 1863. Killed in action at Chickamauga, Ga., September 19, 1863. Buried in National Cemetery, Chattanooga, Tenn. Grave No. 11249. Original place of interment, Chickamauga, Ga.

GLINES, JEREMIAH E. (veteran), Pewamo. Enlisted in company F, Thirteenth Infantry, October 5, 1861, at Pewamo for three years, age thirty. Mustered in January 17, 1862. Chief musician June 18, 1862. Transferred to company F March 1863. Sergeant March 3, 1863. Principal musician May 1, 1863. Reenlisted January 18, 1864, at Chattanooga, Tenn. Mustered in January 28, 1864. Discharged to accept promotion June 16, 1865. Commissioned second lieutenant, company G, May 14, 1865. Mustered in June 17, 1865. Mustered out at Louisville, Ky., July 25, 1865.

GORDON, LEWIS, Tompkins. Enlisted in company F, Thirteenth Infantry, September 3, 1864, at Monterey for three years, age sixteen. Mustered in September 3, 1864. Discharged at Washington, D.C., June 8, 1865.

JENKS, LORA C., Pewamo. Enlisted in company F, Thirteenth Infantry, as musician, November 26, 1861, at Pewamo for three years, age forty-two. Mustered in January 17, 1862. Principal musician October 1, 1862. Transferred to company F, March 9, 1863. Sergeant April 30, 1862. Reenlisted January 18, 1864, at Chattanooga, Tenn. Mustered in January 28, 1864. Mustered out at Louisville, Ky., July 25, 1865.

LARKIN, ENOS R. (veteran), Browne. Enlisted in company C, Thirteenth Infantry, November 17, 1861, at Browne for three years, age thirty-four. Mustered in January 17, 1862. Reenlisted as corporal January 18, 1864, at Chattanooga, Tenn. Mustered in January 28, 1864. Mustered out at Louisville, Ky., July 25, 1865. Died January 20, 1892. Buried at Rockford, Mich.

MORAN, JAMES, Jackson. Enlisted in company F, Thirteenth Infantry, October 12, 1861, at Parma for three years, age thirty-nine. Mustered in January 17, 1862. Discharged at Louisville, Ky., April 30, 1863.

MURRAY, FRANCIS, Monterey. Enlisted in company C, Thirteenth Infantry, December 24, 1861, at Monterey for three years, age twenty-two. Mustered in January 17, 1862. Died September 21, 1863, of wounds received in action at Chickamauga, Ga., September 19, 1863.

PALMER, THEODORIC R., Kalamazoo. Entered service in company C, Thirteenth Infantry, at organization as Captain, age thirty-two. Commissioned October 3, 1861. Mustered in January 17, 1862. Discharged to accept promotion April 6, 1863. Commissioned major February 26, 1863. Mustered in April 7, 1863. Discharged to accept promotion June 12, 1863. Discharged at expiration of term of service at Savannah, Ga., January 16, 1865.

PRATT, FOSTER, Kalamazoo. Entered service in Thirteenth Infantry as assistant surgeon, age forty-two. Commissioned December 19, 1861. Mustered in January 17, 1862. Commissioned surgeon January 21, 1865. Mustered in May 26, 1865. Discharged at expiration of term of service at Savannah, Ga., January 16, 1865. Recommissioned surgeon on January 21, 1865. Mustered out at Louisville, Ky., July 25, 1865.

RUGGLES, CHARLES H., Prairieville. Enlisted in company A, Thirteenth Infantry, October 23, 1861, at Prairieville for three years. Mustered in January 17, 1862. First sergeant September 1, 1862. Discharged to accept promotion April 6, 1863. Commissioned second lieutenant February 28, 1863. Mustered in April 7, 1863. Commissioned first lieutenant and quartermaster, March 19, 1864. Mustered in March 19, 1864. Mustered out at Louisville, Ky., July 25, 1865.

SHOEMAKER, MICHAEL, Jackson. Entered service in Thirteenth Infantry as colonel. Commissioned January 28, 1862. Mustered in February 1, 1862. Taken prisoner at Tyree Springs, Tenn., September 7, 1862. Exchanged at Richmond, Va., September 27, 1862. Resigned May 26, 1863. Died in Jackson, Mich., November 10, 1895.

SHULTERS, DAVID H., (veteran), Mattawan. Enlisted in company K, Thirteenth Infantry, as Wagoner, November 14, 1861, at Mattawan for three years, age thirty-three. Mustered in January 17, 1862. Reenlisted January 18, 1864, at Chattanooga, Tenn. Mustered in January 28, 1864. Killed in action at Bentonville, N.C., March 19, 1865.

SINCLAIR, JOSEPH. Enlisted in company B, Thirteenth Infantry, for one year, age thirty-six. Mustered in September 3, 1864. Substitute for James Story. Discharged at Washington, D.C., June 8, 1865.

STARKWEATHER, JESSE (veteran), Eaton Rapids. Enlisted in company G, Thirteen Infantry, November 2, 1861, at Eaton Rapids for three years, age nineteen. Mustered in January 17, 1862. Reenlisted January 18, 1864, at Chattanooga, Tenn. Mustered in January 28, 1864. Mustered out at Louisville, Ky., July 25, 1865.

WADE, BENJAMIN S., Hubbardston. Entered in company E, Thirteenth Infantry, for one year, age eighteen. Mustered in September 3, 1864. Substitute for William H. Shutts. Discharged at Washington, D.C., June 8, 1865.

WARD, WILLIAM W. (veteran), Kalamazoo. Enlisted in company G, Thirteenth Infantry, January 7, 1862, at Kalamazoo for three years, age thirty-two. Mustered in January 17, 1862. Reenlisted January 18, 1864, at Chattanooga, Tenn. Mustered in January 28, 1864. Mustered out at Louisville, Ky., July 25, 1865. Deceased. Buried in Oakwood Cemetery, Allegan, Mich.

YERKES, SILAS A., OR E., Lowell. Entered service in company C, Thirteenth Infantry, as second lieutenant, age twenty-seven. Commissioned October 3, 1861. Mustered in January 17, 1862. Discharged to accept promotion May 20, 1862. Commissioned first lieutenant May 15, 1862. Mustered in May 21, 1862. Discharged to accept promotion April 6, 1863. Commissioned captain February 26, 1863. Mustered in April 7, 1863. Wounded in action at Chickamauga, Ga., September 1863. Brevet major, U.S. Volunteers, March 15, 1865, for meritorious services during the campaign in Georgia and the Carolinas. Commissioned major, May 12, 1865. Discharged because of disability, May 15, 1865.

Appendix II.

Slaves Referred to by McCline

I. McCline's own family
Grandmother Hanna: McCline's maternal grandmother
   A. Hanna's daughter (unnamed, deceased), married to John "Jack" McCline, Sr. (owned by a storekeeper in Wilson County)
      Their children:
      1. Daughter (unnamed, deceased)
      2. Richard McCline "Dick"
      3. Jefferson McCline "Jeff"—cowboy; later—waiter
      4. Armstead McCline
      5. John McCline, Jr.—cowboy
   B. Uncle Richard
      1. Two children (Aunt Hanna is possibly his wife, see below)
      2. Richard's house was where the men met to share news and discuss issues
   C. Uncle Stephen
      1. His wife and four children lived on the McRidley plantation
      2. Stephen was head carpenter and head miller
II. Living in the same house with Grandmother Hanna and her four grandsons
   A. Buck—the shoemaker; the only slave at Clover Bottom who could read
   B. Betsy—Buck's wife
   C. Frank—their son, John McCline's childhood friend
III. Other slaves
   A. Abe—blacksmith, banjo player, storyteller
   B. Aron
   C. Aunt Hanna—head milker (possibly the wife of Uncle Richard)

This genealogy was compiled by Katherine Kitch Hagerman of Sante Fe, New Mexico, the Hagerman family historian and archivist.

D. Austin—assistant to Stephen in carpentering and milling; also did field work
E. Booker
F. Cynthia—assistant gardener; lived with Lawson and his wife
G. Daniel—painter
H. David—foreman in the fields
I. Dilsey—Austin's wife
J. Henry—storyteller
K. Jesse—new coachman
L. Lawson—old coachman (retired)
   1. Laura—waitress at the White House
   2. Betsy
M. Lawson's wife (unnamed)
N. Richard—marketman (retired; succeeded by Zuccorilla, an Italian)
O. Uncle Jordan—head gardener (widower)
P. Vann—fiddle player, singer, storyteller
Q. Wyatt—in charge of breeding mules and feeding hogs for slaughter; herb doctor and conjurer

Appendix III.

McCline's Will, Remembrances, and Obituary Notices

Letter from Jesse L. Nusbaum

c/o Region 3, National Park Service
Santa Fe, New Mexico
dated: January, 23, 1948

To: Percy Hagerman, Colorado Springs, Colorado [Herbert J. Hagerman's brother]

Dear Percy:
The attached editorial in a recent issue of the *New Mexican* will hold interest. I wanted to send the fuller account of Johnny's life but that paper got out of hand.

For years after his service with Bert, most of the more socially active and important women here just had to have Johnny handle the catering service for their guest [*sic*].

Hope all goes well for you. All the best. As ever, Sincerely,

Jess Nusbaum

Letter from Percy Hagerman, Colorado Springs

dated January 27, 1948

To: Jesse L. Nusbaum, Santa Fe

Dear Jess:
I thank you very much for sending me the newspaper clipping about the death

of old McCline. He was about the finest member of his race I have ever known. It is considerably more than fifty years since I first knew him and for at least forty years he was with my family, first with my father, then for a long time with me and lastly with Bert in Santa Fe. He was always faithful, loyal and efficient.

On my visits to Santa Fe I always called on him and the last time I saw him I came away with the feeling that he could not last much longer, though he said he expected to live to a hundred. He was indeed a credit to the human race.

I hope things go well with you. We have been having quite a siege of real winter here and are fed up on it. With best regards,
Sincerely yours,
Percy Hagerman

[Percy's 1947 diary records that he was in Santa Fe in January, May, and August of that year. One of these times must have been "the last time" he saw John McCline (note from Katherine Kitch Hagerman)]. These letters are a courtesy of the Hagerman Family Archives.

Obituary Notices

A Splendid Gentleman

A fine human being died here Monday after 95 years of a useful life. He was John H. McCline, a Negro born in Slavery, but dignified in freedom.

Friends were recalling today a story which the late territorial Gov. Herbert J. Hagerman, in whose house-hold Mr. McCline served for years, liked to tell of him.

One day, Mr. McCline approached the then governor.

"Sir," he said, "with your permission, I should like to have next Tuesday off."

"Certainly," the governor replied, "but why?"

"That, sir," answered Mr. McCline, "is the anniversary of the day I first came to your home."

Those who knew Mr. McCline agree he was a splendid gentleman—a person of devoted loyalty—a credit to the human race.

—*Santa Fe New Mexican*, January 21, 1948

Ex-Slave Buried Here During Service Today

John H. McCline, onetime slave whose funeral was held this afternoon, accompanied Sherman's army on its march from Atlanta "to the sea," according to Deputy City Building Inspector A. S. Alvord.

McCline, then about 9, was a personal servant to the captain of Company C, 13th Michigan infantry. Alvord's father, Pfc. Ceborn Ensigne Alvord, was a member of that company.

As Michigan troops were passing the plantation near Nashville, Tenn. where McCline was herding cattle, a Michigander called out, "Come on, boy," Alvord related. McCline promptly accepting the invitation, remained with the Michigan outfit until the end of the war.

He then went back to Michigan with the captain and remained there until the officer died.

McCline, who was "major domo" at the executive mansion when the late Herbert J. Hagerman was governor died Monday morning. Funeral services were held this afternoon at the First Presbyterian church, where he had been janitor for 12 years, and burial was in Fairview cemetery

He was 95 years old.

—*Santa Fe New Mexican*, January 20, 1948

Last Will and Testament

of

John H. McCline.

****

I, John H. McCline, a resident of the City of Santa Fe, County of Santa Fe, State of New Mexico, make this my Last Will and Testament, and do hereby revoke any and all wills by me heretofore at any time made.

FIRST: I direct that my just debts and funeral expenses be paid as soon after my death as practicable.

SECOND: I give, devise and bequeath to my wife, Bertha McCline, all property owned by me at the time of my death, real, personal or mixed, and wheresoever situate.

THIRD: I designate and appoint my wife, Bertha McCline, Executrix of this my Last Will and Testament, and direct that no bond be required of her as such Executrix.

IN WITNESS WHEREOF I have executed this instrument as my Last Will and Testament at Santa Fe, New Mexico, this _13_ day of November, 1943.

John H. McCline

The foregoing instrument was at the place and on the date specified therein, signed, published and declared by the testator named therein to be his Last Will and Testament in the presence of each of us, and we thereupon, at his request and in his presence and in the presence of each other, at said time and place, have hereunto subscribed our names as attesting witnesses thereto.

Helen L. Quintana Residing at Santa Fe, New Mexico.

John N. Jones Residing at Santa Fe, New Mexico.

First page of Last Will and Testament of John McCline.

NOTES

Editor's Introduction

1. Two pioneering scholars disagree over the authorship of Briton Hammon's narrative. Marion Wilson Starling believes parts of the work were written by someone else. See *The Slave's Narrative: Its Place in American History* (Boston: G. K. Hall, 1981). Francis Smith Foster assumes that Hammon wrote his own story. See *Witnessing Slavery: Development of the Ante-Bellum Slave Narrative* (Westport: Greenwood Press, 1979).
2. Frederick Douglass, *Narrative of the Life of Frederick Douglass, An American Slave, Written by Himself* (Boston: published at the Anti-Slavery Office, 1845).
3. Classic slave narrative developed between 1830 and 1865, when more than half of the approximately 115 separately published narratives in the United State and Great Britain appeared. (Marion Wilson Starling estimates that more than 6,000 slaves' stories appeared in interviews, essays, and biographies.) Very similar in their episodic structure, ironic voice, development of theme and plantation characters, these nearly uniform works make up the body of classic slave narrative literature.
4. Extensive scholarship has been done on the distinguishing literary characteristics and historical influences of classic antebellum narrative and on the development of postbellum narrative. See, for example, William Andrews, *To Tell a Free Story: The First Century of Afro-American Autobiography, 1760–1864* (Urbana: Univ. of Illinois Press, 1986), and Andrews, "The Representation of Slavery and the Rise of Afro-American Literary Realism, 1865–1920," in *Slavery and the Literary Imagination,* ed. Deborah E. McDowell and Arnold Rampersad (Baltimore: Johns Hopkins Univ. Press, 1989). See also Starling, *The Slave's Narrative*, and Foster, *Witnessing Slavery.*
5. In 1860 Tennessee had a total of 275,719 slaves, most of them working relatively small farms in West and Middle Tennessee. Shelby County, where Memphis is located, and Fayette County, both in West Tennessee, ranked first and

second respectively with 16,953 and 15,473 slaves. Davidson County in Middle Tennessee (which includes Nashville) where McCline lived had 14,790 slaves. East Tennesseeans held a small percentage of the slave population. For a comprehensive study of slavery in Tennessee, see Bobby L. Lovett, "The Negro in Tennessee, 1861–1866: A Socio-Military History of the Civil War Era" (Ph.D. diss., Univ. of Arkansas, 1978).

6. Ira Berlin, Joseph P. Reidy, and Leslie S. Rowland, eds., *Freedom, A Documentary History of Emancipation 1861–1867: Series II, The Black Military Experience* (New York: Cambridge Univ. Press, 1982), 12.

7. The first two regiments of ex-slaves had both an official date of enlistment and an official date of muster. Raised by generals in the field, but unrecognized by the war department, the First Kansas Colored and the First South Carolina Volunteers date enlistments as early as August 6, 1862, and May 9, 1862, respectively. The earliest muster dates are January 13, 1863, for the Kansas regiment and November 7, 1862, for the Carolina regiment. A third nonwhite regiment of this early period was the Louisiana Native Guards, composed of free mulattos.

8. Howard C. Westwood, *Black Troops, White Commanders, and Freedmen During the Civil War* (Carbondale: Southern Illinois Univ. Press, 1992), 9.

9. Berlin, Reidy, and Rowland, *Freedom,* 252.

10. Ibid., 176.

11. Ibid., 12.

12. Lovett, "The Negro in Tennessee," 12, 10.

13. See Edwin S. Redkey's chapter "Black Soldiers in White Regiments," in *A Grand Army of Black Men: Letters from African-American Soldiers in the Union Army, 1861–1965* (New York: Cambridge Univ. Press, 1992), 9–26.

14. James M. McPherson, *The Negro's Civil War: How American Blacks Felt and Acted During the War for the Union* (New York: Ballantine Books, 1991), 21.

15. Frederick Douglass, "Address for the Promotion of Colored Enlistments, Delivered at a Mass Meeting in Philadelphia, July 6, 1863," *The Life and Writings of Frederick Douglass,* vol. 3: The Civil War 1861–1865, ed. Philip S. Foner (New York: International Publishers, 1975), 370.

16. Douglass, "Another Word to Colored Men," in *Life and Writings,* 344.

17. I do not mean to suggest that not many black soldiers were combatants. For an account of blacks in battle, see Dudley Taylor Cornish, *The Sable Arm: Negro Troops in the Union Army, 1861–1865* (New York: W. W. Norton, 1966).

18. Berlin, Reidy, and Rowland, *Freedom,* 491.

19. Ibid., 388.

20. William A. Gladstone, *Men of Color* (Gettysburg: Thomas Publications, 1993).

21. Lovett, "The Negro in Tennessee," 36.

22. Stephen Butterfield addresses this subject of collective identity in *Black Autobiography in America* (Amherst: Univ. of Massachusetts Press, 1974).

INTRODUCTION BY H. J. HAGERMAN

1. Later in the introduction, Hagerman strongly implicates Llewelyn (who became U.S. attorney for New Mexico) in Hagerman's resignation from the office of territorial governor.
2. Hagerman is undoubtedly referring to Edward Oliver *Wolcott*, elected to the U.S. Senate in 1895 from Colorado.
3. William McKinley (1843–1901) was shot by an assassin, Leon F. Czolgosz, on September 6, 1901, while attending a public reception for the Pan-American Exposition in Buffalo, New York. He died on September 14.
4. Nicholas II, the last czar of Russia, came to power in 1894, presiding during the next twenty-three years over a conflicting period of industrial growth and political unrest as students, workers, and peasants protested economic depression. St. Petersburg (since 1918 Leningrad and recently St. Petersburg again), where Hagerman resided, was also the location of the czar's winter home and the capital of Russia. Foreign embassies, theaters, museums, palaces, bejeweled churches, all contributed to the city's character. It was what Hagerman calls "brilliant" as the first western-style city in Russia and the center of intellectual and social life. Hagerman's diplomatic duties as second secretary of the United States Embassy were marked by the pageantry of royal life, and his social circle included various members of the extended royal family. But in the 1890s when Hagerman worked there and into the twentieth century St. Petersburg was also the scene of political revolt. Hagerman was aware of the economic extremes: the wealth and privilege of an upper class and the deprivations suffered by peasants in the countryside and even in some areas of St. Petersburg. It is interesting that 1898, the year that Hagerman joined the embassy in Russia, was the same year Marxists formed the Russian Social Democratic Labor Party, the parent organization of Lenin's Bolsheviks, who overthrew Nicholas in the 1917 revolution. Hagerman's letters during this period present his view of Russian life and of American politics in relation to Russian affairs. See his *Letters of a Young Diplomat* (Santa Fe: The Rydal Press, 1937).
5. Described as well-educated, genteel, and politically naive, Herbert James Hagerman (1871–1935) was a progressive Republican (in opposition to the Republican old guard) appointed by Roosevelt in January 1906 to curb corruption—political patronage, land fraud—in New Mexico. When Hagerman removed Holm O. Bursum, chairman of the Territorial Republican Committee from his position as superintendent of prisons for misappropriating money, his political opponents evened the score by taking advantage of a public controversy over Hagerman's alleged involvement in land grant fraud. The charge was that Hagerman had sold ten thousand acres of timberland, without the knowledge and consent of the commissioner of Public Lands, at an undervalued price to the Pennsylvania Development Company. In purchasing the land, the development company had circumvented a law restricting sale of public

land to one-quarter of a section per person or corporation. Believing that he was the victim of a conspiracy by those who wanted him out, Hagerman wrote a series of letters to President Roosevelt, explaining his position in the transaction. But, apparently hoping to restore order to the Republican party in New Mexico, Roosevelt demanded Hagerman's resignation in April 1907 and appointed a former Rough Rider, George Curry, to the office. Later, Hagerman was able to demonstrate that Curry had been offered the post before the land sale controversy, suggesting that Hagerman was right about behind-the-scenes efforts to remove him from office. For a detailed discussion of the controversy, see Carol Larson, *Forgotten Frontier: The Story of Southeastern New Mexico* (Albuquerque: Univ. of New Mexico Press). For more information on Hagerman's tenure as governor, see Hagerman, *A Statement in Regard to Certain Matters Concerning the Governorship and Political Affairs in New Mexico in 1906–1907* (Roswell, N.Mex., 1908); Robert A Larson, "The Profile of a New Mexico Progressive," *New Mexico Historical Review* 45 (July 1970): 233–44; Thomas McMullin and David Walker, *Biographical Directory of American Territorial Governors* (Westport, Conn.: Meckler Publishing, 1984), 257–58. The Hagerman Papers are located in the state of New Mexico Records Center and Archives in Santa Fe, in the National Archives in Washington, and in the Rio Grande Historical Collections of the library at New Mexico State University, Las Cruces.

6.　Theodore Roosevelt, a colonel during the Spanish-American War (April 1898 to August 1898), commanded the First Volunteer Calvary Regiment, about one thousand men, including William Llewelyn, popularly known as the Rough Riders. Roosevelt led the charge near San Juan Hill in Cuba, which helped win the war and which caused his regiment to be hailed as heroes.

7.　McCline's occupation is variously recorded in census records as domestic, servant, and gardener. He was also a popular cook and caterer in Santa Fe.

8.　Hagerman's meaning here is unclear. He certainly respected McCline and thought him intellectually capable of writing his memoir, and if McCline was bicycling to work daily, as Hagerman reports later in his introduction, infirmity was not Hagerman's concern. Perhaps Hagerman is referring to what could have been a problem with dexterity. McCline's signature on his last will and testament (see Appendix III) in 1943 reveals a barely legible scrawl, not the kind that results from the writer's haste or indifference, but one marked by the painstaking deliberateness of a child and that would have made writing slow and perhaps difficult. (Of course, probably almost two decades had lapsed between writing the memoir and signing his will. The illegible signature might possibly have been caused by the infirmities of a ninety-year-old man.) McCline was also left-handed, and Hagerman may have believed this to be a handicap.

9.　Hagerman became special commissioner to the Navajos in January 1923 during a period of growing Native American rights activism. The Pueblos and their supporters were fighting assaults on their culture and land. Most notably, in 1922, the year before Hagerman's appointment, the Bursum Bill, introduced in the Congress by Hagerman's old political enemy Holm O. Bursum, then Senator from New Mexico, threatened Pueblo land rights by favoring claims to Indian land made by white squatters. Appointed by Secretary of the Interior Albert Fall, Hagerman's official job was to negotiate land use, primarily oil development, on the Navajo reservation. Unofficially, he also served to counter Bursum's activity by organizing a Navajo tribal council to manage land leases to outsiders. Initially viewed with skepticism by reformers, in time Hagerman was considered a dedicated public servant who greatly improved supervision of the Indian Service. See Lawrence C. Kelly, *The Assault on Assimilation* (Albuquerque: Univ. of New Mexico Press, 1983), 276–78. Although a political appointee and by association aligned with federal policy, which was generally unsympathetic to Indian affairs, Hagerman was apparently sincere in his efforts to deal equitably with the Pueblos. Nevertheless, by 1932 Hagerman had fallen victim to those—like John Collier, founder of the American Indian Defense Association (AIDA)—who accused him of intrusion into the internal affairs of the Pueblos. And once again he was implicated in a land fraud case. This time, Hagerman was the subject of Senate hearings over whether his salary should be withheld for allegedly selling an oil lease for one thousand dollars that later turned out to be valuable. The hearings went in his favor. It seems that the land in question was sold at public auction with no prior knowledge of its potential worth. In fact, records show that the buyer, who had bid a thousand dollars just to get the auction going, had tried unsuccessfully after the auction to find another buyer.

10. Walapi is a Hopi Indian village.

11. In the 1930s approximately six black families lived in Santa Fe, enough to support an African Methodist Episcopal (AME) church. In the summer the population grew with servants who accompanied employers to summer residences.

12. Algernon and Jessie Slaughter lived with McCline. Bertha Slaughter and her daughter, Ben Ethel, apparently also boarded in McCline's house, and in 1937 McCline, age eighty-six, married Bertha, age forty-six. Bertha, originally from St. Genevieve, Missouri, had been widowed twice. Her first husband, Benjamin Bondurant of St. Louis, with whom she had her daughter, died in 1913. Two years later Bertha moved to Santa Fe and married Ernest Slaughter, Algernon's brother, who died in 1936. The following year she married McCline. Bertha McCline died in 1990 at age ninety-nine.

In addition to his "inference" here, early in his introduction Hagerman records McCline's comment about having finished with weddings, suggesting that McCline may have been married prior to 1937. I have found, however, no public record or any other evidence of a previous marriage.

I. BEFORE THE WAR

1. James Hoggatt (1798–1863) was a wealthy planter by Middle Tennessee standards. He was ranked eleventh among 125 farmers in Davidson County with at least 20 slaves and 100 acres of improved farm land and first among the 13 farmers in his district. See Samuel D. Smith, ed., *Woodlawn Mansion: History, Architecture, Archeology* (Nashville: Printed with funds provided by Northern Telecom, 1985), 5–17. As McCline recalls, Hoggatt's slave population and land holdings were quite extensive. In 1860 he owned 4,030 acres and 203 slaves in 3 counties: 1,500 acres and 60 slaves in Davidson County where McCline was held, 1,530 acres and 107 slaves in Rutherford County, and 1,000 acres and 30 slaves in Wilson County. In addition to the Tennessee property, Hoggatt owned one-half interest in a cotton plantation in Yazoo, Mississippi. Clover Bottom (without the "s"), encompassing an area much broader than Hoggatt's plantation, was named by the earliest settlers in the 1700s for the white clover they found growing all over the bottomland. For more information on the history of Clover Bottom, see Benjamin C. Nance, "Historical Background and Archeological Assessment of the Clover Bottom Mansion" (Department of Environment and Conservation, Tennessee Division of Archeology, Mar. 1993) and Paul Clements, *A Past Remembered: A Collection of Antebellum Houses in Davidson County* (Nashville: Clearview Press, 1987).
2. Clover Bottom plantation is eight miles *east* of Nashville.
3. As Steve Rogers, Historic Preservation Specialist with the Department of Environment and Conservation at the Tennessee Historical Commission, has pointed out, the main entrance to Clover Bottom faces west and not north, as McCline writes. Beginning with this placement, McCline's cardinal mapping of the house and outbuildings at Clover Bottom is consistently ninety degrees off. For accurate placements, see the line-drawn map of the plantation. In the interest of clarity, from here on, when documentation of the correct placement exists, I have silently corrected McCline's directional references except where otherwise noted.
4. Hoggatt's first wife, Mary Jane Walker, died in 1829, and in 1834 he married Mary Ann Saunders (1813–1887), fifteen years his junior, whose family was prominent in the area.
5. Emily and Delia Gentry, daughters of Mary Ann Hoggatt's sister Emily, came to live at Clover Bottom after their mother's death.
6. The Hoggatt plantation was "bounded" on the *south* by Stewart's Ferry Pike and on the *east* by the river. From here on, where appropriate, I will silently replace Murfreesboro Pike with Stewart's Ferry. I am indebted to Steve Rogers for this and subsequent revisions in McCline's plantation geography.
7. On the 1871 Davidson County map, this toll gate is located at the intersection of Lebanon and Stewart's Ferry Pikes. The course of Lebanon Pike toward the bridge is *northeast*.

8. Here and later, there is a discrepancy between McCline's count of Hoggatt's chattel and other property at Clover Bottom and the 1860 census. According to the census, Hoggatt's holdings peaked at about 60 slaves, 20 horses, 40 mules, 80 cows, 6 oxen, 150 sheep, and 200 swine. Half of Hoggatt's 1,500 acres was cultivated. A census taken after the sale and winter harvest of animals could partly account for McCline's numbers. Of course, the total sum of Hoggatt's holdings at the 3 Tennessee plantations greatly exceeds McCline's estimates.

9. That Hoggatt was a planter and not a slavetrader is demonstrated by the number of extended slave families at Clover Bottom and at the plantation in Mississippi. (In an apparent attempt to keep at least one family together, for example, Hoggatt left to his niece Emily Gentry the slaves Yellow John, his wife, and their children.) In addition to the livestock enumerated earlier, Hoggatt raised agricultural crops. According to the 1860 Davidson County Agricultural Census, these included an annual harvest of 600 bushels of wheat, 4,000 bushels of Indian corn, 100 bushels of oats, 100 of peas and beans, 400 of Irish potatoes, 600 of sweet potatoes, and 2,000 pounds of butter.

10. No record of the smokehouse exists, but taking into account McCline's ninety degree rotation in direction, it would have been *east* of the main house.

11. Hoggatt's overseer during this period was a man named *Richard* Phillips.

12. McCline is more than likely describing the cash garden, which earned about $1,000 annually.

13. The 1860 Davidson County slave census lists only twelve houses on the farm.

14. Hoggatt was apparently the kind of slaveholder who took a scientific approach to plantation management. Slaveholders in this class attended agricultural fairs and discussed papers on, among other subjects, building the best slave quarters. McCline's description of the new quarters is similar to instructions given in the October 6, 1857, issue of the *Practical Farmer and Mechanic,* published at Somerville, Tennessee: "His [the planter's] negro quarters should be placed a convenient distance from his dwelling on a dry, airy ridge—raised two feet from the ground—so they can be thoroughly ventilated underneath, and placed at distances apart of at least fifty yards to ensure health. In this construction, they should be sufficiently spacious so as not to crowd the family intended to occupy them—with brick chimneys and large fire-places to impart warmth to every part of the room." Caleb Perry Patterson, *The Negro in Tennessee, 1790– 1865* (Austin: Univ. of Texas Bulletin, 1922), 65. The "saddlebag" construction—two rooms with a centrally located fireplace between the rooms—was the most common type of Big House slave quarter. See John Michael Vlach, *Back of the Big House: The Architecture of Plantation Slavery* (Chapel Hill: Univ. of North Carolina Press, 1993), 22.

15. McCline's date of birth and his age during the prewar period of the narrative is unclear. As a child, McCline, like most slaves, did not know when he was born. As an adult, he settled on 1852 as his birth year, and the 1860 slave census would seem to support this year of birth. Listed on the census, in succes-

sion, are four males, ages 17, 13, 11, and 8. These are more than likely McCline (born in 1852 and 8 years old in 1860) and his three older brothers. With an 1852 birth year, McCline would have been 9 or 10 in 1861–62, and what he refers to as the "beginning of this history" would be the same year he left the plantation. Although much of the story he relates takes place before 1861, McCline is most probably marking his beginning as 1862, the year he left, and not the year of his earliest recollection.

16. McCline's grandmother's house is more likely *west* of Lebanon Pike. An 1871 map shows a house on the west side about a mile from the river.

17. This reference and a later one are most likely to James Dodson, who owned a plantation north of Hoggatt's.

18. The plantation wife has emerged as a complex figure in history and literature. In classic slave narrative, she is a poignant symbol of systemic decay in plantation life. Powerless and dependent in her role as southern lady, she becomes as much a victim of her husband's authority as the (other) slaves. Her defense is often a desperate enthusiasm for cruelty, which she directs not toward her husband, but toward the house servants, especially the women, whom she perceives as rivals. In narrative literature, so persistent is the decay that even compassionate northern women who marry into a plantation life are soon tainted beyond the ability to show compassion. (It must be said that, from McCline's description of her, Mrs. Hoggatt was not the least bit ambivalent about her authority.) Historical studies of the plantation mistress incorporate the slave narrative persona, but are not so reductive. See, for example, Elizabeth Fox-Genovese, *Within the Plantation Household: Black and White Women of the Old South,* Chapel Hill: Univ. of North Carolina Press, 1988.

19. Tennessee state laws made trade with slaves illegal and punishable by a series of graduated fines and imprisonment. On selling whiskey and weapons, for example, the law read: "Any person who sells, loans, or delivers to any slave, except for his master or owner, and then only in such owner or master's presence, or upon his written order, any liquor, gun, or weapon . . . is guilty of a misdemeanor, and shall be fined not less than fifty dollars, and imprisoned in the county jail at the discretion of the court." Patterson, *The Negro in Tennessee, 1790–1865,* 47–48. Trade laws, however, were uniformly ignored. Slaves sold game, vegetables, and, when permitted, their services, among other things, and used the money, as McCline says, for purchases. For an account of slaves' financial status, see Ira Berlin and Philip Morgan, eds., *The Slaves' Economy: Independent Production by Slaves in the Americas* (London: Frank Cuss & Co., LTD, 1991).

20. The Hoggatts built a house in the Greek Revival style around 1854 which burned a few years later. Several extensive studies of the Clover Bottom area, including a published history of the plantation house (see, for example, Nance, "Historical Background and Archeological Assessment," 17 and Clements, *A Past Remembered,* 193), cite 1856 as the year the house burned.

McCline, however, places the loss as February 1859, and his date is corroborated by a brief notice in the February 12, 1859, issue of the *Nashville Union and American Paper*. According to the paper: "The Origin of the fire which destroyed the . . . residence of Dr. Hoggatt, on the Lebanon Pike, on the 7th [of February], has not yet been satisfactorily ascertained we believe. We learn from the Lebanon *Herald* that the Doctor suceeded [*sic*] in saving his furniture, and that his loss will not exceed eight or ten thousand dollars."

21. The time was most likely between 1857 and 1859. John Brown, an abolitionist, began formulating his plans in 1857 to invade the South at Harpers Ferry, Virginia, (now West Virginia) in 1859. Brown initially intended to raid the United States arsenal at Harpers Ferry and send raiders out to arm slaves in the vicinity, who would join him at a colony in the mountains. A revised scheme outlined successive raids throughout the South, freeing slaves and gathering recruits as he went. Despite moral and financial support among many leading black and white abolitionists in the North, the plan failed, and Brown was captured and later hanged on December 21, 1859.

22. News of Brown's plan probably reached slaves through free blacks and abolitionists in the state. Prior to 1834, Tennessee had as many as four antislavery societies. After that year, antislavery activity, though less organized, continued, especially in East Tennessee. In some instances, abolitionists from other states were active in Tennessee. In 1835, for example, Rev. Amos Dresser of Ohio was arrested and flogged in Nashville for publishing and distributing abolitionist pamphlets among slaves. Patterson, *The Negro in Tennessee*, 196.

23. The new house in the Italianate style was more elaborate than the one which burned.

24. Synor Zuccorilla (McCline's version is close), age twenty-seven in 1860, and his wife, Isabella, age twenty-four, lived at Clover Bottom with their three children, ages six, four and two. From here, the correct spelling will be used.

25. The house which McCline describes here has been designated "Old Blue Brick" (because one wall was painted blue) and is one of the oldest brick houses in Middle Tennessee. Built around 1790 in that part of Tennessee which was still part of North Carolina, the house was on a twelve-acre parcel of land purchased by Hoggatt in 1850. Andrew Jackson is reported to have mustered his troops on the front yard of Old Blue Brick before riding to New Orleans during the war of 1812. For more details on the history of the house, see Leona Taylor Aiken, *Donelson, Tennessee: Its History and Landmarks* (Nashville, 1968), 69–71.

26. Abraham Lincoln was the antislavery Republican party candidate for the 1860 presidential election. He had argued against slavery as a moral evil during debates with Stephen Douglas two years earlier and was supported by those favoring the abolition of slavery. Yet, as president, Lincoln was a moderate on the politics of slavery, giving priority to maintaining the union of states over abolition. "A House divided against itself cannot stand. I believe this government cannot endure, permanently half slave and half free," he had said in 1858.

Douglas, who supported the Union but did not oppose slavery and who supported a territory's right to choose or reject slavery, a policy he called "popular sovereignty," was nominated by northern Democrats to run for president in 1860. Proslavery Democrats in the South nominated John Breckinridge.

27. Vann's rendition is one clever variation on a familiar American folktale/ballad about love and death. Another version in ballad form is titled *Banks of the Ohio:*

> I asked my love to go with me,
> I held a knife against her breast,
> to take a walk a little way.
> And gently in my arms she pressed,
> And as we walked, and as we talked
> Crying: Willie, oh Willie, don't murder me,
> about our golden wedding day.
> For I'm unprepared for eternity.
>
> Then only say that you'll be mine,
> I took her by her lily white hand,
> In no other arms entwined.
> Led her down where the waters stand.
> Down beside where the waters flow,
> I picked her up and I pitched her in,
> On the banks of the Ohio.
> Watched her as she floated down.
>
> I asked your mother for you, dear,
> I started back home twixt twelve and one,
> And she said you were too young;
> Crying, My God, what have I done?
> Only say that you'll be mine—
> I've murdered the only woman I love,
> Happiness in my home you'll find.
> Because she would not be my bride.

In yet another ballad, an old woman, who wants to be with her lover, blinds her husband by feeding him "Eggs and Marrowbone" (which is also the song's title). Once he is blind, the husband decides to drown himself, but the wife offers to push him into the water:

> The old woman took a running jump
> For to push the old man in,

The old man he stepped to one side
And the old woman she falls in.

She cried for help, screamed for help.
Loudly she did bawl.
The old man said, "I'm so goshdern blind
I can't see you at all."

28. The oldest female noted on the 1860 slave census was ninety; she is unlikely to be McCline's active and fully employed grandmother. Two sixty-year-old women were also listed.

29. The only known public reference to John McCline Sr. was in 1868–69, when he was a student at Fisk Normal School (now Fisk University) for freedmen in Nashville.

30. Andrew Jackson's (1767–1845) home, the Hermitage, a two-story brick house, is located four and one-quarter miles from Clover Bottom. Not surprisingly, Jackson exerted a strong presence in the area. In the early part of the century, he was part owner of the Clover Bottom Turf, a racetrack and site of the famous race between Jackson's horse, Truxton, and Joseph Erwin's horse, Ploughboy. Later Jackson killed Erwin's son-in-law, Charles Dickinson, in a duel over Dickinson's insults to Jackson and his wife, Rachel. In 1804 Jackson opened a store and tavern with his business partner at which John Hoggatt, James Hoggatt's father, shopped. See "The History of Clover Bottom Mansion," an unpublished account compiled by Middle Tennessee State University.

31. McCline seems to be describing a French wallpaper that was distributed by Jean Zuber. First issued in 1852, the paper was called "The War of American Independence" and used thirty-two sheets for a complete scene. Among the images were General Lafayette in the midst of battle, General Cornwallis in Yorktown, and General Washington triumphantly entering the city of Boston.

32. McCline may be referring to Comet Pons-Winnecke. First seen in 1816, it has a period of orbit around the sun every 5.6 to 6.3 years and would have been visible around 1860.

33. Phillips remained at Clover Bottom plantation at least until 1862, the year McCline left. Hoggatt employed three overseers, one at each of his plantations: Phillips, Williamson Birthright, and H. H. Hanes. Hoggatt left Hanes real estate in Rutherford County and a slave named Milly. He also released Hanes from any standing debt. Phillips was not named in his will, but Zuccorilla was bequeathed $2,000 "for his faithful service to me and my family" (Davidson County Wills, Book 19:189). Phillips either remained in the area during the war or returned to Clover Bottom after the war. According to the 1870 census many of Hoggatt's former slaves were still living on the plantation, all having taken the name Hoggatt, and Phillips is listed as the overseer.

34. Confederate shelling of Fort Sumter, located in the Charleston, South Carolina harbor, on April 12 and 13, 1861, ignited the war. South Carolina had been the first state to secede from the Union in December 1860. By February of the next year, Mississippi, Alabama, and Georgia had voted to secede, and several other state conventions were considering the question of secession. It was also in February that Jefferson Davis of Mississippi was elected president of the Confederate States of America.

35. Tennessee was not of one mind on the questions of secession and war. In February 1861, when Davis was elected to the Confederate presidency, Tennessee chose not to hold a state convention on secession by a popular vote of 68,282 to 59,449. By May, however, the Tennessee legislature in Nashville voted 66–25 in favor of secession; a popular referendum in June upheld the legislature with 104,913 in favor and 47,238 against (*The Civil War Almanac* [New York: World Almanac Publication, 1983], 45). Tennessee was the last state to secede and the first to be readmitted.

36. During February 1862, the Union carried out plans to take Confederate positions in Kentucky and Tennessee. This included an infantry and naval attack on Fort Donelson at Dover, Tennessee. General Grant declared: "No terms except unconditional and immediate surrender can be accepted" (*Civil War Almanac*, 85). The fort fell on February 16, and the Cumberland and Tennessee Rivers were in Union control. In anticipation of federal occupation of Nashville, Confederate Governor Harris moved the capital from Nashville to Memphis. Throughout this period, civilians were fleeing the area, resulting, no doubt, in the chaos that McCline describes.

37. In late 1862 General Crittenden and General Morgan camped at Clover Bottom for five weeks and eight to ten days respectively. On May 16, 1867, the Hoggatt family filed a claim with the federal government for reimbursement of property taken by the encamped troops. They wanted payment for 21,000 bushels of corn, 22,500 pounds of fodder, 80,000 pounds of hay at 20 dollars a ton, 500 bushels of seed millet at $1 a bushel, 500 bushels of oats, 8,000 feet of lumber, 28,678 feet of plank fence at 25 cents per unit (the unit isn't specified, but this is most probably the fence to which McCline is referring), 160 cords of wood, 850 pounds of nails, 4 mules, 4,000 cords of fire wood. The total claim came to $15,904.70, of which $6,437 was approved by the government. See Office of the Quartermaster General-Claims Branch 1861–1889; Documents File-Miscellaneous Claims Box 325, Claims (#765–#840), Claims #767.

38. Masters (and mistresses) tried a variety of measures to keep slaves on plantations during the war, including moral conversion. John Cimprich points out that a "small number of slaveholders, mostly unionists, underwent a change of heart and began compensating their slaves before any signs of disloyalty appeared. In 1864 Joseph B. Killebrew, of Montgomery County, started paying a generous annual wage of $200 for men and $96–$120 for women, plus room and board for all. A Shelby County planter offered his slaves half the crop

that year. James P. Lyon had gone even further the year before by dividing his Madison County plantation into tenant farms for his slaves" (John Cimprich, *Slavery's End in Tennessee, 1861–1865* [University, Ala.: Univ. of Alabama Press, 1985], 27). McCline takes a more cynical view of Mrs. Hoggatt's sudden generosity.

39. The red stripe indicates that he was an artillery officer.

40. On July 21 and 22 (not late August), Gen. Nathan Bedford Forrest and his 1,000 troops were in the Clover Bottom area.

41. General Forrest's official report of his activities during this period confirms McCline's account: "I remained at Lebanon until Monday morning, and moved then with my command toward Nashville. On reaching the vicinity of Nashville, say 5 or 6 miles, I captured 3 of the enemy's pickets. I moved them around the city, semicircling it and the Nashville and Chattanooga Railroad, passing within 3 miles of the city, and capturing on the way 2 additional pickets" (Report of Brig. Gen. Nathan B. Forrest, C.S. Army, including operations July 18–24, *Official Records*, ser. I, vol. 16, pt. 1: 818).

42. Like their grandmother, Richard and Armstead McCline were considered mulatto, the category given them in the 1870 census in Tennessee. Similarly, John was placed in the same color category in the 1870 census in Michigan.

43. The date is likely September 1862; McCline had left the plantation by 1863.

II. During the War

1. See Appendix I for more information on the military service of individual soldiers in the Michigan Thirteenth Infantry.

2. The Michigan Thirteenth Infantry was organized at Kalamazoo, Michigan, and mustered into service January 17, 1862. The total enrollment in its ten companies (A through K; there is no J) was 2,092. It was engaged in Alabama with General Buell's army during the summer of 1862 and in Tennessee and Kentucky with General Smith's division of Buell's army during the fall. In December the regiment belonged to the Third Brigade, First Division, General Thomas's corps, and joined the army commanded by General Rosecrans on its advance upon Murfreesboro, Tennessee. McCline left Clover Bottom with the regiment on December 18. On that date, the regiment was ordered out with a forage train and marched to within five miles of Andrew Jackson's Hermitage, placing the Thirteenth at Clover Bottom. The regiment marched a total of thirty miles that day. "Diary of Captain Clement C. Webb 13th Mich. Inf, February 1862 December 1862," Stones River National Battlefield Archives, 17.

3. Theodoric Palmer of Kalamazoo, Michigan, was apparently a "War Democrat" who supported Lincoln's policies. His was one of three party views on war and slavery: northern Democrats generally opposed slavery, and southern Democrats, not surprisingly, supported it. During the war, northern Democrats were further split between those who opposed Lincoln and war, preferring a com-

promise of the kind Stephen Douglas supported that would allow states to choose or reject slavery, and those Democrats, like Palmer, who accepted war.

4. McCline does not give Dick's last name, but the reference is probably (despite the age discrepancy) to Richard Chirgwin. See Appendix I for more information.

5. Lora C. Jenks (McCline refers to him correctly later in the narrative) was a principal musician in Company F.

6. The wagon train reached *La Vergne.* From here on, I have corrected McCline's spelling.

7. These were cedar trees, *Juniperus virginiana,* and not pine, which are not native to this area. Pines were introduced much later. I am indebted to Steve Rogers at the Tennessee Historical Commission for this information.

8. Hagerman consistently typed "lead" for "led." In the interest of clarity, from this point forward I will use "led" when it is appropriate.

9. McCline is no doubt describing the aftermath of the Battle of Murfreesboro, where Federal General Rosecrans, advancing south from Nashville met General Bragg on Stones River. The armies fought for three days, from December 31, 1862, to January 3, 1863, when Bragg retreated. Each side lost about one-third of its soldiers, giving this battle the highest casualty rate of the war. In a letter to the adjutant general, dated January 3, 1867, Colonel Culver of the Thirteenth describes Stones River and Chickamauga (a later battle) as the battles in which the regiment most distinguished itself:

> In the battle of Stones River the 13th supported the 6th Ohio Independent Battery. Early on the morning of the memorable 31st of December our Brigade was detached by verbal orders of Gnl- Rosecrans and directed to go to the support of Gnl- R. M. Johnson of McCook's corps who was on the extreme right of the line and was being forced back by overwhelming numbers of the enemy—the order was promptly executed and while getting into position we were attacked by the advancing columns of the Rebel Gnl- Hanson's Division which we stubbornly resisted for 15 or 20 minutes when other Regiments of the Brigade retired in disorder leaving the 13th to protect the Battery. Our position was in a cotton field without protection. We fell back about 200 yards to the edge of the cedar thicket formed on the left of the Battery and delivered such a destructive fire that an entire Brigade . . . were held in check for over 20 minutes, but we were again compelled to retire leaving one third of the Regiment dead or wounded and two guns from the Battery. We reformed again about 150 yards to the rear of the second position and being opportunity [sic] by the gallant 51st Illinois . . . we made a dashing charge with the bayonet, broke . . . the Rebel line, retook the two guns and captured 100 prisoners and defeated the purposes of the enemy on this part of the field . . . getting possession of the Murfreesboro Pike. (Regimental Service Records, Thirteenth Michigan Infantry, Michigan State Archives, Civil War Collection)

10. When Fort Donelson, forty miles northwest of Nashville, fell to the Union, Confederates decided to abandon Nashville without a fight. However, the transition

was not as tranquil as McCline asserts. He had forgotten the chaotic retreats from the city he described earlier. In fact, as the Federals advanced, many Nashville residents fled in fear. Under the Federal military governor, Andrew Johnson, new public officials were appointed, commerce was halted, and schools were closed as Nashville became an occupied city. See Walter T. Durham, *Nashville: The Occupied City* (Nashville: Tennessee Historical Society, 1985).

11. Two Osborns appear on the Thirteenth's roster. But one Osborn joined too late to fit McCline's reference, and the other died soon after McCline joined the regiment. It is likely that McCline misremembered the name.

12. General Albert Sidney Johnston's Confederates attacked General Grant's forces at Shiloh on April 6, 1862. In two days of fighting, thousands were killed—13,047 Union and 10,694 Confederates, including General Johnston—but the North held its position. Shiloh was the Thirteenth's first major battle. Since McCline did not join the regiment until the close of 1862, he did not witness the fight, but based on this account, Aron apparently did.

13. In a letter to Adj. Gen. John Robertson of Michigan dated May 24, 1863, Lt. Col. Culver gives no reason for Colonel Shoemaker's resignation. (McCline's spelling of the colonel's name, incidentally, is incorrect.) He writes simply: "I have to inform you that Col Michael Shoemaker has resigned the command of this Regiment." The letter to Robertson continues with a promotion recommendation for another officer: "At a meeting of the commissioned officers of this Regiment Capt Willard G Eaton was unanimously Nominated for the Majority, and I cheerfully approve of this selection." Two days later, Eaton was promoted to major, and Culver was promoted to colonel. Regimental Service Records, Thirteenth Michigan Infantry, Michigan State Historical Center.

14. Michael Shoemaker described some details of his capture and imprisonment in a letter now located in the Regimental Services Records, Thirteenth Michigan Infantry, Michigan Historical Center. The letter, written from Jackson, Michigan, in February 1880, was addressed to General Robertson in Lansing:

> Dear General
>   In compliance with your request I give you date of my capture during the war of the rebellion, of my confinement in Libby Prison, and of my exchange.
> I was taken prisoner on Sunday night the 7th of September 1862, in Tennessee, near Tyree Springs, was taken by way of Carthage, Athens, and Knoxville, to Richmond, Virginia, arriving there on the 23rd of September. On the 24th I was immured in Libby prison, and was fortunate in being exchanged on Sunday the 27th of September, just two weeks from the day I was captured, and eleven hundred miles from the place.
> Yours Very Truly
> M. Shoemaker

15. As part of General Rosecrans's forces, the Thirteenth was on the offensive against General Bragg's Confederates, attempting to push them out of Middle

Tennessee. After retreating from Tullahoma, Bragg's forces had taken a stand behind the Tennessee River.

16. General Bragg, driven out of West Tennessee, moved his troops to Chattanooga. Rosecrans's army pursued.

17. *Civil War Almanac* quite appropriately describes the Chickamauga campaign on Chickamauga Creek as "The bloodiest battle of the war in the Western Theater" between Bragg's Confederate Army and Rosecrans's Army of the Cumberland. "It is prophetic," the *Almanac* continues, "that the ancient Cherokee Indian name for this creek is Chickamauga, meaning 'River of Death'!" (168). In two days of combat the Union had 16,169 casualties—1,656 killed, 9,756 wounded, and 4,757 missing. The Confederates had 18,274 casualties—2,132 dead, 14,674 wounded, and 1,468 missing.

18. Rosecrans, a West Point graduate and civil engineer, took charge of the Army of the Cumberland at age forty-three, a few months before McCline joined the Thirteenth. Here McCline reports seeing General Rosecrans on the afternoon of September 16, which is the same day the general set up headquarters at the Gordon-Lee Mansion at Chickamauga. See Peter Cozzens, *This Terrible Sound: The Battle of Chickamauga* (Urbana: Univ. of Illinois Press, 1992), 94. The same day, according to McCline, his regiment "went into camp in an open field just north of the strip of woods in which the great battle was raging." Officially, the Thirteenth was camped at Lee and Gordon's Mills on September 17–18 (Frederick H. Dyer, *A Compendium of the War of the Rebellion* [New York: Thomas Yoseloff, 1959], 3: 1287), certainly creating the opportunity for McCline to see the general. Whether the encounter took place on September 16 or 17, however, is uncertain.

19. On the evening of September 16, in anticipation of an attack, all corps commanders were ordered to give each soldier three days' rations and about twenty pounds plus a cartridge box full of ammunition (Cozzens, *This Terrible Sound*, 94). McCline's errand on the same evening was no doubt related to these orders.

20. Rosecrans thought, in error, that Bragg was in retreat, when in fact he was creating a clever trap designed to divide and conquer the three sections of Union troops spread out over forty miles of mountains.

21. This number was lost from 217, the total number of officers and men the regiment carried into action.

22. McCline foreshortens time in estimating the period between Chickamauga in September and this description (which he introduces as "a few days later") of Missionary Ridge in November.

23. From the end of November 1863 to February 17, 1864, the Thirteenth was on picket duty and engaged in cutting timber for warehouses in Chattanooga.

24. After the war Mrs. Hoggatt lived at Clover Bottom. In the 1870 Davidson County census she was staying in the plantation house with McCline's grandmother, Hanna. Hanna's sons (and McCline's uncles), Richard and Stephen;

Wyatt, the hoodoo; Buck (whom McCline recounts in Part I had been sent to the Louisiana plantation as punishment for hiding a runaway from another plantation, and who apparently returned to his family after the war), his wife Betsy and their son Frank; and many other former slaves are living at Clover Bottom, and all have taken the Hoggatt surname. Richard Phillips is still listed as the overseer.

25. According to the "Descriptive Roll" of Company C, John C. Colton had been sick since July 8, 1864, and died of "chronic diarrhea" on September 7. If McCline is right, his may be the only surviving account of the injury leading to Colton's death.

26. Future misspellings of this word will be corrected.

27. Black troops participated in every major Union campaign in 1864–65 except Sherman's invasion of Georgia. McPherson, *The Negro's Civil War*, 227. It is curious that McCline, who has near-total recall of most other events in his story, cannot remember the name of this black battalion. Clearly, the passage has personal significance for him beyond its place in his chronology. The great pains he takes to assert the men's professional and military presence demonstrates a desire to emphasize the black soldiers' contribution to the war.

28. During the spring and summer of 1864, the Thirteenth had been on engineering duty in Chattanooga and, as McCline relates, constructing hospitals on Lookout Mountain, Georgia. Relieved of engineering duty in late September, the regiment returned to Middle Tennessee in pursuit of Gen. Nathan B. Forrest's army.

29. McCline seems to be referring to events in fall 1864. By then, command of the two great armies fighting in Tennessee had changed. Gen. Ulysses S. Grant, who had been in charge of the Department of Ohio, Cumberland and Tennessee and had replaced Rosecrans as commander of the Army of the Cumberland with Gen. George Thomas, was commander of all Union forces. William T. Sherman had succeeded Grant as commander of all Union forces in the West, including McCline's regiment, which was part of the Fourteenth Army Corps. General Bragg, who resigned as commander of the Confederate Army of Tennessee in November 1863, had been succeeded by Gen. Joseph Johnston. McCline's unit was apparently on the alert for General Forrest's army. Forrest's force was active in northern Mississippi and in western Tennessee, where it was pirating gunboats and disrupting Union supply and communication lines along the Tennessee River. Even as McCline and the Thirteenth went west, Sherman, with other parts of his army, was headquartered in Atlanta, having begun his advance upon the city several months before.

30. Lincoln received overwhelming support from the soldiers on active duty. Out of approximately 154,000 votes, 119,754 went to Lincoln. *Civil War Almanac*, 233.

31. McCline temporarily forgets that Culver and Eaton were promoted to colo-

nel and major, respectively, in May 1863, less than six months after he joined the Thirteenth.

32. As noted in my introduction, pay inequity condemned black soldiers to a fraction of white soldiers' total wages: $10 per month minus $3 for clothing for the former and $10 *plus* $3.50 for clothing for the latter. After much political debate, Congress granted equal pay on June 15, 1864, retroactive to April 19, 1861, for those who had enlisted as free men on that date and to the beginning of 1864 for all others. Approximately four months after the equal pay legislation, McCline received only $8 per month. From McCline's perspective, however, any wages were gratuitous, since his was not an official enlistment. (Dating this event is difficult: troop movements and other story markers suggest McCline's pay begins late fall 1864; yet, McCline recalls the event as coincidental to Captain Yerkes's promotion to major which, according to official records, did not occur until March 15, 1865. McCline also says his pay began a year and three months after he joined the regiment, which would place the commencement of his pay in March–April 1864.)

33. This is no doubt a reference to Lt. G. Edwin Dunbar, who is mentioned later.

34. Perhaps this is Lieutenant Clark referred to earlier. There is no officer named Clark on the official roster.

35. Since McCline had received his first pay the day before this incident, what he used to pay for the knife which he purchased "a few days before" is not clear. For dramatic effect, he may have condensed the time between being paid and having this confrontation with Lieutenant Flint.

36. The year is 1864.

37. In preparation for the march to Savannah, all garrisons in the vicinity of Atlanta between Chattahoochee and Chattanooga were ordered to Atlanta and given instructions to leave behind attachments "to destroy every bridge and trestle along the Western and Atlantic" (Albert Castel, *Decision in the West: The Atlanta Campaign of 1864* [Lawrence: Univ. Press of Kansas, 1992], 554). In the wake of such destruction, "The army stood detached from all friends," according to General Sherman, "dependent on its own resources and supplies" (William Tecumseh Sherman, *Memoirs of General W. T. Sherman* [New York: Library of America, 1990], 646).

38. This should be the Chattahoochee River.

39. There is no official record of Dr. Owens or Chaplin Ellis.

40. Colonel Poe, United States engineer on Sherman's staff, was given the special assignment of "destroying the buildings of Atlanta which could be converted to hostile uses." Accordingly, Poe's forces leveled the depot, roundhouse, and railroad machine shops and fired them. The fire spread to the block of stores near the depot and "the heart of the city was in flames all night" (Sherman, *Memoirs,* 654). McCline's sequencing of events is reversed. He reports that the depot was leveled when he entered the city and the roundhouse was torched later.

41. Taking only a 20-day food supply (1,200,000 rations), Sherman planned to have his army of approximately 60,598 live off the land during its Georgia campaign. He ordered the army to "forage liberally on the country during the march," to gather "corn or forage of any kind, meat of any kind, vegetables, corn-meal, or whatever is needed by the command, aiming at all times to keep in the wagons at least ten days' provisions . . . and three days' forage" (Sherman, *Memoirs,* 652). Troops were told to take what they found among local residents and to meet any resistance with relentless force.

42. When Sherman left Chattanooga in May 1864 to begin his march to Atlanta and from there to the sea, his primary adversary was Gen. Joseph Eggleston Johnston, commander of the Army of Tennessee, with about 60,000 troops camped at Dalton, Georgia. As Sherman advanced, Johnston retreated. Not considered aggressive enough, Johnson was replaced by General Hood on July 17 and was not reassigned until February 1865. During the period in October–November which McCline recounts, Hood and not Johnston was in command of the Confederate force.

43. John Daniels, a soldier in the Michigan Thirteenth, remembers the march south through Georgia in much the same way as McCline: "We get our living by foraging on the country. We are in the lap of plenty except bread. We get meat fresh and salt, sorghum, honey, sweet potatoes, and meal. The camp is full of provisions." Once in Savannah, Daniels reports that rations were low. Entry of Friday, Nov. 25, 1864, Diary of John Daniels, Bentley Library, Michigan Historical Collections.

44. From November 16, 1864, when Sherman left Atlanta, to November 23, when he reached Milledgeville, the Confederate capital, Sherman traveled with the Fourteenth Corps, which included the Michigan Thirteenth. Sherman's army had begun the seven-day march to Milledgeville on November 15, but the general and his staff had delayed their start, staying behind with the Fourteenth to "complete the loading of the trains, and the destruction of the buildings of Atlanta" (Sherman, *Memoirs,* 654).

45. McCline is no doubt referring to Gen. Hugh Judson Kilpatrick. In subsequent references, Fitzpatrick will be changed to Kilpatrick.

46. On December 10, 1864, Sherman and his 60,000 men approached Savannah where Hardee was encamped with 18,000 Confederate troops.

47. As Sherman advanced, Hardee and his army escaped toward South Carolina, leaving behind 250 heavy guns. *Civil War Almanac,* 241.

48. John Daniels notes in his diary that rations in Savannah were scanty: "We moved camp this afternoon within a mile and a half of the city. We draw scanty rations and buy rice so that we have nearly enough to eat though the meal is very bad yet. It is beef that has been driven through the swamps and rivers of GA. And was poor when it was first foraged" (entry of Friday, Dec. 23, 1864, Diary of John Daniels).

49. Six or seven thousand refugees are said to have followed Sherman to Savan-

nah (Sherman at one time counted them at 17,000). Union strategy was to weaken the South by encouraging slaves to leave plantations. Once off the plantation, however, Sherman apparently did not care about their welfare and did not want responsibility for them. In Savannah Sherman met with representative blacks who told him that the refugee problem would be solved with grants of land. Accordingly, on January 16, 1865, Sherman issued Special Field Order No. 15, which provided that the "islands from Charleston south, the abandoned rice-fields along the rivers for thirty miles back from the sea, and the country bordering the Saint John's River, Fla., are reserved and set apart for the settlement of the negroes now made free by the acts of war and the proclamation of the President of the United States" (Howard C. Westwood, *Black Troops, White Commanders, and Freedmen During the Civil War* [Carbondale: Southern Illinois Univ. Press, 1992], 112). This measure proved to be temporary and eventually the land went back to its original owners. Refugees posed the same problem for Sherman in the Carolinas.

50. McCline's trajectory goes awry here. The Thirteenth Michigan, in the Second Brigade of Gen. Jefferson C. Davis's Fourteenth Corps, left Savannah on January 20, 1865, crossed the Savannah River, and then proceeded through South Carolina to Fayetteville, North Carolina (and not to Charlotte, which is some distance to the west). Four days after arriving in Fayetteville, the Fourteenth left on March 15 and headed northeast toward Goldsboro, North Carolina, by way of Averasboro and Bentonville, where it arrived on March 23.

51. McCline gets two events out of sequence here. The Battle of Bentonville, which he is about to recount, took place as McCline says on March 19–21, 1865, but it was after Bentonville, on April 13 (not before, as McCline writes) that Sherman entered Raleigh, North Carolina.

52. McCline overestimates the size of the Confederate force, which was 22,500 in the Carolinas.

53. At Bentonville on March 19 the regiment was engaged all day and suffered 110 men killed, wounded, and missing. Among the killed was Colonel Eaton, described by Colonel Culver as "gallant and noble . . . than whom a better soldier or kinder gentleman never lived" (Regimental Service Records, Thirteenth Michigan Infantry, Michigan Historical Center). In his account of the battle of Bentonville, Mark L. Bradley recounts that Major Eaton was killed by a bullet to the brain. "After the battle, several men of the 13th Michigan would return to this area [the battlefield] to recover the bodies of their fallen comrades, and would find Major Eaton's corpse stripped to its underwear [plundered by Confederate soldiers] and lying in a mass grave" (Mark L. Bradley, *Last Stand in the Carolinas: The Battle of Bentonville,* 2d ed. [Campbell, Calif.: Savas Woodbury Publishers, 1996], 187, 189).

54. On the evening of April 14, 1865, President Lincoln was shot at Ford's theater by John Wilkes Booth. The next morning Lincoln died and two days later,

on April 17, Generals Sherman and Johnston met at Durham Station, North Carolina, to discuss peace.

55. Daniels corroborates McCline's account of the soldiers' behavior: "The Boys are robbing the sutlers and peddlers who come within our lines to speculate" (entry of Tuesday, Apr. 9, 1865, Diary of John Daniels). According to Daniels, General Halleck "ordered that none of Sherman's men should camp within 3 miles of town." Two days later Daniels records that Halleck "characterizes us as thieves and cut-throats."

56. Foraging for provisions was military policy during the march through Georgia, and the return through the Carolinas. Sherman attempted initially to organize foraging details, but this proved inefficient as competition for resources made hunting chaotic. At one time or other, as McCline illustrates, all troops were foragers. But the consistent groups going forth every day were Sherman's Bummers, described by one Union officer as fearless and loyal:

> I doubt whether the history of war shows an organization equal to it in scientific and authorized stealing. These squads are composed of about twenty men each, selected for their great personal bravery and reliable character as soldiers. They are always commanded by picked officers, whose duty it is to scout the country and gather everything that can be used by the Army.
>
> Nothing escapes them; they go miles in every direction from the main column, and never hesitate to fight wherever the enemy can be found and very frequently whip ten times their own number. A column of troops always stops to reconnoiter if they find the enemy skirmishers in their front as the presumption is that the enemy will not appear at the head of a column unless in considerable force. The Bummers pitch in at once, and either whip the enemy, or as soon as they find the enemy too heavy for them, retreat.

The officer concludes, "There is, however, of necessity a strong demoralizing tendency connected with this work" (Richard Harwell and Philip N. Racine, eds., *The Fiery Trail: A Union Officer's Account of Sherman's Last Campaigns* [Knoxville: Univ. of Tennessee Press, 1986], 107). That demoralizing tendency was the Bummers' reckless disregard for private property. By all accounts, these nonmilitary soldiers could have been prototypes for the Dirty Dozen.

57. Also called chuck-luck, this is a gambling game in which players bet on the role of dice.

III. After the War

1. Of the four who went to Paw Paw (Culver, Bart, Osborn, McCline), only McCline is listed in the 1870 census for Paw Paw Village.

When the war ended, McCline's grandmother was still at Clover Bottom. Maybe McCline did not know this or had no way of getting back to Tennessee on his own. It is more likely, however, that he simply took the most immediate and familiar course: continuing on with his companions.

If McCline thought that his best future lay in moving forward, in continuing the adventure, he may have been right. In Tennessee, the transition from slave to freedman was dangerous and difficult. Overseeing this change was the Freedman's Bureau, a new federal agency charged with establishing schools, hospitals, orphanages, supervising legal affairs, and with ensuring the safety as well as the discipline of blacks. One of the bureau's major goals was securing employment for freedmen living in urban areas and in contraband camps, which had been created during the war. To do this, the bureau urged blacks to return or remain in rural areas to work for planters. Although the bureau established a wage scale and work rules, these were not systematically enforced, and the immediate consequence was a labor system that closely resembled the slave system.

Opposition to the bureau's policy of not alienating whites and not reacting to white violence and discrimination came from prominent black free men, assertive freedmen, and from former black soldiers, who demanded economic and political justice. Gradually, the Tennessee legislature passed laws granting blacks legal status: the right to give testimony in course, legalized marriages, "the right to enter into contracts, sue, inherit property, and have legal protection of life and property" (Lovett, *The Negro in Tennessee*, 201). But these rights were not comprehensive, and they could not outlaw white bitterness over the loss of a way of life. John Cimprich offers an illuminating summary of the condition of freedmen in Tennessee in the months following war: "Neither Reconstruction nor slavery died easily, and both left vestiges behind. Freedmen gained a large zone of privacy because emancipation weakened several institutional controls that whites had exercised over them. Poverty, the numerical superiority of whites, caste barriers, and racial prejudices continued to set outer bounds upon black lives" (Cimprich, *Slavery's End in Tennessee*, 131).

2. On the 1870 Paw Paw Village, Van Buren County, census, J. M. Longwell is listed as a hotel keeper who seems to have employed several young people. McCline is identified as a porter at Longwell's hotel.

3. The year was most certainly 1874.

4. When McCline went to Chicago in 1874, just three years after the 1871 fire, the city was still in ruins. The fire had burned for more than twenty-four hours and destroyed the downtown with its wooden buildings. Two hundred million dollars in property was lost and ninety thousand people lost homes. McCline was one of the throng of skilled, unskilled, and professional workers who went to Chicago seeking creative and economic opportunity.

5. Marshall Field (1834–1906) was a philanthropist and retail merchandizing innovator who began Marshall Field and Company, the famous Chicago department store.

6. On the 1880 Davidson County census, four years after McCline's return to Tennessee, Armstead, twenty-nine, was married to Kate, twenty-five, and they had two daughters, Hannah, six, and Ellen, one. In the same period, another brother, Richard, thirty-four, was married to Ellen, twenty-nine, and they had an adopted son, Jesse Harris, age ten.

7. McCline is using a shortened version of The Nashville Normal and Theological Institute, founded in 1864 to prepare freedmen as teachers and ministers. In 1884 the school was incorporated as Roger Williams University. For a more detailed history, see Bobby L. Lovett, "Leaders of Afro-American Nashville," (published by the 1984 Nashville Conference on Afro-American Culture and History), and Bobby L. Lovett and Linda T. Wynn, "Profiles of African Americans in Tennessee," (published by the 1996 Annual Local Conference on Afro-American Culture and History, Nashville, Tennessee). School catalogues for the years 1877–78, 1878–79, and 1880–81 record John and his brother Charmin Jefferson (as the school lists him) McCline as first-, second-, and third-year students respectively. (In the second year, Jefferson is still recorded as a first-year student while McCline is listed as a second-year student.) For some reason the school continued to list John as an official student even though, by his own account, he had returned to St. Louis by early 1878. Nashville Institute, *Catalogue,* 1877–78, 1878–79, Dargan-Carver Library, Nashville, Tennessee.

8. McCline lived with Bishop and Sarah Donoho and their sons, Jonathan, age six, William, age four, and Brown, age 3. Trousdale County 1880 census, 1st Civil District, Enumeration District 223, p. 5).

9. In 1885 McCline is listed in *Gould's St. Louis Directory* as a waiter at the Lindell Hotel. In 1887–88 and 1889–90, he is listed in the St. Louis edition of *City Directories of the United States* as a waiter and porter, respectively. According to McCline, he lived in St. Louis for twelve years, from 1878, when he was twenty-six years old, to 1890, when he moved to Colorado Springs. Although it would seem that he might have married or begun a family during this period, no official marriage license exists.

10. Mary Elizabeth Braddon (1835–1915) was a commercially successful Victorian novelist. She wrote eighty books between 1861 and 1911, when she was seventy-four. Her last novel was published posthumously in 1916. McCline was not alone in liking her "sensation" novels about bigamy, murder, and other betrayals and predictable adventure. Many of Braddon's titles appeared during the 1880s when McCline was in St. Louis, including *Just As I Am* (1880), *The Missing Witness* (1880), *The Story of Barbara* (1880), *Wyllard's Weird* (1885), *One Thing Needful* (1886), *Like and Unlike* (1887), *The Fatal Three* (1888), *The Day Will Come* (1889), and many others.

SELECTED BIBLIOGRAPHY

ARCHIVAL RECORDS

Census records. Tennessee State Library and Archives, Nashville, Tennessee.

Chicago Historical Society. Prints and Photographs. Chicago, Illinois.

"Diary of Captain Clement C. Webb 13th Mich. Inf. Feb. 1862 December 1862." Stones River National Battlefield Archives.

Fisk Normal School Catalogues. Fisk Univ. Archives, Nashville, Tennessee.

"Marching Through Georgia: Diary of John Daniels 13th Michigan Infantry, Company C 3 Sept. 1864 to 20 June 1865." Bentley Library, Michigan Historical Collections, Ann Arbor, Michigan.

Missouri Historical Society. Photographs and Prints. St. Louis, Missouri.

Nashville Normal and Theological Institute Catalogues. Dargan-Carver Library, Historical Commission and Sunday School Board of the Southern Baptist Commission, Nashville, Tennessee.

National Archives. Office of the Quartermaster General Claims Branch, 1861–1889.

Regimental Service Records, Thirteenth Michigan. State Archives, Michigan Library and Historical Center, Lansing, Michigan.

Rio Grande Historical Collection. Photographic Archives, New Mexico State Univ. Library, Las Cruces, New Mexico.

St. Louis Archives. St. Louis, Missouri.

Territorial Archives of New Mexico. Herbert J. Hagerman, 1906–1907. State of New Mexico Records Center and Archives, Santa Fe, New Mexico.

U.S. Army Military History Institute. Photographs. Carlisle Barracks, Carlisle, Pennsylvania.

UNPUBLISHED STUDIES

Lovett, Bobby L. "The Negro in Tennessee, 1861–1866: A Socio-Military History of the Civil War Era." Ph.D. diss., Univ. of Arkansas, 1978.

Nance, Benjamin C. "Historical Background and Archaeological Assessment of the Clover Bottom Mansion." Nashville: Dept. of Environment and Conservation, Tennessee Division of Archaeology, Mar. 1993.

"The History of Clover Bottom Mansion" by Middle Tennessee State Univ.

NEWSPAPERS

Nashville Union and American Paper, Feb. 14, 1859.
Santa Fe New Mexican, 20 January 1948; Jan. 21, 1948.

BOOKS AND ARTICLES

Aiken, Leona Taylor. *Donelson, Tennessee: Its History and Landmarks.* Nashville, 1968.
Andrews, William. *To Tell A Free Story: The First Century of Afro-American Autobiography,
      1760–1865.* Urbana: Univ. of Illinois Press, 1986.
———. "The Representation of Slavery and the Rise of Afro-American Literary Realism,
      1865–1920." In *Slavery and the Literary Imagination,* ed. Deborah E. McDowell and
      Arnold Rampersad. Baltimore: Johns Hopkins Univ. Press, 1987.
Berlin, Ira, ed. *Freedom, A Documentary History of Emancipation 1861–1867: Series II. The
      Black Military Experience.* Cambridge: Cambridge Univ. Press, 1982.
Berlin, Ira, and Philip D. Morgan, ed. *The Slaves' Economy: Independent Production by Slaves
      in the Americas.* London: Frank Cass, 1991.
Bradley, Mark L. *Last Stand in the Carolinas: The Battle of Bentonville,* 2d ed. Campbell,
      Calif.: Savas Woodbury Publishers, 1996.
Butterfield, Stephen. *Black Autobiography in American.* Amherst: Univ. of Massachusetts
      Press, 1974.
Castel, Albert. *Decision in the West: The Atlanta Campaign of 1864.* Lawrence: Univ. Press
      of Kansas, 1992.
Cimprich, John. *Slavery's End in Tennessee, 1861–1865.* University, Ala.: Univ. of Alabama
      Press, 1985.
The Civil War Almanac. Introduction by Henry Steele Commager. New York: World Alma-
      nac Publication, 1983.
Clements, Paul. *A Past Remembered: Antebellum Houses in Davidson County,* vol. 1. Nash-
      ville: Clearview Press, 1987.
Cozzens, Peter. *No Better Place to Die: The Battle of Stones River.* Urbana: Univ. of Illinois
      Press, 1990.
———. *This Terrible Sound: The Battle of Chickamauga.* Urbana: Univ. of Illinois Press,
      1992.
Durham, Walter T. *Nashville: The Occupied City.* Nashville: Tennessee Historical Society,
      1985.
Dyer, Frederick. *A Compendium of the War of the Rebellion,* vol. 3. New York: Thomas
      Yoseloff, 1959.
Foster, Francis Smith. *Witnessing Slavery: Development of the Ante-Bellum Slave Narrative.*
      Westport, Conn.: Greenwood Press, 1979.
Fox-Genovese, Elizabeth. *Within the Plantation Household: Black and White Women of the
      Old South.* Chapel Hill: Univ. of North Carolina Press, 1988.
Glatthaar, Joseph T. *Forged in Battle: The Civil War Alliance of Black Soldiers and White
      Officers.* New York: The Free Press, 1990.
Hagerman, Herbert J. *A Statement in Regard to Certain Matters Covering the Governorship
      and Political Affairs in New Mexico in 1906–1907.* Roswell, New Mexico, 1908.
———. *The Letters of a Young Diplomat.* Santa Fe: The Rydal Press, 1937.

Harwell, Richard, and Philip N. Racine, eds. *The Fiery Trail: A Union Officer's Account of Sherman's Last Campaigns.* Knoxville: Univ. of Tennessee Press, 1986.

Higgins, Thomas Wentworth. *Army Life in a Black Regiment.* Boston, 1890. Reprinted with a new introduction by Howard Mumford Jones. East Lansing: Michigan State Univ. Press, 1960.

Kelly, Lawrence. *The Assault on Assimilation: John Collier and the Origins of Indian Policy Reform.* Albuquerque: Univ. of New Mexico Press, 1983.

Larson, Carole. *Forgotten Frontier: The Story of Southeastern New Mexico.* Albuquerque: Univ. of New Mexico Press, 1993.

Larson, Robert W. "The Profile of a New Mexico Progressive." *New Mexico Historical Review* (July 1970): 231–45.

McPherson, James M. *The Negro's Civil War.* New York: Ballentine Books, 1965.

Patterson, Caleb Perry. *The Negro in Tennessee, 1790–1865.* Austin, Univ. of Texas Bulletin, 1922.

Rodkey, Edwin S., ed. *A Grand Army of Black Men.* Cambridge: Cambridge Univ. Press, 1992.

Sherman, William T. *Memoirs of General William T. Sherman,* 2 vols. New York: Library of America, 1990.

Starling, Marion Wilson. *The Slave's Narrative: Its Place in American History.* Boston: G. K. Hall, 1981.

Smith, Samuel D., ed. *Woodlawn Mansion: History, Architecture, Archeology.* Nashville: Printed with funds provided by Northern Telecom, 1985.

Vlach, John Michael. *Back of the Big House: The Architecture of Plantation Slavery.* Chapel Hill: Univ. of North Carolina Press, 1993.

Westwood, Howard C. *Black Troops, White Commanders, and Freedmen During the Civil War.* Carbondale: Southern Illinois Univ. Press, 1992.

INDEX

Andrew, John A., xxii
Atlanta, 91–92, 93, 142n 40; *see also* Thirteenth
    Michigan Infantry
Autobiography, xv

Black Civil War soldiers, xvii passim, xix–xxiv,
    81–82, 126n, 141n 27; in Confederate
    army, xxi; education of, xxxiii; Fifty-
    fourth Massachusetts, xxi, xxii; as former
    slaves, xviii, xxi; Fourteenth U.S. Colored
    Infantry, xxii; Hannibal Guards of
    Philadelphia, xxi; Home Guards of
    Cincinnati, xxi; impressment of, xviii–
    xix, xx; northern recruitment of, xxi–
    xxii; number of, xxi; in Tennessee, xxi,
    xxii; wages of, xxii, 142n 32; *see also*
    Bureau of Colored Troops
Black civilian laborers, xxiii
Bragg, Henry S., 46, 75, 77, 138n 9, 139–40n 15,
    140n 20, 141n 29
Breckinridge, John, 30, 134n 26
Brown, John, 26–27, 37, 133nn 21, 22
Brown, William Wells, xxii
Buell, Don Carlos, 137n 2
Bureau of Colored Troops, xx; *see also* black
    Civil War soldiers

Carolinas, 98, 99–101
Chattanooga, 9, 74–75, 78, 79, 80
Chicamauga Creek, xvii, 75; *see also* Thirteenth
    Michigan Infantry at Chicamauga Creek
Clover Bottom plantation, xviii, 11, 13, 14–20,
    21–22, 23, 39, 40, 130nn 1, 2, 3, 5, 131n 8,
    135nn 30, 33, 136n 37, 140n 24, 141n 24,
    145n 1; James Anderson as overseer, xvi,

16, 17; burning of the house, 25–26, 28–
    29, 132–33n 20; Mrs. Phillips, 17, 20, 22,
    40; Richard Phillips as overseer, xvi, 9, 17–
    18, 19, 22, 23, 26, 27, 28, 29, 30, 38, 45,
    131n 11, 135n 33, 141n 24; slave census
    for, 15, 39; slave life there, 19–20, 21–22,
    24–25, 34; Synor Zuccorilla as market
    man, 28, 38, 29, 133n 24
Clover Bottom plantation: roster of slaves, 119–
    20
    Abe, 18, 22, 32, 37
    Armstead; *see* McCline, John
    Aron, 33
    Austin, 18, 25, 30, 38
    Betsy, 21, 23, 141n 24
    Betsy (Jordon's daughter), 22
    Booker, 46
    Buck, 21, 39 passim, 141n 24
    Cynthia, 31–32
    Daniel, 18
    David, 18
    Dilsey, 38
    Frank, 21, 23, 39, 44, 47, 141n 24
    Hanna (aunt), 18
    Hanna (grandmother); *see* McCline, John
    Jefferson; *see* McCline, John
    Jesse, 30, 32, 37
    John; *see* McCline, John
    Jordon, 31, 32
    Laura, 31, 32
    Lawson, 29, 32
    Richard (marketman), 28, 29
    Richard (uncle); *see* McCline, John
    Stephen (brother); *see* McCline, John
    Stephen (uncle); *see* McCline, John

Clover Bottom plantation: roster of slaves, *cont.*
  Vann, 32–33
  Wyatt, 18, 39, 40, 141n 24
Confederate troops, xix, 41, 43, 45, 62, 65, 66, 79,
  80, 86, 92, 93, 94, 95, 97, 101, 103, 136nn
  34, 36, 138n 10, 143nn 42, 46, 144n 52
Confiscation Act of 1861, xix; of 1862, xx
Crittenden, Thomas L., 136

Davis, Jefferson, 136n 34
Delaney, Martin R., xxii
Douglass Frederick, xv, xxi, xxii, 125n 2, 126nn
  15, 16
Douglass, Stephen, 30, 133–34n 26, 138n 3

Foote, Andrew H., 43
Forrest, Nathan Bedford, 45, 46, 85, 137nn 40,
  41, 141n 28

Grant, Ullyses S., 43, 77

Hagerman, Herbert James, xvii, xxiv passim, 2–
  9, 11–13, 16, 26, 30, 32, 40, 51, 127–29,
  138n 8; as agent to the Pueblos, 7, 129n 9;
  and Holm O. Bursum, 127n 5; and
  William Llewelyn, 3, 5, 7, 127n 1, 128n 6;
  and McCline, 2–3, 4, 5–9; and William
  McKinley, 4, 127n 3; as president of the
  tax payers association in New Mexico, 7;
  and Theodore Roosevelt, 4, 5, 7, 128nn 5,
  6; as Russian diplomat, 3–4, 5, 127n 4; as
  territorial governor, xxiv, 127nn 1, 5
Hagerman, John James, 3
Hagerman, Lowry, 4
Hammon, Britton, xv
Hardee, William J., 94, 143n 47
Hermitage, the, 35, 135n 30
Hoggatt, James, xvi, xviii, 11–13, 16, 38, 78,
  130n 1, 4, 131nn 8, 9, 11, 12, 133n 20,
  135n 33
Hoggatt, Mary, xvi, 12, 13–14, 17, 18 passim, 19,
  23–24, 29, 31, 34, 38, 39, 40, 43, 44, 45, 51,
  78, 109, 130nn 4, 5, 132n 18, 137n 38
Hood, John B., 143n 42

Jackson, Andrew, 35, 133n 25, 135n 30
Johnston, Albert Sidney, 139n 12
Johnston, Joseph E., xvii, 92, 93, 100, 141n 29,
  143, 145n 54

Kilpatrick, Hugh Judson, 93, 96, 143n 45

Lavergne, Tenn., 59, 63
Lincoln, Abraham, xix, 30, 38, 39, 40, 88, 100,
  133n 26, 141n 30, 144n 54
Longstreet, James, 75
Lookout Mountain, 9, 71, 74, 77, 79, 84, 141n 28

McClellan, George B., 88
McCline, Bertha, xxiv, 129n 12; her niece Berje
  Barrow, xxiv
McCline, John, xv–xviii, 2–3, 4, 5–9, 20, 22–23,
  35–36, 40–41, 42, 131–32nn, 15, 16, 137nn
  38, 42, 140nn 18, 24, 147nn 6, 9; his
  brother Armstead, 20, 110, 137n 42, 147n
  6; his brother Jefferson, xvii, 20, 22, 23, 36,
  37, 42 passim, 44, 78–79, 109, 110, 147n 7;
  his brother Richard, 20, 110, 137n 42, 147n
  7; in Chicago, xxiv, 107–10, 111, 146n 4;
  and the Civil War, xvii; in Colorado
  Springs, xxiv, 112, 147n 9; his death, xxiv,
  121–23; his father John McCline, Sr., xvi,
  20, 34; his grandmother Hanna, xvi, 17, 20,
  22, 23, 24, 25, 28, 33, 40, 52, 60, 78, 82,
  132n 16, 135n 28, 137n 42, 140n 24, 145n
  1; in Michigan, xxiv, 107; at the Nashville
  Institute, 110, 111; in Santa Fe, xxiv, xxvi
  (*see also* Hagerman and McCline); in St.
  Louis, xviii, 111–12, 147n 10; and the
  Thirteenth Michigan, xvii, 51–105 (*see also*
  Thirteenth Michigan Infantry); his uncle
  Richard, 47, 140n 24; his uncle Stephen,
  18, 27, 47, 140nn 24, 34; after the war,
  xxiv–xxvii; *see also* Hagerman and McCline
Militia Act, xx
Milledgeville, 92–93
Morgan, Edward D., 136
Murfreesboro, xvii; *see also* Thirteenth
  Michigan Infantry at Murfreesboro

Nashville, 11, 14, 18, 20, 26, 30, 34, 35, 37, 41,
  42, 46, 51, 60, 61, 62, 64, 67, 83, 87, 110,
  111, 137n 41, 139n 10

Paw Paw, Mich., 77

Rosecrans, William S., 75, 137n 2, 139n 15,
  140nn 16, 20, 141n 29

Savannah, 93, 94–99
Sherman, William T., xvii, 9, 79, 92, 93, 100,
  141nn 27, 29, 142nn 37, 40, 143nn 41, 44,
  46, 47, 49, 144–45nn 54–56; and McCline,

93; treatment of blacks, 99, 143–44nn 49–51

Sherman's Bummers, 102, 145n 56

Slavery, xvi, xviii; at Clover Bottom plantation, 18, 21, 126n 5, 132n 19, 146n 1; emancipation, xix, xx; in Kentucky, xx; in Tennessee, xviii, xix, xx–xxi, 132n 19, 136n 137–38; *see also* Hoggatt, James

Stearns, Major George L., xix, xx

Stones River, 14; *see also* Thirteenth Michigan Infantry at Stones River

Thirteenth Michigan Infantry, 53, 79, 93, 137nn 1, 2, 144nn 50, 53; at Chicamauga Creek, 75, 76–77, 138n 9, 140nn 17–22 (*see also* Chicamauga Creek); at Missionary Ridge, 77; at Murfreesboro, 59–60, 61, 66, 138n 9 (*see also* Murfreesboro); at Shiloh, 64, 139n 12; in Atlanta, 90, 91–92 (*see also* Atlanta); at Stones River, 138n 9 (*see also* Stones River)

Thirteenth Michigan Infantry, black servants in:
Aron, 54, 55–57, 63, 64, 65, 68, 70, 72, 77
Bradley "Bart" Brown, 88, 90, 91

Thirteenth Michigan Infantry, enlisted members of, 113–17
Chat Baker, 53, 58
Thomas Bissinger, 91
Richard "Dick" Chirgwin, 57, 58, 60, 61, 62, 68, 70, 71, 72–73, 74, 76, 78, 81, 138n 4
Clark (sergeant), 89, 90
John Colton, 80, 141n 25
Joshua Culver, xvii, 54, 55, 68, 76, 77, 88, 91, 107, 138n 9, 139n 13, 141n 31, 144n 53, 145n 1

John Daniels, ,143nn 43, 48, 145n 55
G. Edwin Dunbar, 88, 91, 142n 33
Horace Easton, 71, 104
Williard Eaton, 88, 91, 100, 139n 13, 141n 31, 144n 53
Charles Flint, 11, 88, 89, 90, 91, 95, 100, 142n 35
Clark Fox, 76
Jeremiah Glines, 66, 67, 78, 84
Louis Gordon, 75
Lora Jenks, 58, 66, 67, 138n 5
Jordan (the quartermaster), 58, 60
Enos Larkin, 82, 83, 87, 89, 90, 91, 96, 97
James Moran, 63–64
Francis Murray, 76
Dave Osborn, 63
Theodoric Palmer, 54, 80, 137n 3
Foster Pratt, 53, 55, 56, 80, 91, 93
Charles Ruggles, 72
Michael Shoemaker, 54, 55, 64, 68, 139nn 13, 14
David Shulters, 61, 70, 100
Joseph Sinclair, 84
Jesse Starkweather, 58, 70
James Story, 84
Benjamin Wade, 75
William Ward, 88, 91
Clement Webb, 137n 2;
Silas Yerkes, 81, 82, 83, 88, 89, 90, 91, 142n 32

Tullahoma, Tenn., 65

Union Army, xviii, 43–44, 45, 46, 62, 66, 102

Westwood, Howard, xx

Slavery in the Clover Bottoms was designed and typeset on a Macintosh computer system using PageMaker software. The text is set in Minion with Adobe Woodtype Ornaments; the titles are set in Copperplate. This book was designed by Todd Duren, composed by Kimberly Scarbrough, and manufactured by Thomson-Shore, Inc. The recycled paper used in this book is designed for an effective life of at least three hundred years.